GOVERNING FROM THE CENTER

KEN GLADDISH

Governing from the Center

Politics and Policy-Making in the Netherlands

NORTHERN ILLINOIS UNIVERSITY PRESS
DeKALB
1991

Published simultaneously by Northern Illinois University Press,
DeKalb, Illinois 60115, and C. Hurst & Co. (Publishers) Ltd., London

Library of Congress Cataloging-in-Publication Data

Gladdish, Ken.
    Governing from the center : politics and policy-making in the
Netherlands / Ken Gladdish.
        p.   cm.
    'First published in the United Kingdom by C. Hurst . . . London'—
    Includes bibliographical references (p.   ) and index.
    ISBN 0-87580-580-9   ISBN 978-0-87580-162-9 (HC)
    1. Netherlands—Politics and government—1948–   I. Title
    JNB801.B53   1991
    220.9492—dc20   90–21363
                                                              CIP

FOREWORD

Since the 1960s, an abundance of material has been published in English about the government and politics of the Netherlands. An excellent resumé of this output has recently been compiled by Professor Hans Daalder as an Appendix to an edition of *West European Politics* (vol. 12, no. 1, January 1989), which has now appeared in volume form under the title 'Politics in the Netherlands'. He records however that 'there are no real systematic textbooks on Dutch politics in English'. This book is a modest attempt to remedy that deficiency.

It is, of course, impossible in a single, short work to cover adequately every aspect of Dutch political practice. I have therefore operated on the selective principle that there are certain central features which are indispensable to an understanding of the system. These involve giving some account of the historical development of the Dutch state, and the evolution of its highly successful democracy. The first four chapters endeavour to provide an outline of this process to date. Each of the remaining six chapters highlights a vital aspect of Dutch institutions and policy-making, concluding with a review of the relations between the Netherlands and the international community.

In compiling the book, I have naturally drawn extensively on the work of many scholars in the field, and therefore have numerous debts to discharge. I must begin by paying tribute to my first mentor, the late Dr Ernest van Raalte, whose distinguished volume *The Parliament of the Kingdom of the Netherlands*, published in 1959, was my introduction to the complex nexus between representation, the legislature and the cabinet. It was he who promoted my initial contacts with Dutch politicians and public figures, and his wisdom and enthusiasm were invaluable to my early steps in an unfamiliar polity.

Thereafter three eminent political scientists – Professors Hans Daudt, Hans Daalder and Peter Baehr – opened up for me the whole realm of academic discourse on which I have since fed. These early encouragements were followed by a flow of equally sustaining advice and assistance from a host of scholars, most notably Professors Jan Kooiman, Alfred van Staden, Rinus van Schendelen, and Rudy Andeweg, Drs Ruud Koole and Dr Theo van der Tak. These last four have very gallantly scrutinised various chapters of the book. This does not leave them with the least responsibility for its content. But I have used their insights and comments unsparingly in my effort to offer an account which respects the data, even though my interpretations are inevitably those of an observer, not a citizen.

I have also received considerable help with recent information from Ms Carien Laken, of the Royal Netherlands Embassy in London. It was from one of her predecessors Dr D.J. van Wijnen, that I gained my introduction to Ernest van Raalte, and a copy (gratis) of his important book.

At the local end of my lengthy research, I owe much to my late wife Enid, who patiently endured my frequent absences in the Netherlands, and to my wife Margaret, who has proofed my chapters and improved both their style and their spelling. The processing of the words was distributed among several valiant secretaries in the department of politics at this University: Mrs Margaret Paul, Mrs Sheila Baxter, Mrs Ann Cade and Mrs Marjorie McNamara. Finally the index has been assiduously prepared by Dr Christine Howell, an alumna of the university.

There is one further general acknowledgement. It is to the good sense, hospitality and civilised values of all those in the Netherlands with whom I have discussed, over the years, so many facets of political life. They have been unfailingly generous with their time and tolerant of both my intellectual uncertainties and linguistic deficiencies. It is scarcely fashionable to applaud élites, but my experience of the Dutch political and academic élite has done much to help me understand the remarkable stability and decency of their democracy.

University of Reading   KEN GLADDISH
June 1990

The map on page xi is reproduced, with permission, from *The Netherlands* (World Bibliographical Series), Oxford: Clio Press, 1988.

CONTENTS

TABLES

The Netherlands

1

THE SHAPING OF THE STATE

In fact, the separation of the Low Countries from the German Empire . . .
their combination into a single state, the speedy break-up into two – the free
North and the Spanish South – none of these can be explained by general
factors of whatever kind. The actual and assignable cause of all this was the
policy and fate of the House of Burgundy, from the first Philip, towards the
end of the 14th Century, to Charles V and Philip II in the sixteenth.
  — J.H. Huizinga, *Dutch Civilisation in the Seventeenth Century* (1935,
  repr. 1968), p. 107

. . . there was nothing in the earlier history of the country, in the history of
the mutual relations between the provinces, that would lead the
unprejudiced observer to expect the North-South cleavage that actually came
about . . . brought about initially by the interference of the military power
of Spain, by the campaigns of the Duke of Parma and by the counter-
campaigns of the Stadholder Maurice, the outcome of which was determined, not by the inclinations of the people or any supposed divergent
tendencies as between North and South, but by the strategic importance of
the geographical configuration of the country, especially of the great rivers.
  — P. Geyl, *The Netherlands in the Seventeenth Century* (1964), p. 23

The origins of the polity

Two questions dominate the origins of the contemporary kingdom of
the Netherlands: the first is how an independent polity managed to
emerge from the late mediaeval imperial tapestry of individual towns and
provinces which constituted the Low Countries in the mid-sixteenth
century: the second is how it came to assume the particular shape which
it has effectively retained ever since.

The quotations which preface this chapter suggest some at least of the
essential facts. Dynastic history, physical geography and military
fortunes all played crucial parts in the political outcome, as they have
throughout the European experience. That two eminent Dutch
historians should be at such pains to stress the fortuitous aspects of Dutch
independence is highly significant. In part they were reacting to a long-
term current of more deterministic historiography which held that some

1

form of Dutch identity had been primordial. But the necessary point is that there could well have been different outcomes.

One alternative scenario would have been the emergence of a polity which incorporated all the Dutch-speaking and linguistically cognate provinces, even though such neatness is rare in the development of states. By contrast the Low Countries might have remained fragmented but unpartitioned, to attain statehood when self-determination was a more fashionable concept. To air these prospects risks back-dating much later parameters; safer to note that in the circumstances of late sixteenth-century Europe there were no clear determinants of political identity. Thus very particular forces had to be at work to produce a new, non-monarchical state in a universe of empires, dynasties, and historic entities unrelated to cultural homogeneity or popular sovereignty.

The process of incorporating the diverse units which lay between the French kingdom and the German empire had begun, as Huizinga suggests, under Burgundian rule in the late fourteenth century. From the 1420s, a central assembly, the States-General, met triennially in Brussels to transact matters of taxation and conferments of privilege, the two being closely inter-related. Burgundian rule gave way to Habsburg towards the end of the fifteenth century. The progress of unification was accelerated by the Emperor Charles V, and this imperial consolidation was to become a vital element in the origins of an independent Netherlands. Less than twenty years before the first anti-Spanish revolt in 1566, the Habsburgs had persuaded the Imperial Diet to concede separate jurisdiction to the Low Countries. A year later, in 1549, the Pragmatic Sanction bound the seventeen provinces to a united acceptance of succession by a single ruler.

Many issues contributed to the series of revolts which eventually crystallised into an independence movement within the northern provinces. The Habsburg consolidation of power provoked local pride and particularism. The cost of consolidation, most graphically in terms of increased taxation to service the imperial army, provoked a sense of financial exploitation. To this brew was added religious divergence which became militant on the part of the Calvinist minority. Once a rebellion had been triggered, élites were caught between local loyalties and interests and allegiance to the Spanish crown. Initially there was little if any conception of autonomous political identity. This emerged slowly and painfully as the economic depredations, the physical destruction and the casualty figures induced new thinking about the best way out of a maze of confusion and suffering. Dispossessed emigres came to believe that only permanent separation from Spain would restore their lost fortunes and deliver religious toleration.

Yet there were profound difficulties in the path of conceiving how a distinct political entity could be forged from the diverse claims and interests of the various units. One besetting problem was that of sovereignty. There seemed no obvious focus of authority which might replace the Spanish crown, and, given sixteenth-century views of legitimacy, no clear course which might win assent from the European powers. Without their own monarch the dissenting provinces seemed inchoate and acephalous, and they turned successively to France, to Germany, even to England to supply that vital credential. All eventually turned them down, reluctant to risk prolonged warfare for the sake of a dubious suzerainty over a rebellious, disputatious population, itself divided between competing faiths and conflicting interests.

Having failed to find a substitute for Habsburg lordship, the Dutch were eventually compelled to navigate without a master. A new state emerged which came to describe itself as a republic, though one without either a central constitution or a clear-cut political executive. The polity was in essence confederal, a loose-knit union of seven provinces, each of which retained considerable autonomy. Within the confederation, two conflicting principles converged, though not harmoniously. One principle was that of oligarchy, represented by the mercantile Regents who controlled the major towns. The other was that of aristocratic, military command represented by the office of the provincial *Stadholder*. The *Stadholder*, whose basic role was that of military intendant, was an imperial officer whose office survived the transformation to independence. It was invariably held by a member of the high nobility. The lower ranks of the nobility tended to align themselves with the Regents, so that the operation of the two principles was asymmetrical.

The revolt which gradually grew into a war of independence forms an extremely complex chronicle, extending, in its various manifestations, over some sixty years.[1] Even then the final settlement had to await the end of the Thirty Years War in Europe; so that the entire process stretched from the first disturbances in the southern provinces, which broke out in 1566, to the Peace of Munster in 1648.

The rebellion in the northern provinces took shape in 1572 with the capture of the port of Brill in Zealand by the Sea Beggars' fleet, and remained active until the ceasefire of 1607, which two years later was converted into a twelve year truce. The truce marked the reluctant Spanish recognition of the de facto independence of the seven northern provinces – Holland, Zeeland, Utrecht, Friesland, Guelderland, Overijssel and the Ommerlanden (later Groningen).[2] The fortunes of the rebels at each stage swung precariously between triumphs and disasters, frequently hinging upon external events which drew off the Spanish forces and offered either a breathing space or an opportunity to recover lost ground. Thus in 1590 a long sequence of recapture by the Spanish army in the south and north-east was curbed only by events in France which took the Duke of Parma away to deny Paris to Henry of Navarre.

Equally crucial, and affecting both sides, was the continuous drain of resources into the escalating costs of protracted war. In 1575, at a relatively early stage, Philip II declared his treasury bankrupt. On many subsequent occasions campaigns had to be curtailed because of lack of funds to pay the troops, which set off successive mutinies by unpaid Spanish soldiers. The devastations of the mutineers, notoriously in Antwerp in 1576, added greatly to the chaos, and although in the short term they spread terror, in the long term they stiffened the republican conviction that the Spaniards had to be overthrown.

In any review of major events, the career of William of Orange, an imperial prince and *Stadholder*, is of critical importance in the period from 1567 until his assassination in 1584. It was he who financed and led successive expeditions against the Spanish, frequently without great success and, until 1579, without renouncing his allegiance to the King of Spain. In that year he belatedly put his name to the Union of Utrecht joining six of the northern provinces in an alliance which formed the basis of eventual independence.

Another crucial element in the struggle was the militancy of the mounting number of Calvinists who formed an irreconcilable spearhead of resistance to subjugation by the Habsburgs. For as the Counter-Reformation gathered momentum it was clear that it was not simply their freedom of worship which was at stake, but, in the most literal sense, their very lives. Initially few in number, even among the various Protestant sects, they were fervent recruiters, expanding in influence until by 1579 the Union of Utrecht elected to dissociate from Catholicism. Yet the United Provinces never became predominantly Calvinist and had eventually to tolerate all faiths to preserve order and unity.

After the assassination of William of Orange, the overall military command passed to Count Maurice of Nassau who by 1597 had won the entire north-east for the nascent republic. The death of Philip II in 1598, the closing of the 'Spanish road' from Italy in 1601, the corridor through which Spanish troops could be supplied to the Low Countries, and the ferocity of the epidemic of bubonic plague in Spain in 1600, all made signal contributions to the waning of the imperial capacity to continue the war.

Given the drawn out character of the struggle a definitive date for the establishment of an independent Dutch state is not easy to specify. But from 1579 on, the operations of the Union of Utrecht came to constitute a pattern of concerted action which represents the gestation of both an autonomous polity and a system of political practice. By 1587 the States-General of the seven provinces was acting in lieu of a sovereign authority; and in 1590, in a significant formulation, it declared itself 'the sovereign institution of the country [which] has no overlord except the deputies of the provincial estates themselves'.[3]

At this point the office of *Stadholder* in five of the provinces was vested in Count Maurice of Nassau whose cousin subsequently became *Stadholder* in the remaining two. This concentration of executive cum military authority was paralleled within the States-General, which in the 1590s had slimmed down to an average attendance smaller than that of the modern Dutch cabinet.[4] It thus operated not as an assembly but as a deliberative committee of delegates from the provincial estates, within which Holland had the dominant voice. Indeed, it shared the same building in The Hague as the States of Holland, the Binnenhof, which still houses the Dutch parliament or States-General.

The States of Holland was itself a compact body comprising two representatives from each of the eighteen voting towns and one member of the provincial nobility. Apart from Friesland, which had wider participation in its provincial body, the other provinces were equally oligarchic.[5] Underneath the formal apparatus of government, political control was in the hands of a small number of families who preserved their powers against all rivals. Holland was run by a network of town councils whose total composition amounted to some 700 men who were neither elected by nor accountable to the rest of the citizenry.[6]

The new republic was clearly no kind of democracy. The pattern of oligarchy which had grown up under Burgundian and Spanish rule was perpetuated, even intensified under conditions of independence. This may throw light on a problem of terminology. The Dutch campaign which culminated in self-determination has never been referred to as a revolution. Historians have instead settled on the term revolt, often capitalised as the Revolt, to characterise the separation from Spain. In terms of the preservation of almost all aspects of the preceding order – social, political and economic – this seems an apt choice.

For substantial political change within, the Netherlands had to wait until the nineteenth century when political institutions afforded scope for open competition and extensive participation. The regent class which presided at the formation of the state was to survive the life of the republic and to lay down a geology of attitudes and practices which confronted the centralising monarchy in the nineteenth century.

The republican performance

The Dutch republic lasted for more than two centuries. From 1795 to 1806 it went through a so-called revolutionary phase, having come under French control, and then became extinct. Its fortunes were dominated by three dimensions: economic development, external imperatives and constitutional confusion. It functioned as a state largely in terms of its impact upon the rest of the world. Internally it remained disunited, to an extent which makes remarkable not its eventual collapse but its prolonged survival.

In so far as it possessed a formal political structure, a hierarchy of government extended from the councils of the numerous towns, through the provincial estates to the States-General. But this hierarchy, itself uneven, was cross-cut by further features. One was the diversity of mechanisms within the separate provinces. Another was the overwhelming pre-eminence of Holland at the inter-provincial level; and a third was the existence of a para-monarchical office, that of the *Stadholder*, which although a provincial appointment could embrace several or all of the provinces according to circumstance.

To reduce this mosaic to a clear account of government and politics during the two centuries of the republic is scarcely possible. At different stages the principal lines of force centred variously upon the Amsterdam Regents, the Grand Pensionaries (the chief officer of the States of Holland) and the *Stadholders*. Each phase was affected as much by external events and relations as by internal dynamics. Under conditions of relative peace, civilian forces tended to prevail. For instance, during the truce with Spain which began in 1609, the Grand Pensionary Johan van Oldenbarnevelt was effectively the republic's chief executive – until his execution in 1619.[7] There followed a period of *Stadholder* control which ended in 1650 with the death of William II of Orange. In Holland and the leading provinces he was not replaced and again a Grand Pensionary, Johan de Witt, gained the ascendancy until he was assassinated in 1672. Half the country having been occupied by the French and the British, William III re-asserted the role of *Stadholder* until his death in 1702, whereupon the maritime provinces once more did without a *Stadholder* until 1747, when yet another French invasion required military control, and William IV was appointed to command all seven provinces.[8]

These complex oscillations at what in modern parlance might be termed national level were the top dressing upon an underlying pattern which had its own variations and continuities. The most palpable concentration of sub-national power was in the hands of the permanent controllers of the major towns – the mercantile Regents, above all in the province of Holland. The Regents were, as their title implies, the seigneurs of a republican oligarchy based upon wealth and commercial infuence, rather in the manner of the Italian city states of the late middle ages. The absence of a court, other than the entourages of the periodic *Stadholders*, meant that there was no central source of patronage or arbitration. The regent class was therefore drawn to institute its own modes of demarcation, exclusion and accommodation. Unregulated and unrestricted competition between the most powerful families would have generated endless internecine strife, with no means of peaceful mediation. For in a pre-democratic age the idea of the populace as mediator, through some form of electoral determination, was clearly unthinkable.

So the practice of élite management through a fixed allocation of offices and rewards became the effective political system. In the absence of coherent formal structures, this pattern provided a measure of order and stability and also linked the economic and social systems to the political. The populace, in so far as it was able to exert any influence upon regent hegemony, did so by supporting the House of Orange – the major countervailing institution – and, in less directly political realms, the Calvinist churches. Towards the end of the republican era, in its revolutionary phase, the lower middle classes attempted to assert democratic claims without aristocratic reinforcement.

During much of the first century of independence, the impact of the new republic upon the external world verged upon the miraculous. Having closed the port of Antwerp, which remained within Spanish territory, the Dutch proceeded to exert a profound grip upon intra-European trade. Able to finance a staple market, which could both hold and release at favourable prices the major commodities traded between northern and southern Europe, the merchants of Holland made Amsterdam the principal continental entrepôt. Over and beyond its

European operations, the republic's seafaring capacity opened up trans-oceanic commerce on a world scale. The Dutch East India Company pioneered the routes to South-East Asia, displacing *en passant* the Portuguese, and establishing what would eventually become the core of a colonial empire. Settlements were founded in virtually every continent, from North America to Brazil, and South Africa to India. For a time Dutch sea-power could challenge that of England, and inflict defeats upon its navy.

But the resources which sustained these far flung operations remained inherently slender. The total population of the republic, only a minority of which was maritime, was some 1.5 million in 1600, rising to only 2 million by 1800.[9] Also the Netherlands, unlike its major trading rival, was not an island, and had therefore to look to its land defences as well as its naval prowess. The existence of a hostile empire to its south under Spanish and later Austrian control was a perennial problem. The proximity of a major military power – France – was even more minatory.

Throughout the seventeenth and eighteenth centuries, the French made successive inroads into the Low Countries, which the republic alone was unable to staunch. This meant that the Dutch required a continuously active and supple foreign policy to ensure that alliances could be formed to repel French invasions. Britain was the obvious ally, but Dutch maritime interests were endemically at odds with British ambitions. The external power game had deep internal repercussions given the divisions of interest within the polity. The dynastic links between the Netherlands and Britain, which were to converge in William III, led in the eighteenth century to conflict between anglophile Orangists and anglophobe Regents; which in the final phase of the republican experience was to verge upon civil war.

Two cosmic international phenomena eventually sealed the fate of the Dutch republic. The first was the American war of independence, the second the French Revolution and its aftermath. The precariousness of the Dutch state was by the 1770s self-evident; and the failure to resolve basic internal conflicts was to leave it powerless in the face of mounting global tensions.

The American rebellion drove the republic into a debilitating war with Britain from 1780–4. During the war, internal dissent escalated as a quasi-democratic movement of the excluded middle classes challenged the traditional contest between Regents and Orangists. A Prussian invasion from the east ostensibly shored up the House of Orange by silencing the Regents and driving several thousand 'Patriot' democrats into exile.[10] But the result was to leave the Netherlands at the mercy of France. A French invasion in 1793 was headed off by the Austrians, who held the southern Netherlands. But in 1795, a French republican army, charged with the revolutionary fervour which was to carry French arms across Europe over the next two decades, overcame all Dutch resistance and installed a Patriot regime in the seven provinces. The oligarchs were either dismissed or converted, and the Prince of Orange, the last of the *Stadholders*, was driven into exile in England.

The confederal republic which had emerged somewhat gratuitously from the war with Spain two centuries earlier, thus joined the long chronicle of defunct regimes. The autonomy of the towns and the sovereignty of the provinces were extinguished. A unitary republic was proclaimed on the French model and a national convention eventually produced a constitution which was adopted by plebiscite in 1797–8. The political transformation of France, from a citizen's state to an imperial autocracy, was progressively extended to the Netherlands. Thus by 1806 the Batavian republic had been replaced by the kingdom of Holland, ruled over by Napoleon's brother Louis Bonaparte. Even this vestigial form of nationhood proved short-lived, for in 1810 Louis was de-throned and Dutch territory was formally incorporated into France.

As the Napoleonic imperium neared its end, the French defeat at the battle of Leipzig in 1813 opened the Netherlands to the advancing allied armies; and local risings against the departing French troops completed the process of liberation. The son of the last *Stadholder* assumed control of the country and was installed as its King, to rule over a now unitary state. Twenty years of convulsive world events had converted the Dutch political system from an assemblage of municipal and provincial entities into an executive monarchy.

A political scientist attempting to identify long-term factors in political development might be tempted to conclude that throughout the history of the republic, a monarchical spirit had been lurking in the wings of the Dutch experience. Certainly at least one early *Stadholder*, Frederick Henry, had monarchical pretensions. However, it is more plausible to contend that the eventual installation of monarchy represented not a teleological process, but rather an empirical failure of republicanism. The American case offers a useful contrast. For there republicanism grew out of the failure of a long-range monarchical system. The United States did not however become fastened to a patrician republic. Within two generations a complex of factors had driven the system on towards democracy.

The Dutch republic came about too early in the history of European development for a transition from oligarchy to popular sovereignty to be feasible. Surrounded by authoritarian monarchies, its principals could not risk, nor even visualise such a progression. The weakness of a power the size of the seven provinces, the ultimate fragility of its economy and the indefensibility of its frontiers made the republican endeavour almost certainly mortal.[11] By the end of the Napoleonic period the question was whether a Dutch state could survive, rather than whether the republic might have endured.

The adoption of monarchy

To the great powers who presided over Europe after Napoleon's defeat, the creation of a unified buffer state in the Low Countries seemed both an obvious and a necessary antidote to future French imperialism. The establishment of a monarchy with its roots in the northern Dutch provinces seemed the presumptive focus of such an entity, and by 1814 this had become part of the agenda for the post-war settlement. By March 1814, William of Orange was installed as King William I, ruling as an excutive monarch in The Hague according to a constitution, or fundamental law, compiled by his associates. Under its provision a States-General, elected by the now nine Dutch provinces, shared in the legislative processes of initiative and veto. But the monarch alone was to exercise all governmental powers, appointing and dismissing his ministers, declaring war and making peace, controlling the state finances and administering exclusively the overseas possessions. Religious freedom was guaranteed but the monarchy itself was committed to the Dutch Reformed Protestant Church.[12]

In June 1814 the great powers signed a protocol uniting the southern provinces of the Low Countries with the northern. William promptly produced his own articles of incorporation and had the fundamental law amended to take account of the amalgamation.[13] The States-General was now to consist of two chambers: the first composed of notables appointed for life by the King, the second to consist of equal numbers of provincial representatives from north and south, elected by the provincial estates. This did not confer any governmental status upon the provinces. The fundamental law made it clear that sovereignty was vested wholly and solely in the monarch.

From the outset the southern provinces were largely opposed to the union. A majority of the Belgian notables summoned to endorse the royal articles rejected them, only to be over-ruled by the King. Thereafter the underlying objections of the Belgian élite were nourished by royal policies, in particular the distribution of the national debt, the Dutch domination of the bureaucracy, the harsh press laws, the promotion of the Dutch language in Flanders and interference with Catholic education. By 1828 Belgian grievances had begun to undermine royal control of the States-General, culminating in the rejection of the budget. In the autumn of 1830, soon after the July revolution in France, disturbances broke out in the south. Despite the despatch of royal troops, a provisional government was formed in Brussels which called for a separate Belgian state. William's appeal for support to the great powers led to a conference in London which opted for an independent Belgium. A further Dutch invasion was turned back by French troops, and by the autumn of 1831 a Belgian monarchy had been installed. (The new Belgian King was Prince Leopold of Saxe-Coburg, widower of Princess Charlotte of Great Britain.)

The bid to unite the Low Countries had collapsed a mere fifteen years after the Congress of Vienna. Historians have offered their explanations why the attempt to establish a single state did not succeed. Kossmann has blamed the lack of a strong centre for the debacle and has suggested that 'unification came too early'.[14] But more fundamental was the failure to win the consent of the southern provinces to either the strategy or the method of unification, given the disparities of religion, culture, social structure and economic development between the two halves of the ephemeral polity.[15]

William himself took seven further years to accept the fact of Belgian independence. When, in 1838, he finally chose to do so, a tidying of the fundamental law produced a provision which induced his abdication in favour of his son William II in 1840. It was that henceforth royal decisions would require the counter signature of ministers, who would then be responsible in law for their consequences. The provision was a logical development of royal immunity, but proved unacceptable to the King. His own acceptability to the people had in any case been jeopardised by his decision to take a Belgian Catholic aristocrat for his second wife. The monarchy itself did not come under challenge, but its initial authoritarian period had come to an end. Under William II and his successor the next phase of government and politics would be increasingly parliamentary.

The 1840s saw the Netherlands exposed to mounting economic and political pressures. On the economic front an ancient system of controls, subsidies and tariffs was under challenge from the more enterprising members of the merchant class which was coming to advocate freer trade. Its contentions were advanced in a context of debilitating public debt, increasing poverty as a growing population confronted an unmodernised economy, and an uncomfortable dependence upon colonial exploitation in the East Indies. Against this background, new political forces were assembling. Political liberals, grouped around J.R. Thorbecke, a Leiden law professor from a shopkeeping family, were pressing for constitutional change which would open the system to the middle classes. Elements of the Catholic élite were prepared to support Thorbecke in return for ecclesiastical and educational concessions, while within the anti-liberal camp a revitalised Calvinism was beginning to crystallise into what would become the 'anti-revolutionary' position.

The appointment in 1842 of a skilful Minister of Finance, van Hall, greatly improved the fiscal picture. Political reform remained stalled, however, until 1848 when the February revolution in France moved William II to commission a constitutional revision. His principal commissioner was Thorbecke who within weeks delivered a draft of ideas which he had pondered over many years. There followed a crisis in which the anti-liberal cabinet under Schimmelpenninck resigned, and an augmented Second Chamber opposed the draft proposals. They were nevertheless pushed through, with royal support, and adopted in November 1848.

The new constitution was an astute balance of traditional and progressive provisions. Unlike the new constitution of France, it did not plunge the nation into a premature outburst of radical democracy. The royal prerogative was retained in foreign affairs, war and peace, the command of the armed forces and the administration of the colonies, alongside the appointment of ministers and the power to summon and dissolve the States-General. But the principle of ministerial responsibility to the States-General was affirmed, the Second Chamber secured the right to approve or reject the annual budget and, most significantly for the future, the Lower House was now to be directly elected on a national basis.[16]

The new franchise was admittedly somewhat modest in its scope. Eligibility to vote was restricted to males paying a relatively high level of direct taxes, which produced an initial electorate of around 10% of the adult male population.[17] But as affluence extended (or taxation increased) so would the number of voters. The scaffolding for a mass electorate had at least been erected. The First Chamber also became more representative, and would henceforth be elected by the provincial estates, instead of being appointed by the King. There was however no provision requiring ministers either to be or to have been members of the States-General, a dissociation which would continue to characterise cabinet-parliamentary relations up to the present.

Indeed the 1848 constitution set the mould of the Dutch political structure thereafter: 140 years later, ministers and their deputies are precluded from sitting in parliament, the Second Chamber is directly elected on a national basis, and the First Chamber is elected by the provincial assemblies. Apart from the introduction of universal suffrage, and strict proportional representation, the only deep operational change has been the gradual transfer of the entire prerogative from the monarch to the cabinet. But this is to apply a long perspective to the sheer anatomy of the constitutional system, whereas it is the changes in political physiology which make an account of developments since 1848 worth compiling. The first States-General under the new constitution was opened by William II in February 1849. A month later he was dead, leaving the throne to his son, William III, and to Thorbecke the task of leading the first cabinet of the parliamentary era.

NOTES

1. Many historians would question the implication that the various phases of the revolt can be viewed as a unified phenomenon. Parker (1979) observes in his Foreword: 'Most contemporaries were able to see that there was not one Dutch revolt but three.'
2. To the original seven provinces were later added Limburg, North Brabant and Drenthe.
3. Parker (1979), pp. 243–7.
4. Parker, ibid.
5. Parker, ibid.
6. Parker, ibid.
7. Oldenbarnevelt had in fact become chief spokesman for the States of Holland as early as 1586, two years after the assassination of William I. To the English who knew him as Mr Barnfield, he soon came to speak for the entire republic. Parker (1979), pp. 247–9.
8. Kossman (1978), p. 20.
9. Ibid., p. 17.
10. Vlekke (1945), p. 273.

11. This view is contested by Rudy Andeweg who sees the republic as having consider-
    able viability.
12. Edmundson (1922), pp. 367–8.
13. Ibid., p. 369. The protocol to the articles included a clause that asserted jurisdictior
    over Belgium 'by virtue of right of conquest'.
14. Kossman (1978), p. 150.
15. There was opposition to the union in the north as well as the south, strongl)
    expressed in the Amsterdam newspaper, *De Noordstar*, edited by F.A. Van Hall,
    later to be a minister and cabinet leader. Van Tijn (1971).
16. Vlekke (1945) (p. 307): 'The constitutional revision of 1848 shifted the center of
    political gravity from the Crown to the States-General.'
17. Kossmann (1978), p. 194, and Vlekke (1945), p. 308. The two estimates range
    from 75,000 to 100,000 voters.

2

PARLIAMENTARY POLITICS

The Netherlands . . . chose the "Scientific method" for reforming the State and it was one of the few nations that could boast that it needed neither revolutionary nor conservative doctrines
— Van Limburg-Brouwer, *De Gids* (1854), quoted in E.H. Kossman, *The Low Countries, 1780-1940* (1978), p. 263

Responsible government

Thorbecke began his first ministry in November 1849. On his accession, William III maintained in office the cabinet under de Kempenaer which had been formed the previous year, and only when it was defeated in the Second Chamber did the King summon the architect of the new constitution. Ministers were now responsible to parliament; but direct royal influence over the appointment of cabinets was to continue for at least a further generation.

The implementation of the 1848 constitution did not effect a sudden change in the complexion of the presiding élite. Even the electorate was little different from that which, indirectly via the provincial estates, had previously determined the membership of the Lower House. There was a substantial turnover of members in the 1850 election with three-quarters of the seats going to new incumbents. But the chamber remained predominantly staffed by aristocrats and patricians who had been educated in law and destined for public office.[1] Over the next thirty years four-fifths of all ministers would have this identical background.[2]

The principal lacuna in the assertion of parliamentary control over public policy was the absence of a party system. The two leading figures of the post 1849 generation, Thorbecke and his 'anti-revolutionary' rival, Groen van Prinsterer, made no attempt to form organised groups with political programmes; although they did endeavour to influence the choice of parliamentary candidates.[3] Thorbecke, a temperamental pragmatist, believed that the constitutional balance, in other words its uncertainty, precluded the formation of parties. This allowed for considerable flexibility in staffing cabinets; it also helped to preserve a continuing political role for the monarch.

15

There seems little doubt that the possibility of regimenting parliamentarians at this stage would have been quite unrealistic. This was not because either the members themselves or the local associations formed to orchestrate the new system of direct elections lacked clear sentiments. Van Tijn's work on the composition of the Second Chamber from 1848 till 1897 discloses definite constellations of opinion and indeed he uses the term 'party structure'.[4] But the machinery of representation was entirely local. There were no national party organisations. As the small electorate slowly expanded in size, the dominance of particular allegiances shifted within districts, and MPs depended upon those allegiances and not the patronage of non-existent party machines.

There were nevertheless groupings within the chamber which could be described in terms of political positions. There was, first and foremost, the Liberals, who until the 1870s tended to support Thorbecke and earned the soubriquet the 'doctrinaires'. The doctrine rested upon two key principles: one the campaign for freer trade and economic modernisation; the other a belief in complete religious emancipation allied with a clear separation of church and state in public matters. In the 1850s and '60s the majority of Liberals came from the 'outer provinces'.[5] Socially they were predominantly upper-middle-class, though they represented voters who were less exalted, given that some 12% of males over twenty-five had the franchise.[6] They were also supported by Catholic voters until 1868 when members elected as Catholics entered the chamber.

In 1850, at the first election under the new constitution, Liberals accounted for approximately forty-four of the sixty-eight seats in the Lower House (see Table 2.1). They suffered severe reverses in the election of 1853 but they recovered their majority in 1860. Thereafter they were able to exert considerable control of parliamentary business until the 1880s when their relative unity dissolved, and the confessionals were able to challenge their dominance. The other major grouping in this period was the Conservatives, who had ties with the pre-parliamentary system but accepted the new constitution so long as 'the old élite could stay in charge'.[7] They received strong support in Holland, Utrecht and Guelderland where traditional élites continued to control local affairs. In the 1853 election they out-performed the Liberals and were almost as successful in 1866. But in the 1870s they declined in the face of confessional mobilisation, finally vanishing in the 1890s.

Two smaller contingents completed the parliamentary ranks. One was an intermediate grouping, styled by commentators as Conservative-

Table 2.1
POLITICAL ORIENTATIONS IN THE SECOND CHAMBER, 1850–88

	1850	1860	1871	1878	1888
Liberals	44	40	43	51	45
Conservative-Liberal	8	10	4	-	-
Conservative	13	18	15	8	1
Anti-revolutionary	3	4	5	10	27
Catholic	-	-	13	17	26
Socialist	-	-	-	-	1
Total seats	68	72	75	86	100

Note: The table is derived from Van Tijn (1971). The evolving pattern should be considered in relation to both the expanding electorate, which rose from 84,000 in 1853 to 295,000 in 1890,[8] and also the increasing size of the chamber. Thus although Liberal seats did not diminish, by 1888 they no longer constituted a majority.

Liberals, the most prominent of whom was van Hall, who led cabinets in 1853–6 and 1860–1. The other was the small cohort of Anti-Revolutionaries led by van Prinsterer, which constituted the spearhead of Calvinist opinion and had influence well beyond its numbers in the chamber. This group formed the initial nucleus of what, in the 1870s under different management, would become the great Anti-Revolutionary Party.

At the governmental level, cabinet formations and changes during the period show a pattern of some complexity. There were seventeen administrations in the forty years 1848–88 under twelve different chairmen. The longest tenure of cabinet leadership was that of Thorbecke who held office for a total of nine years, ending in 1872. There was no formal title of premier during this era. Instead cabinet chairmen operated from key ministries – the Interior, Foreign Affairs, and less frequently Justice, Finance and the Colonies. In some cases political labels could be attached to cabinets, in others not. In the second half of the period the formation of cabinets was more closely related to election results, and there were fewer changes of government. The four decades of pre-mass politics which elapsed after 1849 were thus somewhat intricate from the standpoint of dynamic analysis. Of the range of issues and preoccupations, three realms predominate: the economic, the religious and the colonial. Economic historians emphasise the retardation of development in the Netherlands in the nineteenth century in comparison with the surrounding states of Western Europe.[9] The most immediate and vivid contrast is provided by Belgium, which by the 1840s was second only to Britain in the extent and volume of its industrialisation. Kraemer cites figures for the number of industrial enterprises powered by steam, and for kilometres of railway track, which show that by 1850, Belgium exceeded the Netherlands by a ratio of 5 to 1 in each case.[10]

Differential development was of course a factor which helped to fuel the separation of the two political entities in 1830. Belgian industrialisation was based upon the massive reserves of coal and iron in the Liège-Namur region. The Netherlands had no comparable resources, and indeed until the discovery of natural gas around 1960 was devoid of the raw materials of industry, apart from modest deposits of soft coal in Limburg. The Belgian infrastructure, in terms of roads and railways, was infinitely easier to expand than that of the Netherlands, where the terrain was chequered by waterways and the water table too close to the surface for the cheap construction of modern land routes.

William I is credited with an energetic concern for advancing the Dutch economy. But up till the latter 1840s, the finances of the state were too precarious to sustain systematic government investment, though some new shipping canals were constructed. The parliamentary era in the Netherlands was therefore inaugurated in the context of a relatively backward economy. Since industrial enterprise seemed unpropitious, the recipe for improvement came to be increasingly perceived in terms of freer trade, and a whole series of measures to this end were enacted by Thorbecke and his successors.[11] But these measures, though not without their effects, were unable to bring about a rapid transformation of either the infrastructure or the economy. The gradual elimination of export taxes helped to stimulate the overseas trade in agricultural products. The removal of restrictions on the carrying trade conversely undermined the Dutch merchant marine.[12] Not till 1890 was a comprehensive railway system in place, which was also the point when a national pattern of waterways was completed.[13]

At the first national census in 1830, the population of the Dutch provinces totalled 2.6 million. This figure increased steadily through the nineteenth century, although not at the rate of more industrialised countries, to reach 5.2 million in 1900. But the resources were lacking to provide the rising numbers with either adequate services or, for the majority, tolerable levels of income. There were therefore mounting social problems. Such problems were of course generic to Europe in the nineteenth century. In the Netherlands, given the absence of substantial industrial growth, they took the form of rural poverty rather than urban squalor.[14] In the last quarter of the century there was an increase of industrial activity. By 1890 one-third of the Dutch labour force was employed in some form of industry, which was a higher proportion than in the United States at that point, and twice as high as in Sweden.[15] But the units were small, machinery was primitive and productivity was low.

Up till the 1880s, these social problems remained sub-political. In the rural areas, relations between proprietors and labourers were generally relaxed, though the Calvinist revival among the lower middle classes seems to have intensified their antipathies towards the lowest strata.[16] In the towns the bourgeoisie had weak connections with the workers, since its incomes were derived either from trade or from government bonds and colonial investments.[17] There was pauperisation, in both the towns and the countryside. But until the latter part of the nineteenth century it did not attract great political concern. Instead controversy was channelled into sectarian debates, and in particular the battle between the confessionals and the Liberals over the terms and character of public education.

Various strands converge upon the grand debate over schooling which was to dominate Dutch politics right through the crucial stage of political mass mobilisation. One strand was the momentum of Catholic emancipation which began in the 1790s and achieved formal success with the re-establishment of the church structure in the 1850s. That 'concession' helped to bring down a Liberal government. But Catholic gratitude was short-lived as the Liberals came to be identified with an educational system which denied the right to free, public, denominational schools. And in 1868 the Dutch Catholic bishops, taking their cue from the *Quanta Cura* encyclical of 1864, anathematised liberalism in an episcopal letter.

A second strand was the Calvinist revival which had its roots in the Orthodox secession from the Reformed Church in 1843. The dissent progressed, through separate congregations, until by the 1870s the seeds of a mass based movement, both religious and political, had been sown. As with the Catholics, the Calvinists campaigned for the financing of sectarian schools by the state. This meant outright opposition to the Liberal position, which was that although state schools should teach broadly Christian values, sectarian schools should not be financed out of state revenue.

Both confessional movements were implicitly a reflection of social concerns. For sectarian education was essentially the preoccupation of the hitherto non-participating lower middle classes, who were asserting their political muscle in an increasingly open competition for power and influence. From the outset the Dutch polity had grounded much of its political discourse in quasi-theological controversy. Religion was therefore a well-tested source of mobilisation and advocacy. This may help to explain why agitation, which might have been translated into broader social conflict, could become so obsessively focussed upon such a specific institutional issue.

Thorbecke's first cabinet, which took office in 1849, ended with his resignation after the election of 1853, which reduced the Liberal contingent in the Lower House from forty-four to twenty-five members. The succeeding cabinet, formed by the Conservative Liberal van Hall, brought in a schools bill permitting sectarian schools if they were privately financed. It was defeated at the instigation of the Anti-Revolutionary Members of Parliament.* In 1857 the next administration managed to enact a law which allowed for some state assistance to sectarian schools. But the confessional demands for full equality of provision were unappeased.

The third realm of major policy debate, the colonial question, transsected the pattern of parliamentary positions on economic and religious affairs. Dutch colonisation in the seventeenth and eighteenth centuries had been extensive rather than intensive. Settlements had in all cases been ancillary to commerce, and not until the nineteenth century was there any disposition towards systematic exploitation of the overseas possessions. After 1815 the colonial presence was concentrated upon the West and East Indies, the latter consisting mainly of Java until the British redistribution of territory in South-East Asia added Sumatra and other islands in Indonesia.

Under the 1814 constitution, colonial matters were reserved exclusively to the monarch. After 1849, although the royal prerogative was reaffirmed, the States-General acquired full control of the budget, which meant that colonial finance, and therefore policy, became part of the parliamentary agenda. The politicians thereby inherited a policy known as the Javanese 'culture system' which relied upon the expropriation of

* The Dutch expression for a Member of Parliament is *Lid* (pl. *Leden*) *van de Tweede Kamer* (= Member of the Second Chamber). It has no recognised abbreviation, and therefore the British abbreviation 'MP' is used throughout.

indigenous produce by indirect rule via the native authorities. The balancing of the national books in the 1840s depended significantly upon the culture system making large regular contributions to the treasury. Given the programme of trade de-restriction which the Thorbecke Liberals embarked upon in the 1850s, the mercantilist approach to the East Indian possessions came under scrutiny. But a reform of colonial methods was gravely inhibited by fears of the possible effects on the national revenue. Both humanitarians and free-traders urged new policies; but in 1866 a bill of the van de Putte cabinet to abolish the culture system was defeated in the Lower House.

Four years later the culture system was modified. But arguments about colonial policy continued to disturb parliamentary coalitions. In the 1870s military measures against local rulers in the East Indies reversed the flow of colonial revenue into the treasury. In 1874 the problems of managing the Asian territories brought down a cabinet and went on to fuel the political uncertainties of the 1880s. During this decade agitation was mounting both inside and outside parliament. The schools question was uniting the sectarian forces. Social problems were becoming more overt as the first socialist movement was launched. The Liberals were dissolving into factions which made parliamentary alignments even less vertebrate, and the nature of the franchise was coming under critical examination.

In 1886 elections failed to provide a basis for a new ministry despite the unpopularity of the government. A round of somewhat half-hearted constitutional reform was undertaken. The size of the two chambers was now fixed at fifty members for the first, and 100 members for the second;[18] and the electorate was extended to include all males over twenty-three with a residence and 'signs of capability and prosperity'. Although this was not viewed as a radical widening of the suffrage, the subsequent enabling law trebled the number of electors. At the following election in 1888, the Anti-Revolutionaries and the Catholics were able to achieve a small combined majority and form the first confessional government.

The advent of party government

The assumption of office by the Mackay cabinet in April 1888 is generally regarded as a watershed in the evolution of modern party government in the Netherlands.[19] What it represents is the point at which an organised party, the Anti-Revolutionaries (ARP), was able to

stamp part of a cabinet with a clear political label. But this was a forma-
tive, not a conclusive, stage in a transitional process. Apart from the
ARP and the Liberal Union, set up in 1885 but without either a
programme or a mass following, groupings in the Second Chamber were
still largely informal.

Support for the Mackay cabinet was, equally, only partly defined in
organised party terms. In the Lower House it was backed by twenty-
seven Anti-Revolutionary members and twenty-five Catholics
representing various local electoral associations. Not till 1897 was a
common programme drawn up for these Catholic associations, and only
in 1904 were they partly welded into a General League. Also the traditional pattern of government by notables was not disrupted. Mackay was
a baron, and his team of seven ministers included four aristocrats, two
more than in the previous cabinet.[20]

If the claims of governments post 1888 to be considered as modern
party administrations remained incomplete, the complexion of parliament in the 1890s was similarly provisional. In all some eight tendencies
of varying solidity are discernible. The Anti-Revolutionaries were themselves divided between a major faction led by Kuyper and a more
conservative wing gathered around de Savornin Lohman, which
between 1898 and 1909 was to emerge as a separate party – the Christian
Historical Union.[21] The Liberals, after Thorbecke's death in 1872, had
gradually dispersed into three distinct strands. There were Free Liberals,
the remnant of the former doctrinaires, Progressive Unionists, a centre
grouping, and the more radical Liberal Democratic Bund.[22] Catholic
members, like the Protestants, comprised a mainstream, led by the
priest-poet Schaepman, and an aristocratic rearguard. Finally there was
the small but growing Socialist group with two seats in 1897, rising to
fifteen seats by 1913.

A further index of the still invertebrate nature of parliamentary alignments was that formations could be cross-cut by issues. The 1894
election, for example, was contested not on party lines but according to
positions on the franchise bill of the Interior Minister, Tak van
Poortvliet. The opponents won and a new ministry, nominally liberal,
was formed to frame a more restrictive voting provision. The evidence
that the 1890s were transitional is augmented by the extent of continuity
in the style of government. Cabinets remained committees of public
figures within which the chief minister behaved as primus inter pares.
Kuyper, as a new model party leader, sought a more vigorous role for the
cabinet chairman from 1901 till 1905, but this was not immediately
followed by a new trend. Until 1937, chief ministers continued to have

Table 2.2
POLITICAL COMPOSITION OF THE LOWER HOUSE, 1888–1918

Elections	1888	1891	1894	1897	1901	1905	1909	1913
Liberals	46	53	57					
Conservative Liberal				13	8	9	4	10
Progressive Unionists				35	18	25	20	22
Radicals		1	3	4	9	11	9	7
Anti-Revolutionaries	27	21	15	17	23	15	25	11
Christian Historicals				6	9	8	10	10
Catholics	25	25	25	22	25	25	25	25
Socialists	1	-	-	2	6	6	7	15
Others	1	-	-	1	2	1	-	-
Total seats	100	100	100	100	100	100	100	100

Note: Derived from Daalder (1966), pp. 418–19. During this period, elections were organised on the basis of single-member constituencies with provision for a second ballot when there was no absolute majority on the first round. It was therefore a majoritarian but not a proportional system.

Table 2.3
CABINETS, 1888–1918

	Leader	Ministers
1888–91	Mackay (AR)	AR, RC, C, Ind.
1891–4	van Tienhoven (L)	L, I
1894–7	Roëll (L)	L, I
1897–1901	Pierson (L)	L, I
1901–5	Kuyper (AR)	AR, RC, I
1905–8	De Meester (L)	L, I
1908–13	Heemskerk (AR)	AR, RC, I
1913–18	van der Linden (L)	L, I

Source: Derived from *Parlement en Kiezer* and Kossmann (1978), Appendix II.
Abbreviations: AR = Anti-Revolutionary; RC = Roman Catholic; L = Liberal; I = Independent; C = Conservative.

no personal office and to operate as the holders of portfolios within the cabinet.

Governments in the 1890s were however beginning to face the social challenges of the time with more structured programmes of legislation. This is particularly true of the Pierson cabinet of 1897–1901. As Finance Minister in the van Tienhoven government (1891–4) Pierson had steered through parliament both a progressive income and a wealth tax. As chief minister, still holding the finance portfolio, he promoted a left-liberal slate of measures. These included the introduction of compulsory education up to the age of thirteen, a public health service, workmen's compensation and a reorganisation of the army. Thereafter social reform would figure in the promises of most cabinets up to 1918, though not always with great effectiveness.

On the confessional front the Mackay cabinet had achieved its principal aim with the School Law of 1889. State support was now made available to private denominational schools though on a basis still some way short of complete equality. In 1901 after a decade of ostensibly liberal governments, a Christian coalition of Calvinists and Catholics won a decisive majority in the Second Chamber. Although its leader, Kuyper, presented a progressive image, the dock and railway strike of 1903 drove him to restrict the use of the strike weapon by employees in the public, albeit privately-owned, utilities. When the confessionals returned to office in 1908, Kuyper was supplanted as chief minister by Heemskerk. Social reform was now given a corporatist flavour by Talma, the Minister for Agriculture, Industry and Commerce. The confessionals were coming into increasingly direct competition with the expanding socialist movement, the outcome of which would be the pattern of *verzuiling* or pillarisation. One measure of this competition was the formation, from 1905 onwards, of three separate trade union federations – the social democratic NVV, the Calvinist CNV and the Catholic NKV.[23]

The first socialist organisation had been set up in Amsterdam in 1878. In 1881 a national Social Democratic Bund was formed by Domela Nieuwenhuis, a Protestant pastor, which in the fashion of the period adopted the Gotha programme of the German SDP. But it remained a miniscule, marginal movement until the foundation of the Social Democratic Workers Party (SDAP) in 1894. The progression from a mere reflection of socialism elsewhere in the late 1870s to a genuine party in the mid-1890s marked the emergence of an urban industrial working class. In the early 1880s, economic depression had fuelled a dramatic increase in migration from the rural areas to the cities.[24] Unemployment thus became more vivid, and social tensions provoked disturbances, notably the 'eel revolt' of 1886 when the police opened fire in the Jordaan district of Amsterdam and left twenty-six dead and 100 wounded.[25]

The initial clientele of the SDAP was small[26] but it rose slowly to some 25,000 members by 1914, by which time it had significant representation in the Lower House and had become a key element in the national debate about the mechanics of the electoral system. In 1913 Socialist MPs had been invited to join the minority Liberal government of van der Linden, since they held the balance of seats in the Second Chamber. The party declined the invitation though they gave general support to the cabinet during the First World War.

The 'pacification', 1913-18

Three issues dominated the political agenda in the quarter-century before the First World War: the franchise, the schools question and social legislation. An extension of the franchise had been accepted by parliament in 1887, though the details were not settled until 1896. The schools question had been tackled in the law of 1889, though its dénouement had to wait a further twenty-five years. Social legislation had been carried forward sporadically from the early 1890s, but it still fell well short of a comprehensive programme. The final rounds of the debate about the franchise and education were presided over by what was to be the last non-confessional cabinet, that of Cort van der Linden in 1913-18. The ensuing settlement would be known as the 'pacification'.

Before the war began, van der Linden had embarked upon a programme which included the introduction of universal suffrage and a system of old age pensions. By 1915 the process of a constitutional revision was in train, to be completed by 1917. Its principal ingredients were:

1. universal male suffrage;
2. provision for female suffrage (enacted in 1919);
3. equalisation of the qualifications for membership of the First and Second Chambers of parliament;
4. proportional representation within the frame of a single national constituency;
5. complete equality in governmental provision for public and denominational schools;
6. compulsory attendance at the polls.

The adoption of national proportional representation (PR) was a response to the difficulties of operating a constituency electoral system where a number of parties were contending.[27] Electoral pacts had served with decreasing efficiency, and the rise of the Socialists threatened to exacerbate the problems of effective representation. The major consequences of the new electoral system, which was employed in the elections of 1918, were an increase of Catholic seats but a decimation of the Liberals, though they may have fared even less well without PR. From thirty-nine seats in 1913, they fell to twenty in 1918 and thereafter were to dwindle to ten seats by 1939. Nevertheless, Liberals in their various guises managed to exert a continuing influence upon public affairs, from their positions as senior civil servants, judges, educationalists and industrialists.

As the elements in the pacification process were debated, the government, though supported by all major parties including the Socialists, had to wrestle with the problems of neutrality in a highly threatening environment. The army was mobilised at the end of July 1914, only to reveal its inadequacy as a defence force given the scale of the military build-up of the great powers. Faith in the protection of the Dutch heartland rested, as unrealistically as it still did in 1940, upon schemes for flooding parts of the country if invasion occurred. Attitudes towards the two sides in the war were both ambiguous and divided. Many feared a German victory which might result in the Netherlands being swallowed by the Second Reich. But antagonism towards Britain lingered on from the Boer War, when the Kuyper government had given moral support to the Boers. As the war dragged on and calculations of survival became paramount, the commander-in-chief, General Snijders, held that if the Netherlands were drawn into the conflict it should align itself with Germany. Even Troelstra, the Socialist leader, thought it would be folly to try to oppose a German invasion. The effects of the war included shortages, price inflation and shipping losses, all of which imposed considerable deprivation on the mass of the people.[28]

In the autumn of 1918, as the German western front collapsed and revolutionary disturbances broke out in German cities, reverberations of discontent on the part of the less privileged were felt in Holland. There were mutinies in the armed forces, and popular agitation was met by military action and marked by casualties. Troelstra made a rash, ambivalent call for the establishment of a socialist state. His summons proved abortive. Although the SDAP won twenty-two seats in the 1918 election, to become the second largest party in the Lower House, and the

Communist party entered parliament, there was no mass support for the overthrow of the regime. A confessional government under a Catholic noble, Ruys de Beerenbrouck (the first Catholic to lead a Dutch cabinet) took office and held it till 1925.

The inter-war period

From 1918 the political structure which would extend up to the present period was essentially in place. Its key components had been assembled and tested in the course of the evolution of parliamentary government which had begun in 1849. The roles of the two legislative chambers had been refined;[29] the position of the monarch had become clarified as that of a constitutional prompt and witness; and the institutional relationship between the cabinet and parliament had been settled.

The operational style of the system was of course very much dependent upon party configuration and behaviour. This would remain a dynamic factor, subject to variation and change over the next seventy years. It would in the long term express the outcome of social change,

Table 2.4

POLITICAL COMPOSITION OF THE LOWER HOUSE, 1918–40

Elections	1918	1922	1925	1929	1933	1937
Liberals		10	9	8	7	4
Conservative-Lib.	9	-				
Centre	6	-				
Radicals	5	5	7	7	6	6
Anti-Revolutionaries	13	16	13	12	14	17
Christian Historicals	7	11	11	11	10	8
Catholics	30	32	30	30	28	31
Socialists	22	20	24	24	22	23
Communists	2	2	1	2	4	3
Others	6	4	5	6	9	8
Total seats	100	100	100	100	100	100

Note: Derived from Daalder (1966), pp. 419–20. These elections were held within a system of proportional representation with effectively a single national constituency. The allocation of seats therefore reflects as accurately as possible the distribution of votes nationally.

although radical developments in the attitudes and mores of society at large would not become dramatic until the latter 1960s. The new and indeed novel provisions for representation adopted in 1917 had the major effect of stabilising the pattern of electoral support for the major parties. This was in part a function of the socio-cultural balance, but it was cemented by the meticulous translation of votes into seats which national PR guaranteed. Between 1918 and 1937, the SDAP, the fastest growing pre-war party, remained within a range of twenty to twenty-four seats. The Catholic party in the same period varied only from twenty-eight to thirty-one seats.

The system could readily admit new parties to the Lower House of parliament by virtue of having no threshold other than the purely arithmetical hurdle of the distribution of the total national vote among 100 seats. This aspect helped pro-Nazi support to surface in the legislature during the 1930s.[30] It also encouraged a plethora of minute movements to participate in elections, reaching an apogee of fifty-four contending parties in the 1937 election. Above all the new electoral system recognised, reflected and reinforced the crystallisation of political sub-cultures known as *verzuiling*, or pillarisation. Originating in the 1880s when the confessional movements sought to mobilise their followers into self-conscious communities, this process became in the 1920s the dominant and most conspicuous feature of social organisation. Trade unions, educational bodies, welfare schemes, cultural associations and the media, all became orchestrated on the basis of would-be hermetic pillars topped by political parties. Catholics and Protestants especially, although generally allied at parliamentary level, maintained separate social phylae from which their members were expected neither to emerge nor escape. This was paralleled by the assembly of a socialist pillar, and less concertedly by a latitudinarian liberal sphere.

In its political form, *verzuiling* suggested a distinctive genus of democratic consolidation, which was to be subsequently christened 'consociationalism', and would become a focus of intense debate post 1945. The underlying rationale of the phenomenon, as later propounded by Lijphart[31] and others[32] was that deep divisions within Dutch society could be best resolved by apartness at mass level and accommodation at élite level on the basis of a proportional distribution of resources. The counter-theory was that *verzuiling* did not express deep divisions in society, but merely served to consolidate support for contending élites.[33]

Over and beyond *verzuiling*, there were other cross currents in the political climate of the inter-war period. The ephemeral outburst of National Socialism was but one example of impatience with the laborious operations of élite democracy. In fact the years after 1918 were marginally less patrician, in terms of the backgrounds of parliamentarians, than either the preceding era or the period from the 1950s onwards. Fewer MPs had benefited from higher education and fewer had fathers from the highest professional ranks.[34]

But outright frustration with the system was provoked more by economic circumstance than by procedural unease. After the vicissitudes of post-war readjustment, the Dutch economy enjoyed relative prosperity from 1925–31. Then the international depression struck with devastating consequences. More than a third of the merchant fleet was laid up; between 1931 and 1934 gross national income fell by 25%, and by 1935 unemployment had reached half a million.[35] Having struggled to survive by deflation and adherence to the gold standard, the second Colijn ministry (1933–7) was forced to abandon gold in 1936 (one of the last countries to do so) and devalue the guilder.[36]

Although two of the three parties in the Colijn coalition gained seats in the 1937 election, counter philosophies were attracting interest, notably among Catholic corporatists who praised the approaches of Dollfuss in Austria and Salazar in Portugal. On the left, the SDAP advocated planning, nationalisation and deficit-financed public works, but, alerted by National Socialism, was careful not to propound authoritarian solutions.

Throughout the inter-war period, the confessionals were dominant at both governmental and parliamentary levels. The three chief ministers from 1918 to 1940 were, respectively, Roman Catholic (Ruys de Beerenbrouck), Christian Historical (de Geer) and Anti-Revolutionary (Colijn). Until 1937, the traditional practice of chief ministers operating from departmental portfolios persisted. In that year Colijn created for himself a new office of 'general affairs' which after 1945 became the minister-presidency or prime-ministership. At all elections between the wars, the major confessional trio were able to achieve at least half the seats in the Second Chamber, which enabled them to field and sustain cabinets of their own complexion. They thus ruled uninterruptedly from 1918 up till 1939, except during the second Colijn government when Liberals were given a token place in cabinet.

The Second World War

In August 1939, three weeks before the German attack on Poland, Colijn's fifth and briefest cabinet was brought down by a parliamentary motion condemning its 'unrepresentativeness in the face of the gathering

Table 2.5
CABINETS, 1918–40

	Leader	Ministers
1918–22	Ruys de Beerenbrouck (RC)	RC, AR, CH, L, I
1922–5	Ruys de Beerenbrouck (RC)	RC, AR, CH, L, I
1925–6	Colijn (AR)	RC, AR, CH, L
1926–9	De Geer (CH)	RC, AR, CH, L, I
1929–33	Ruys de Beerenbrouck (RC)	RC, AR, CH, I
1933–7	Colijn (AR)	RC, AR, CH, L, I
1937–9	Colijn (AR)	RC, AR, CH, I
1939	Colijn (AR)	AR, CH, L, I
1939–40	De Geer (CH)	CH, RC, S, L, AR, I

Source: *Parlement en Kiezer* and Kossman (1978).
Abbreviations: AR = Anti-Revolutionary; RC = Roman Catholic; CH = Christian Historical; L = Liberal; S = Socialist; I = Independent.

crisis in Europe'.[37] It was replaced by an all-party cabinet under de Geer which included a Liberal and two Socialist ministers (the first Socialists to hold office in the Netherlands). The de Geer cabinet served through the German invasion of May 1940, disbanding in September when a war cabinet in exile was formed in London under the former Justice Minister Gerbrandy.

The government had issued a proclamation of neutrality in September 1939, in the hope that, as in the 1914–18 war, the Netherlands could remain outside the conflict. The hope proved false. At dawn on 10 May 1940, the German XVIIIth Army crossed the Dutch border with a total force of eighteen divisions. The invasion was accompanied by parachute drops behind Dutch lines and near The Hague. The maximum force available to resist the invasion was nine first-line divisions, with five divisions in reserve.[38] The outcome of the German assault was never in doubt. The Dutch army remained in the field for four days until on 14 May the commander-in-chief negotiated a formal capitulation. As negotiations were concluded, Rotterdam was bombed, and fighting continued in Zeeland for three more days.

For the next five years the greater part of the Netherlands suffered under German occupation. The initial idea of the Nazi regime was to rule indirectly, as in Denmark, while endeavouring to win over the Dutch to the overall designs of the Third Reich. But the departure of the Queen and part of the cabinet led quickly to the imposition of direct rule under a Commissioner (an Austrian, Seyss-Inquart) who progressively enforced Nazi measures including the deportation and extermination of most of the Jewish population.

From 1941 onwards, the Netherlands was treated as an occupied country within which the ultimate authority was military. The methods of rule were to increase in harshness as the war turned against Germany and the Dutch resistance gained in strength.[39] As resistance became more organised it came to reflect various political lines of force which had implications for the restoration of sovereign rule. Indeed a wide spectrum of views and movements emerged under the stress and pressures of occupation.

Apart from the relatively small groups of Dutch Nazis and SS recruits, plus active collaborators, the rest of the population ranged from monarchists to Communists, and both the resistance forces and the underground press reflected these divisions. The situation was complicated by the separation of the ministers in exile, plus the Queen, from the political leaders and party influentials who remained in the Netherlands. And as a further cross-thread, there was disagreement about the kind of political system which should succeed the ending of the occupation. A return to the politics of sub-cultural dissociation was unpopular with the left, whereas orthodox confessionals generally supported a restoration of *verzuiling*.

As the war neared its end, the government-in-exile sought to both unite and control the resistance by the formation of a central command under Prince Bernhard, husband of the heir presumptive, but divisions remained. During the first year of peace a national government under the joint chairmanship of Schermerhorn, a latitudinarian, and Drees, a Socialist, dealt with the aftermath of occupation until elections in May 1946 restored normal constitutional politics.

NOTES

1. Van den Berg (1983), p. 325.
2. Kossmann (1978), pp. 274–5.
3. Ibid.
4. Van Tijn (1971).
5. Ibid.
6. Daalder (1975), p. 224.
7. Van Tijn (1971), p. 185.
8. Daalder (1966), p. 417.
9. See Griffiths (1979), Mokyr (1976).
10. Kraemer (1966), p. 38.
11. Ibid.
12. Kossmann (1978), p. 265.
13. De Jonge (1971).
14. Kossman (1978), p. 265, observes that the proportion of urban to rural population was the same in 1870 as in 1830.
15. Schiff (1971).
16. Langebroek (*Netherlands Journal of Sociology*).
17. Wilterdink (1985).
18. Kossmann (1978), p. 350.
19. Daalder (1966), p. 422: 'Before 1888 party affiliations and party composition of cabinets were too undefined to permit tabular representation.'
20. *Parlement en Kiezer* (Parliament and Voter) Annual Official Handbook, The Hague.
21. Verkade (1965), pp. 45–7.
22. Ibid.
23. Kraemer (1966), p. 74.
24. Kossman (1978), pp. 315–6.
25. Ibid.
26. Ibid., p. 444: '[The SDAP] totalled 2,200 members in 1898, mainly among the agricultural labourers in Friesland and poor Amsterdam Jews'.
27. Daalder (1975), p. 225.
28. Kossmann (1978), p. 553: 'By the end of the war the condition of the workers, badly clothed, underfed; miserably housed, was desperate.'
29. The First Chamber's powers were reduced to those of formal ratification under the constitutional revision of 1922.
30. See Smit and van der Wusten, 'Dynamics of the Dutch National Socialist Movement (NSB): 1931–35' in S.U. Larsen *et al.* (eds), *Who Were the Fascists?*, Oslo/Bergen, 1980.
31. Lijphart (1968, 1975).
32. See van Schendelen (1984).
33. See Scholten (1980), Kieve (1981) and Stuurman (1983).
34. Daalder and Van den Berg (1982).
35. Kossmann (1978), p. 662.
36. Verkade (1965), p. 118.
37. Vlekke (1945).
38. Maass (1970).
39. See Posthumus (1946), Warmbrunn (1963) and van der Zee (1982).

3

CORPORATIST RECONSTRUCTION

Due to the trauma of the Great Depression and war years there was after 1945 in Western countries great pressure to bring about reforms. In the Netherlands the desire was to obtain some control over economic developments, without resorting to nationalisation as done by the British Labour Government.

— I. Scholten, 'Corporatism and the Neo-Liberal Backlash in the Netherlands' (1987), p. 138

Perspectives in 1945

The ending of the war re-opened the agenda of normal constitutional practice. But there were widespread reservations about a resumption of the previous pattern of national politics. The second largest pre-war party, the Social Democratic Workers Party, had played no part in government until the last few months of the inter-war period. The record of centre-right cabinets during the prolonged depression of the 1930s was regarded by many as having been uninspired and divisive. Office-holders had come to seem out of touch with popular needs, and, as elsewhere, the resistance had brought to the surface somewhat amorphous desires for a more participatory and responsive form of democracy.[1]

Yet the constitutional structure seemed a model of democratic provision. The principal chamber of parliament was elected according to a mathematically impeccable form of proportional representation. Cabinets were compiled with immense deliberation so as to be certain of reliable parliamentary majorities. Governments, albeit separated from the legislature, were directly and exclusively responsible to it, the role of the monarch being ostensibly neutral and residual. What then was lacking in the Dutch arrangements, and what possible remedies might the painful reflections of war and occupation engender?

The most generally expressed unease was directed towards the configuration of the party system and its consequences for the democratic process. At one level the source of the problem was located in the extreme openness and proportionality of the electoral system, which it was felt prevented a consolidation of options and strategies in accord with the needs of modern government. At another level the salience of *verzuiling* was deplored because it resulted in a party system with two conflicting dimensions – confessional and secular – which could not be constructively synthesised or reconciled. Supporters of the secular parties, especially on the left, believed that confessional politics were both sterile and irrelevant to mid twentieth-century issues and problems; and that the unbroken cycle of confessional cabinets promoted frustration and anachronism. At a further level of disenchantment, the whole structure of élite management and the entire tradition of quasi-patriarchal leadership were in question. Two styles of leadership were in fact under attack: the intra-communal in which the notables of each *zuil* handed down the orthodox version of correct behaviour; and the national governmental style, itself an amalgam of bureaucracy and inter-élite accommodation.

Central to the experience of political management during the decade prior to the war was the unresolved conflict between capital and labour, and the gulf between employers and the socially and politically divided working class. The entrenchment of *verzuiling* meant, among other things, a tripartite split of organised labour between three trade union federations, one secular and broadly social-democratic, one Catholic and one Calvinist. The effectiveness of trade unions was further diminished by the relatively low levels of union membership, uncertainty about the legality of strike action and the absence of union structures within the workplace. Finally, at the level of national policy-making, there was no convincing provision for the interests of labour to be represented.

An awareness of this was evident long before 1945. As early as 1919 a Supreme Labour Council had been formed, composed of representatives of labour, employers and government, to advise on industrial relations. In 1933 an Industrial Councils Act had provided for a framework of consultative bodies in all branches of industry, with equal employer and employee membership.[2] The seeds of a corporatist system, in which labour would have an equal voice with management had therefore been sown in the inter-war period. Some writers have indeed seen this development as a natural consequence of the *verzuiling* structure.[3] But the harvest had been largely rhetorical, and attitudes towards corporatism were very much conditioned by political allegiances.

In 1935, the SDAP had put forward a Labour Plan modelled upon the de Man plan of the Belgian Workers Party. It advocated, as a counter to the inertias of the Colijn cabinet, public ownership of key enterprises, public works programmes and direct government intervention in the economy. But the Plan was ignored along with the notion of central, governmentally-directed economic planning. If the dire experience of pre-war failures in public policy-making provided the momentum for a new approach to national management, the catalyst was the massive task of post-war reconstruction. When the Netherlands was finally liberated in May 1945, both industry and the infrastructure were in ruins. It was estimated that 40% of manufacturing plants and over 50% of transport stocks had been destroyed. Housing losses during the war were calculated at 165,000 units, which meant a total shortage of 300,000 dwellings in terms of overall population needs.[4]

In September 1945, a Central Planning Bureau was set up by the socialist Minister of Trade and Industry. Its purposes were to compile statistics which would form the basis of regular economic forecasts, and to provide information for the systematic planning of reconstruction.[5] Alongside this technical initiative went a framework of deliberation between employers and employees stemming from the Foundation of Labour, an unofficial body arising from the war designed to promote co-operation between what would henceforth be known as 'the social partners'.

The Foundation of Labour was the first plank in what would become an elaborate edifice of corporatist provision. The overriding aim of corporatism was to manage the process of reconstruction on the basis of consensus, by means of a three-way system of co-operation between government, labour and the employers. The policy combined two strands of socio-political thinking which had previously been mutually hostile. One was the concern of the confessional movements, especially the Catholic, to harmonise class interests by building up a functional framework in which communal commitments would transcend conflict between different sections. This was in line with papal policy which since the late nineteenth century had advocated corporatism as an antidote to socialism.[6] The other strand was the socialist concern to have labour fully represented in economic decision-making, so that it could contend on equal terms with the representatives of capital.

The corporatist compact was sealed by two further factors. One was the attitude of employers. Co-operation between workers and management had become a matter of both patriotism and survival under conditions of enemy occupation. Also, the demands of reconstruction were likely to produce needs for labour which would result in full employment, circumstances which could greatly strengthen trade union bargaining power. It seemed therefore prudent for employers to welcome the opportunity of continuing co-operation within a framework where government would provide both balance and mediation.

The second factor was the complexion of government, which from the end of the war included a strong social democratic element, willing to work with the confessional parties in a concerted effort to re-build the economy and indeed the nation. Corporatist policies therefore commanded an extremely broad measure of support, and were extended to most sectors of economic life. Fiscal policy, wage agreements, price and profits control were all approached on the basis of tripartite deliberation. In 1950, the whole edifice was capped by the establishment of a Social and Economic Council composed of an equal number of representatives of employers, labour and public servants. Its recommendations went direct to the cabinet, thus by-passing parliament, and until the mid-1960s it was the chief source of policy proposals in the socio-economic sphere.

One measure of the success of these policies is that in the two decades following the war, national income per capita increased fourfold and in relation to a rapidly growing population (see Tables 3.1 and 3.2).[7]

Table 3.1
REAL NATIONAL PER CAPITA INCOME (1953 = 100)

1900	60	1950	92
1930	89	1955	116
1939	82	1960	132
1945	40	1965	160

Source: National Accounts 1965. Abert, p. 8.

Table 3.2
POPULATION GROWTH

1900	5.1m.	1960	11.4m.
1940	8.7m.	1970	13.0m.
1950	10.0m.	1980	14.1m.

Source: Netherlands Statistical Yearbooks.

The post-war party system

Given that the incapacities of the political system pre-war were widely regarded as stemming from lack of articulacy in the party system, one immediate question in 1945 was whether this would undergo significant change. Space for the contemplation of change was afforded by a transitional year (June 1945–May 1946) before the holding of a national election. Two eminent political figures, Willem Drees, the SDAP leader, and Professor Schermerhorn were asked by the Queen to form a temporary administration. The two had worked together in setting up a Dutch National Movement early in 1945, a principal reason for their appointment and for the formula of a pre-election administration.[8] For the period of transition the two chambers of parliament were brought up to strength by a special procedure.

The first group to restructure was the Social Democrats who in February 1946 launched the Labour Party (Partij van de Arbeid) which incorporated the SDAP, the small progressive Liberal Union and some ex-confessionals. This move was shortly followed by a re-naming of the National Roman Catholic Party as the Catholic People's Party (KVP). Two years later the various Liberal groups came together as the Party for Freedom and Democracy (VVD). What was important in these moves was what did not happen; and the most significant non-event was that the confessionals retained their old configuration. Therefore the election of May 1946 produced a parliament whose components and pattern of support were surprisingly similar to the outcome of the last previous election in 1937 (see Table 3.3).

The Communist Party, as elsewhere in Western Europe, achieved a burst of popularity, and the newly-formed Labour Party improved upon the performance of its predecessor, the SDAP. But the confessional trio virtually re-staged its pre-war result and jointly commanded a majority of the 100 seats in the Lower House.

Table 3.3
SEATS IN THE SECOND CHAMBER, 1937–46

	Com.	Soc.	RC.	ARP	CHU	Lib.	Other
1937	3	23	31	17	8	10	8
1946	10	29	32	13	8	6	2

Source: Daalder (1966), pp. 470–1.

What had changed however were the lines of force which dictated the composition of the cabinet. The new Labour Party could no longer be overlooked as a major contender for office. Both its success at the polls (though expectations had been even greater) and the prominence of its leader, Willem Drees, virtually ensured its position in government. Also it was prepared to work closely with the Catholics in an alliance which would come to be known as the Rome-Red coalition. In July 1946 therefore, the first of five successive cabinets featuring this coalition was sworn in. The Catholic Party provided the Minister-President, Beel, but there was a parity of portfolios between the two governing parties.[9]

In 1948 after a further election, the cabinet was widened to take in the two Calvinist confessional parties and the newly inaugurated VVD. This time Drees was at its head, a position he would retain for the next decade. As a grand coalition backed by all but eleven members of the Lower House, it experienced inevitable strains, above all over the problem of decolonisation in the East Indies. The Anti-Revolutionaries were the first to leave, and in 1951, the Liberals broke the coalition over policy towards West New Guinea.[10] It was promptly re-formed, but after the 1952 election the VVD stayed out of government. The third Drees cabinet comprising Labour and the confessional trio served out a full parliamentary term until the 1956 election. After the election, a fourth and final coalition under the Labour leader lasted until a cabinet crisis in December 1958 led to a dissolution of parliament – the first since 1933.[11]

Thus ended the twelve years of the Rome-Red alliance. Its break-up could be regarded as the end of the prime phase of post-war reconstruction. The collapse of the rapport was to have immense repercussions over the ensuing years, because the state of relations between Labour and the Catholic Party had become the most central strand of the parliamentary and governmental tapestry. One immediate effect was to divide organised labour between the confessional unions which retained party representation in cabinet, and the secular labour federation, the NVV, which did not.

The achievements of post-war reconstruction

After the first decade of reconstruction, the Social and Economic Council summarised the main objectives of the national economic strategy. They comprised: equilibrium in the balance of payments (the import-export equation), an equitable income distribution, stable prices, full employment, and a rising standard of living.[12] What is significant is that these

Table 3.4
ELECTIONS TO THE SECOND CHAMBER, 1946–59

	1946 %	1946 Seats	1948 %	1948 Seats	1952 %	1952 Seats	1956* %	1956* Seats	1959 %	1959 Seats
PvdA	28	29	26	27	29	30	33	50	30	48
KVP	31	32	31	32	29	30	32	49	32	49
ARP	13	13	13	13	11	12	10	15	9	14
CHU	8	8	9	9	9	9	8	13	8	12
VVD†	6	6	8	8	8	9	9	13	12	19
CPN	11	10	8	8	6	6	5	7	2	3
SGP	2	2	2	2	2	2	2	3	2	3
KNP	–	–	1	1	3	2	–	–	–	–
PSP	–	–	–	–	–	–	–	–	2	2
Other	1	–	2	–	2	–	2	–	2	–
		100		100		100		150		150
Turnout	93		94		95		96		96	

Percentage figures have been rounded off to the nearest unit.
* Total number of seats increased by 50% after the election.
† Party formed in 1948. Previous figure is for Liberals.
Abbreviations:
PvdA   Labour Party
KVP   Catholic People's Party
ARP   Anti-Revolutionary Party
CHU   Christian Historical Union
VVD   People's Party for Freedom and Democracy (Liberals)
CPN   Communist Party of the Netherlands
SGP   Political Reformed Party (Calvinist)
KNP   Catholic National Party
PSP   Pacifist Socialist Party

goals, which successive governments accepted and endorsed, were set by the economics 'establishment' rather than by the politicians and were implemented through the corporate institutions. Writing in 1968, an American economist observed that '. . . reliance on quantitative economic analysis as a guide to political decisions has reached significant proportions in the Netherlands'.[13]

This distinctive style of government and public management has received much attention from economic historians and political scientists.[14] Explanations of it have been offered at a variety of levels. The importance of consensus looms large in most interpretations, though how and why such consensus was achieved and what lay beneath it are questions which have sustained a continuing debate. The most prolonged and systematic argument has centred upon the concept that the Netherlands was symptomatic during this period of a particular genus of political management which has been termed 'consociational democracy'.[15] What at least is clear is that at the political level no single party was able to impose its own exclusive strategy. Equally clear is that the approach to reconstruction was widely seen in terms of the kind of national unity which the war had induced, even though not all Dutchmen had expressed their patriotism in identical ways.

At the technocratic level, the post-war agenda of economic and social regeneration invited the application of new techniques. Professor Jan Tinbergen, a key figure in this process, had been part author of the SDAP'S Labour Plan of 1935, and was commissioned to produce the first draft for the creation of the Central Planning Bureau in 1945-6. The draft was modified by the Beel cabinet, but the bill setting up the Bureau was passed nem. con. by the Second Chamber.[16] From 1947 onwards the production of ostensibly objective forecasts by the Bureau was generally welcomed by the political parties as the basis on which policies could be settled. It was not possible for all the statistical extrapolations to be carefully monitored by the politicians, and not all sections of the community benefited equally. One interesting consequence was that although the Labour Party had considerable leverage in successive cabinets, wage levels remained distinctly low in relation to other factors. This was a circumstance which by the late 1950s had put Dutch products in a very healthy competitive position internationally.

Perhaps the ultimate secret of the equanimity of the various political forces in the period 1947-58 was that each group placed its own interpretation on the benefits of corporatism and technocracy. The Labour Party leadership saw the process as a means of institutionalising the voice of workers in the policy machine. Thus a cut in real wages in 1951 could be accepted by PvdA ministers because they believed that in the long term corporatist co-operation must be to the advantage of labour interests.[17] The Liberals, who other than from 1948-51 were out of office during the reconstruction, viewed the system as a mode of accommodation which avoided direct imposition by the state and which left scope for employers to determine their tactics in the workplace. In addition, the confessionals found it a convenient way of reconciling divergent interests within their own columns, and, from a Catholic

Table 3.5
CABINET COMPOSITION, 1946–73

Prime Minister		*Ministries*
1946–8	Beel	*KVP(6) PvdA(6)
1948–51	Drees	KVP(6) *PvdA(5) CHU(2) ARP(1) VVD(1)
1951–2	Drees	KVP(6) *PvdA(5) CHU(4) VVD(1)
1952–6	Drees	KVP(6) *PvdA(5) CHU(3) ARP(2)
1956–8	Drees	KVP(5) *PvdA(5) CHU(3) ARP(2)
1958–9	Beel	*KVP(8) CHU(4) ARP(3)
1959–63	de Quay	*KVP(6) CHU(3) ARP(2) VVD(3)
1963–5	Marijnen	*KVP(6) CHU(2) ARP(2) VVD(3)
1965–6	Cals	*KVP(6) PvdA(5) ARP(3)
1966–7	Zijlstra	KVP(8) *ARP(6)
1967–71	de Jong	*KVP(4) ARP(3) CHU(2) VVD(3)
1971–2	Biesheuvel	KVP(6) *ARP(3) CHU(2) VVD(3) DS'70(2)
1971–3	Biesheuvel	KVP(6) *ARP(3) CHU(4) VVD(3)

* Party of the Prime Minister.
Source: Andeweg et al., in Griffiths (1980), pp. 229–30.

standpoint, in accord with long-term papal views on corporate practice. Political consensus at élite level in the 1950s was both a fact and a need. Three successive elections, in 1948, 1952 and 1956, resulted in coalitions commanding the support of 73 to 87% of the Lower House. But these massive majorities were counter-balanced by a mosaic of relations within cabinets. Although each government was headed by the PvdA statesman Drees, in none did the Labour Party hold more than five portfolios out of a total of fifteen or sixteen. The Catholic People's Party averaged six cabinet seats, and the ARP and CHU tended jointly to have almost the same weight in cabinet as Labour. The survival of such extensive coalitions clearly necessitated compromise, and it was therefore hardly surprising that there seemed overall a high degree of policy cohesion. But the individual parties were not anaesthetised by the long experience of accommodation; and when certain decisions seemed to involve some element of ideological choice the forces of fission were aroused. Thus Labour in 1958 found itself unable to go along with a policy of taxation readjustment allied with a reduction of price subsidies.

The breaking of the compact with Labour enabled the confessionals to move slightly to the right in economic policy. In the de Quay cabinet of 1959–63, which included the Liberals, greater variability in wage rates was urged. This was the first deliberate departure from the policy of national wage settlements which had been one of the cornerstones of the corporatist strategy. It was answered on the part of industrial unions, notably the metal-workers, with a more aggressive assertion of sectional demands. So that by the mid-1960s, although the corporate structure remained in place, consensus had given way to a rather less co-operative style of industrial relations.

The corporatist approach to wage determination has been sharply characterised by a Dutch political scientist:

> 'The top managers and executives of the employers associations, as well as the employees organisations, conferred with government authorities, and together, in a completely centralised manner, they decided how much of a wage increase was feasible and where, and the nature and place of budget cuts which might be called for.'[18]

He goes on to cite the view of an American expert that the process came close to 'the furthest borders of what is admissible in a non-authoritarian state'.[19] This judgement invites a misperception. For Dutch corporatism was designed to operate on the basis of agreement between the 'social partners' and these accords were backed by a consensus of democratic parties. They were intended as the opposite of an authoritarian imposition of norms, and shaped to avoid the friction of any such attempt. After 1968 when the Foundation of Labour gave up making annual wage recommendations, governments found themselves having to resort to legislative wage freezes to control the economy, as in other West European democracies.[20] So wage determination by conciliar methods, however centralised, was scarcely a sinister mode of presiding over capitalist development.

Moreover corporatism could claim, in its prime phase, a significant range of achievements, for it did manage to preserve full employment, to guarantee income-levels and to promote the highest rate of industrial investment in Western Europe. It was less resoundingly successful in the field of price stabilisation, but industrial conflict remained uniquely low even though wage costs were kept below those of Holland's competitors.[21]

The decline of confessional politics

As will be clear from the previous chapter, the closeness of the relationship between religion and politics in the Netherlands was evident from the onset of parliamentary government in the mid-nineteenth century. The major religious movements in national politics had, not surprisingly, linkages of varying degrees of complexity and intensity with church organisations; and the nature of these linkages is of crucial importance to an understanding both of confessional politics and of the pattern and significance of its decline. The most straightforward of these connections, from the standpoint of voting behaviour, was that between the Catholic Party (after 1946, the KVP) and the Roman Catholic Church.[22] The overwhelming majority of practising Roman Catholics, grouped predominantly in the southern provinces of Limburg and North Brabant, but also numerically significant in all but the three northernmost provinces, voted solidly and regularly for the Catholic Party. Nonpractising Catholics were prepared to support other parties, notably the PvdA, but in the 1950s some 50% of them still supported the KVP (see Table 3.6).

The case of the Protestants was more complex. The official Calvinist church organisation, though it was not formally a state established church, was the Dutch Reformed (Nederlandse Hervormde Kerk). Reconstructed in 1816 by the government of William I, it subsequently became subject to schism and sectarian disputes, the two most notable being the Secession (*Afscheiding*) of 1834, and the Protest (*Doleantie*) of 1886.[23] The essence of these conflicts was the conviction of fervent Calvinists who thought the official church insufficiently strict, orthodox or traditional, that they would be better served in separate congregations. By 1869 there were more than 300 congregations resulting from the Secession,[24] as well as other separatist groups.

Table 3.6
PARTY PREFERENCES OF MAIN DENOMINATIONS (% *of sample*)

		KVP	ARP	CHU	PvdA	VVD	Other	No.
Catholic	P*	95	0	0	2	0	3	295
	NP*	50	7	0	30	10	3	30
Calvinist	P	0	18	45	23	5	9	121
(*Hervormde*)	NP	0	6	19	52	18	6	200
Calvinist	P	0	90	3	1	0	5	93
(*Gereformeerde*)	NP	0	62	0	29	0	10	21
No denomination		1	1	1	72	12	14	194

*P = practising; NP = non-practising.
Source: NIPO survey, 1956.

Calvinist interests in parliament however were at this point neither differentiated nor organised on party lines. The small number of adherents who were entitled to vote were broadly represented by members supporting the Anti-Revolutionary tendency, headed by the aristocrat Groen van Prinsterer. In 1878, the Anti-Revolutionaries were formed into the first modern political party by a Calvinist minister who would become the principal force within the *Doleantie* movement, Abraham Kuyper. By 1892 Kuyper was able to weld the breakaway churches into a new union – the Reformed Dutch Church (*Gereformeerde Kerken in Nederland*). But the union embraced only a minority of Anti-Revolutionary adherents. Calvinist politicians who remained within the official church eventually broke with the ARP in 1898, on social, political and theological grounds, and in 1908 set up their own political party, the Christian Historical Union.

The proportion of Calvinists who had stayed with the official church was, by 1909, more than five times greater than the fraction who worshipped in *Gereformeerde* congregations (see Table 3.7). But whereas the ARP was able to mobilise the latter as efficiently as the Catholic Party could command its followers, the CHU attracted only a minority of *Hervormde* churchgoers. The majority were willing to support other parties, including the ARP, and as the Socialist party gained ground it drew more and more support from members of the official church.

Although there are little useful electoral data prior to the 1950s, it does not seem that the Second World War had very much effect upon the relationship between religion and voting which had crystallised by 1918.

Table 3.7
POPULATION PERCENTAGES OF RELIGIOUS GROUPS

	No Church	Roman Catholic	Calvinist Hervormde	Calvinist Gereformeerde	Other
1899	2.2	35.1	48.4	7.1	7.2
1909	5.0	35.0	44.2	8.4	7.4
1920	7.8	35.6	41.2	8.3	7.1
1930	14.4	36.4	34.5	8.1	6.6
1947	17.1	38.5	31.0	7.0	6.4
1960	18.3	40.4	28.3	6.9	6.1
1971	23.6	40.4	23.5	7.2	5.3

Source: Central Bureau of Statistics.[25]

Therefore the evidence of a sample survey carried out by the Netherlands Institute of Public Opinion in 1956 provides a snapshot of what might be regarded as the 'traditional' picture (see Table 3.6).

The map of voting and religion sketched by the 1956 survey demonstrates both how the confessionals distributed their support among the parties, and whence the secular parties drew their strength. Only a third of the Labour vote, according to the sample, came from secular electors, and a quarter came from non-practising official Calvinists, who also provided the main source of Liberal support. Among the confessional parties, the KVP had both the most solid and the most exclusive support base; all but 5% of regular attenders at mass endorsed the Catholic Party. The ARP was almost as impressive in its grip on churchgoing *Gereformeerden*. Weakest in its hold on a specific church-following was the CHU, which mobilised less than half the *Hervormde* worshippers.

An album for the snapshot is available from the census returns which disclose the demography of religious adherence from 1899. It is clear from the 'album' that the most significant changes from the war up to 1971 were a further decline in the proportion of official Calvinists and a corresponding increase in the proportion of the population which professed no religion.

In the national election of 1963, the traditional voting configuration seemed firmly in place, for the results were comparable with those of the four preceding post-war contests. The confessional trio collected half the seats in the Lower House, jointly seventy-six, and were able to re-convoke the previous coalition with the Liberals under a Catholic Minister-President, Marijnen. There followed an unusual bout of governmental instability. The Marijnen cabinet broke up in 1965 and Labour replaced the Liberals in a new coalition under Cals, also a Catholic. After seventeen months, the KVP parliamentary group pressured Labour out of the cabinet, and a third administration, this time under Zijlstra, an ARP minister, filled the gap until the next national election.

In the provincial elections of 1966, the overall confessional vote had stood up, and Labour had come off worst with a fall of 15% overall. The PvdA therefore expected to lose support in the 1967 national election, as it did. Not anticipated was a sudden loss of eight seats by the KVP which set off, or at least registered, the first stage in a prolonged decline of support for the confessional parties. Over the next five years the KVP and the CHU would fall to almost half their pre-1967 parliamentary

Table 3.8
ELECTIONS TO THE SECOND CHAMBER, 1963–72

| | 1963 | | 1967 | | 1971 | | 1972 | |
	%	Seats	%	Seats	%	Seats	%	Seats
PvdA	28	43	24	37	25	39	27	43
KVP	32	50	27	42	22	35	18	27
ARP	9	13	10	15	9	13	9	14
CHU	9	13	8	12	6	10	5	7
VVD	10	16	11	17	10	16	14	22
D'66	-	-	5	7	7	11	4	6
CPN	3	4	4	5	4	6	5	7
SGP	2	3	2	3	2	3	2	3
GPV	1	1	1	1	2	2	2	2
PSP	3	4	3	4	1	2	2	2
BP	2	3	5	7	1	1	2	3
PPR	-	-	-	-	2	2	5	7
DS'70	-	-	-	-	5	8	4	6
NMP	-	-	-	-	2	2	0	0
RKPN	-	-	-	-	-	-	1	1
Other	1	-	2	-	2	-	0	-
		150		150		150		150
Turnout	95		95		79*		82	

* Compulsory voting ended in 1970.
Abbreviations:
PvdA   Labour Party
KVP   Catholic People's Party
ARP   Anti-Revolutionary Party
CHU   Christian Historical Union
VVD   People's Party for Freedom and Democracy (Liberals)
D'66   Democrats '66
SGP   Political Reformed Party (Calvinist)
PPR   Radical Party
CPN   Communist Party of the Netherlands
GPV   Reformed Political Union (Calvinist)
PSP   Pacifist Socialist Party
BP   Farmers' Party
DS'70   Democratic Socialists '70
NMP   Small Business Party
RKPN   Roman Catholic Party

strengths; only the ARP would hold its ground to gain a seat in 1972. What accounted for the precipitate drop in adherence to two of the three major confessional parties? Since the collapse of confessional dominance is the most dramatic event in modern Dutch politics, the exegetic literature is abundant.[26] An extensive exploration of the question forms part of Rudy Andeweg's thesis 'Dutch Voters Adrift'[27] In his second chapter 'The Religious Factor', he sets out a conceptual anatomy of the possible causes of confessional party decline, drawing clinical distinctions between demographic change, secularisation, a decline of religious orthodoxy and a detachment of voters from the pattern of *verzuiling*. An elaborate analysis of these various factors concludes: 'In general, however, the enormous increase in deconfessionalisation appears to be due to an erosion of religious orthodoxy, rather than to a wilt of the correlation between religious orthodoxy and voting for a religious party' (p. 70). This is a broad overall conclusion for there were variations between the denominational groups, and of course church attendance itself declined significantly. Also he separates the process of deconfessionalisation from the parallel developments of demographic change and secularisation (p. 41). But we can apply an elementary test to Andeweg's verdict by comparing two sets of data, one for church attendance and the other for the actual electoral performance of the religious parties. The figure for 'combined' church attendance in Table 3.9 is a purely statistical average. Nevertheless the overall drop in church attendance in this period, at 13%, is clearly very much smaller than the 30% overall loss of support by the main confessional parties.

Overall party topography

The first four post-war elections, in 1946, 1948, 1952 and 1956, all produced a Second Chamber with only seven parties represented, despite

Table 3.9
REGULAR CHURCH ATTENDANCE (*% of each denomination*)

	Roman Catholic	Hervormde	Gereformeerde	Combined
1966	86	50	95	77
1977	62	41	90	64

Source: Irwin (1980), pp. 210–11.

Table 3.10
PERCENTAGE OF VOTES WON BY MAJOR
CONFESSIONAL PARTIES

	CDA	KVP	CHU	ARP	TOTAL
1967		28	8	10	46
1977	32				32

the openness of the electoral system. These were the big five (Labour, Liberals and the three major confessionals) plus the Communists and the fundamentalist Calvinist SGP. By 1956 the two latter groups held jointly only six out of the 100 seats, which became ten out of 150 seats when the size of the Lower House was raised by 50%.[28] Thus during the reconstruction period, the five governing parties controlled over 90% of the House and settled between them the political agenda.

After 1956 this fixed spectrum began to refract more minutely. In 1957 an anti-NATO group formed the Pacifist Socialist Party (PSP) which won two seats in the 1959 national election. That same year, a Poujadist formation styled the Farmers' Party (Boerenpartij—BP) opened a campaign which took them into the Chamber with three seats in 1963, rising to seven seats in 1967. A further Calvinist fundamentalist group (GPV) also gained a parliamentary seat in 1963.

But it was in the 1967–71 parliament that the small party explosion was detonated. It began with the success of a new constitutional reform movement, Democrats '66 (D'66) which, the year after its foundation, achieved seven seats in the Lower House. By the end of the term four more groups had materialised: a breakaway confessional Radical Party (PPR), a dissident Labour faction, Democratic Socialists '70 (DS'70), and two ephemeral offshoots of the Farmers' Party. At the 1971 election the combined strength of the small parties vote reached 28.1%, the highest figure since 1918 and a significant barometer of voter volatility as the traditional pattern of *verzuiling* moved into its disintegrative phase.

The effects of this fragmentation of party support upon government formation and political strategy generally will be examined in the next chapter.

NOTES

1. See Blom (1977).
2. Kraemer (1966), pp. 54–5.
3. Scholten (1987).
4. Klein (1980), p. 7.
5. Griffiths (1980a), pp. 135–61.
6. Bank (1981), p. 211.
7. Abert (1969), p. 2, records that 'Between 1950 and 1960 the working population of the Netherlands increased by approximately 12%'.
8. Newton (1978), p. 147.
9. Andeweg *et. al.* (1980).
10. Lijphart (1968, 1975), p. 124.
11. Van Raalte (1959), p. 199.
12. Van Eijk (1980).
13. Abert (1969), p. 39.
14. See Windmuller (1969), Griffiths (1980) and Wolinetz (1983).
15. Lijphart (1968, 1975) van Schendelen (1984).
16. Griffiths (1980a), pp. 137–8.
17. Abert (1969), pp. 134–5.
18. Daudt (1982).
19. Windmuller (1969).
20. Ibid.
21. Gladdish (1983).
22. Bakvis (1981).
23. Wintle (1987).
24. Ibid.
25. Cited by Irwin (1980), p. 210.
26. See van Schendelen (1984).
27. Andeweg (1982).
28. Under the Constitutional Revision of 1956.

4

COMPETITIVE POLITICS

From about 1967 onwards . . . instead of the former rules of the game,
which served to manage or even suppress political conflict, party competition
came to be a main propellant of the political system
— W.E. Bakema and W.P. Secker, 'Ministerial Experience and the
Dutch Case' (1988), p. 162

The crisis of the latter 1960s

The decline of allegiance to the main confessional parties, the rise of new
parties and the inclination of the major secular parties towards clearer
choices within a more polarised system, all served to dislodge the old-
style politics of accommodation. From 1946 to 1963 the pattern of
electoral behaviour had congealed to a point where very little change
occurred from election to election, a position reinforced by the absence of
distortion which the electoral system guaranteed. With the exception of
a Liberal surge in 1959 which hoisted the party's holding in the Second
Chamber by nearly 50%, fluctuations in party strengths had been
relatively small throughout the period.

The loss of eight seats by the Catholic Party in the 1967 election,
which signified a drop in its national vote from 31.9% to 26.5%, was
therefore an unprecedentedly violent swing against a major party. But
this sudden downturn in popularity was not restricted to the KVP.
Labour also experienced a loss of six seats, and with the newly formed
D'66 acquiring seven seats in its first election, there were no
corresponding gains by the other members of the big five. Clearly it was
not merely the primacy of the Catholics which was being challenged.
Both the leading parties, one confessional and one secular, were being
squeezed, and the attraction of voters to new movements threatened the
grip of all the major contenders upon the system.

Despite the successes of corporatist reconstruction, indeed conceivably
because by the mid-1960s the Dutch economy was buoyant and the
population affluent as never before, the entire political system was
coming under severe scrutiny. In some ways it was a recrudescence of
disquiets voiced at the end of the war. Certainly the kinds of dissatisfaction which now surfaced, though clearly influenced by recent events,

50

in particular the governmental musical chairs in 1965 and 1966, had a long perspective.

This feature is well captured by the Appeal issued by the Initiating Committee of Democrats '66 which takes issue with aspects of the political structure going back, as the authors point out, to 1848. It is worth highlighting the most salient of the Appeal's contentions, because they achieved wide currency among intellectuals and percolated through the electorate, even though D'66 never became a massive movement. The starting point of the critique was the dichotomy between representation and government, which is spelled out in graphic terms:

The voters elect the Second Chamber of Parliament. Afterwards, the formation of a cabinet is initiated. You, being the voter, have no influence whatsoever on that formation. No influence with regard to the composition of the government, no influence on its program. Suppose you vote for the Catholic People's Party. With what other parties will KVP form a government? With the Labour party? With the Liberals? With one of the two major protestant parties? Will the new government have a mainly socialist, conservative or religious character? At the time of voting you have no certainty on that point. . . . Only this is certain: the program of the government, which will decide our fate in the next few years, comes into being without any influence or participation by the voters.[1]

The document goes on to attack the atmosphere of compromise surrounding the operations of multi-party government, which it links with lack of principles, unaccountability and an arthritic response to 'unexpected situations'. It then takes issue with the supineness of MPs whose parties participate in the cabinet. This is an interesting angle in a system where cabinet and parliament are less closely aligned than in most European counterparts, though a familiar enough concern to British students of parliament.

The second major onslaught was upon the electoral system. Here three objectionable attributes are discerned: the anonymity of candidates within a list method of national PR; the absence of close, or indeed any perceptible links between MPs and their 'constituents', and what is perceived as 'one big, misty uniformity' which blurs the real distinctions between parties contending for office. The catalogue of defects was a formidable one with implications which resonated through the entire political culture. For the system had attained the qualities now under attack in response to a complex matrix of conditions. Parts of the indictment refer inevitably to problems which seem inseparable from responsible parliamentary government.[2] But undoubtedly Dutch practice was ceasing to commend itself to the more critical of its subjects. Two solutions were put forward to these dilemmas by the initiators of D'66. One was that the Minister-President should be directly elected through a second ballot procedure; the other was that the list method of PR should be replaced by a district or constituency system, conceivably multi-member. The fate of these proposals will be discussed in Chapter 6. What is of interest about them is that they sought by constitutional means to effect radical changes in the way that politics was carried on at national level. Such faith in instrumental solutions, and relatively simple ones at that, could perhaps be regarded as characteristic of the strange combination of scepticism and optimism which made the 1960s so exhilarating.

Labour's response to the crisis

In the 1956 election, Labour, having been in government for more than a decade, won a third of the seats in the Lower House. In each of the three subsequent elections Labour lost ground to reach a low point of thirty-seven seats in 1967, by which year it had been out of office for most of the previous decade. Clearly some re-appraisal of party strategy had become pressing. It was in these circumstances that a movement emerged within the party under the label 'New Left', which took its bearings from a series of publications by younger activists.[3] A discerning account of the 'New Left' phenomenon is given by Wolinetz in his survey of the Dutch Labour Party, compiled in the 1970s.[4] He points out that the movement, perhaps better viewed as a tendency, operated as 'a loose and somewhat fluid collection of individuals who met regularly, wrote books and made public pronouncements'. From 1966 on it gained influence within the party's executive, urging a variety of measures which were intended to sharpen Labour's image, and to revive earlier, more radical aspirations towards greater social and economic equality. When the programme of New Left was subsequently described to this author by several of its promoters,[5] the greatest emphasis was put upon the idea of democratisation both within the PvdA and throughout public life. This undoubtedly coincided with the ambitions of younger party members who believed the old guard to be out of touch with social change, hence the party's somewhat depressing electoral performance during the 1960s.

As Wolinetz observes, the protagonists of New Left tended to come from more intellectual occupations than many of the party's older figures. In 1970 a group of the latter broke away from the PvdA to form the more conservative Democratic Socialists '70, which acquired as its leader the son of Labour's former doyen, Willem Drees. Despite this split, the PvdA did slightly better in the 1971 election, and better still in 1972 when, as the dominant party within a 'progressive alliance', it eventually regained office.

The 1971 election (see Table 3.8) provides a useful vantage-point from which to assess the Dutch party system, after the turmoil of the 1960s, on what seemed to be the threshold of a more adversarial style of politics.[6] In 1969 the Labour Party congress, under New Left pressure, had resolved that the party should not henceforth enter into cabinet coalitions with the Catholic People's Party. In part this was a delayed response to the humilation of 'the night of Schmelzer' in 1966, when the KVP parliamentary group forced Labour out of government. More conceptually it was a commitment to a form of polarisation which many on the left had hoped for as long ago as 1945. This time it was believed that the climate was right for a more radical reorientation of the approach to both electoral competition and cabinet formation. The former highly stable deferential social order which had reflected *verzuiling*, and had both underlain and underpinned the traditional politics of accommodation, was apparently giving way to a more fluid, critical style of social and political behaviour. In these circumstance it seemed possible to revert to the ambitions which had accompanied the early phase of socialist mobilisation before 1914. In that period it had been hoped, indeed assumed, that the socialist party could succeed in mobilising the great mass of lower-income voters, thus undermining the basis of support for both the Catholics and the Anti-Revolutionaries.

From 1970, Labour therefore sought alliances with other left of centre parties, at both local and national levels, in order to increase its leverage upon the system. In both the 1971 and 1972 elections this took the form of a pact with D'66 and the PPR, with a joint programme and a 'shadow cabinet' which was symptomatic of the idea of an alternative government. The odds against achieving an outright secular, left of centre majority in parliament were still extremely high. In the 1971–2 Second Chamber, the entire holding of this segment, including the Communists, totalled only sixty seats against a centre and right with ninety. Nevertheless the strategy of the 'progressive alliance' was maintained, even though influential Labour politicians, including some ex-New Left luminaries, remained convinced that a rapprochement with the confessionals, above all the Catholics, would still be indispensable if Labour wished to regain office.[7]

In the event the forcing apart of the traditional mould proved as difficult as many had foreseen. The 'progressive alliance', under the Labour leader den Uyl, emerged as the largest grouping after the 1972 election but it still held only fifty-six seats out of 150. After what, at that point, was a record formation period of 163 days[8] the resulting cabinet was an elaborate patchwork of parties, two of which, the KVP and ARP, provided ministers who had only qualified support from their parliamentary groups. Labour filled seven of the fifteen ministries; but the policy of not collaborating with the Catholic party had had to be discarded for inexorable logistic reasons.

The confessional response

In the election of 1972, the Anti-Revolutionary vote held up but both the KVP and CHU sustained further heavy losses. The idea of a merger of the confessional trio had first been mooted in a KVP report as early as 1966. It now began to assume the proportions of a life-raft in an increasingly hostile sea. Before the 1971 election, leading figures in the Catholic party were prepared to advocate some form of fusion with the two Calvinist parties, looking to the examples of Christian Democrat parties elsewhere in Europe, particularly those with a strongly Catholic complexion.[9] In the months preceding the 1972 election, a joint committee of the three parties published a report which recommended the formation of a non-confessional Christian party. The following year, despite divergent positions within the trio, each party convention resolved upon unification. After two further years of arduous discussion, an all-party convention under the banner of the Christian Democratic Appeal was held in August 1975. Again there were setbacks in the delineation of a common approach. But for the 1977 election a single programme was adopted, together with a common list leader – van Agt of the former KVP. This marked the demise of separate major confessional parties. The final stages of amalgamation were completed in 1980, by which point ministers with the label CDA had been in office in coalition with the Liberals for three years.

A full analysis of the process, complications and consequences of the confessional amalgamation would capsize any summary of developments in Dutch politics during the 1970s and '80s.[10] For there is no question that it has been by far the most important event in the evolution of the party system during this period. On the issue of how inevitable was the merger, two diametrically different positions can be taken. The first would point to the long history of political, albeit often uneasy, co-operation between the major religious movements going back to the Mackay cabinet of 1888. This co-operation deepened after the 'pacification' of 1915–17 which settled the schools question, brought in universal suffrage and introduced national PR. It survived the Second World War and was firmly embedded in the political culture by the time the turbulence of the 1960s shook the foundations of that culture. In these terms unification can be seen as a logical step and the natural fulfilment of generations of close collaboration. And since non-denominational Christian parties were, by the 1970s, well established elsewhere, there could be little of a case to argue on the grounds of ideological incongruity.

But this long era of collaboration between the Catholic and the two principal Calvinist parties represented co-operation at élite levels only, whether municipal, provincial or national. The great mass of Catholics and Calvinists has been mobilised into entirely separate, indeed hermetic networks which constituted the most solid pillars of the *verzuiling* system. So long as these sub-cultural divisions endured, the whole concept of a unified Christian Democratic movement was hopelessly at odds with the social facts. The demise of *verzuiling* as a dominant feature of Dutch society was therefore indispensable to any all-purpose, throughgoing amalgamation of the parties. So the notion of a long historical prelude to merger was misleading. This was confirmed by the evidence that the religious dimensions of *verzuiling* had not been calmly dismantled by community leaders, but had instead been overtaken by the pressure of social change. What followed at the party level was therefore a largely pragmatic response to events, most of them highly negative in the shape of election losses. On this view amalgamation, far from crowning generations of harmony, could be thought likely to engender immense strain and difficulty below élite level.

The definitive account of this process, almost a decade after complete amalgamation, has still to be compiled. But there is no doubt that from the vantage point of the late 1980s, the establishment of the CDA has rescued the former confessionals from a grave deterioration of popular support and conceivably eventual demise. The verdict could not have been so confident (and it may yet be overtaken by future events) before the Appeal's election triumphs, under the leadership of Ruud Lubbers, in 1986 and 1989. For the CDA's performance in the two preceding elections, in 1981 and 1982, showed a continuing erosion of support. What appears to have happened is that after a period of ambivalence, the

Appeal has been able to assume the role of a popular centre party which can attract voters of no confessional orientation, including new young electors. Given the continuing dynamics of the Dutch party system, a strong centre movement is *ipso facto* in a dominating position, even thought it may only command a third of the parliamentary seats.

Table 4.1
ELECTIONS TO THE SECOND CHAMBER, 1977–89

	1977		1981		1982		1986		1989	
	%	Seats	%	Seats	%	Seats	%	Seats	%	Seats
PvdA	33.8	53	28.2	44	30.4	47	33.3	52	31.9	49
CDA	31.9	49	30.8	48	29.3	45	34.6	54	35.3	54
VVD	17.9	28	17.3	26	23.1	36	17.4	27	14.6	22
D'66	5.4	8	11.0	17	4.3	6	6.1	9	7.9	12
PPR	1.7	3	2.0	3	1.6	2	1.3	2		
CPN	1.7	2	2.1	3	1.8	3	0.6	0	4.1*	6*
PSP	0.9	1	2.1	3	2.2	3	1.2	1		
EVP	–	–	0.5	0	0.7	1	0.2	0		
SGP	2.1	3	2.0	3	1.9	3	1.8	3	1.9	3
GPV	1.0	1	0.8	1	0.8	1	1.0	1	1.2	2
BP	0.8	1	0.2	0	–	–	–	–	–	–
DS'70	0.7	1	0.6	0	–	–	–	–	–	–
RPF	–	–	1.2	2	1.5	2	0.9	1	1.0	1
CP	–	–	0.1	0	0.8	1	0.4	0	0.9†	1†
Turnout	87.6		86.1		80.6		85.7		80.1	

* Joint list as 'Green Left'.
† Renamed *'Janmaat'*.

Abbreviations:

PvdA	Labour Party
CDA	Christian Democratic Appeal
VVD	People's Party for Freedom and Democracy (Liberals)
D'66	Democrats '66
SGP	Political Reformed Party (Calvinist)
PPR	Radical Party
CPN	Communist Party of the Netherlands
GPV	Reformed Political Union (Calvinist)
PSP	Pacifist Socialist Party
BP	Farmers' Party
DS'70	Democratic Socialists '70
RPF	Reformed Political Federation (Calvinist)
EVP	Evangelical People's Party (Calvinist)
CP	Centre Party (Ultra-Right)

The Liberal ascent

The third element in an account of the emergence of more competitive politics since the late 1960s is the performance of the Liberal party. The history of Liberal politics in the Netherlands has much in common with that of the rest of Northern Europe since the mid-nineteenth century. As the secular, constitutionalist élite within the parliamentary arena, politicians of liberal persuasions had presided over the process of democratisation, beginning with the establishment of complete religious freedom and equality, and culminating in the introduction of modern concepts of welfare. They had, however, tended to do this *de haut en bas*, subtending a grandee image and being reluctant to convert their operations into those of a mass-based movement. From the end of the period of Liberal governments in 1918 to the Second World War, Liberal political groups had been fragmented and peripheral to the major national campaigns. Only in 1948 were the various strands gathered up into a concerted party – the People's Party for Freedom and Democracy (VVD) under the leadership of P.J. Oud. Although thereby unifying the secular right of centre position, the party was at that stage unable to attract more than 8% of the national vote. It made little advance on this until the end of the 1950s, and no consolidated progress until the early 1970s.

The absence of a conservative party in the Netherlands, plus the existence of a confessional right-wing, presented the Liberals for much of the post-war period with a problem of party space. This was compounded by a dual persona which combined a humanitarian outlook on social matters with a pro-employer position in economic affairs. The party leadership, until the early 1970s, was marked by a patrician style which served to inhibit the attraction of new or younger voters. The party's fortunes thus remained somewhat static until the emergence of more populist leaders, notably Hans Wiegel who took over the VVD in 1972.

Such leverage as the VVD possessed was a result of the need of the confessional grouping to offset the pressure of the PvdA to be included in cabinet coalitions. Thus from 1959 on, the exclusion of Labour from government meant admitting the Liberals, who for most of the period up to 1973 held three ministries in successive cabinets. Despite this dependence, the Liberal leadership at the beginning of the 1970s welcomed the strategy of polarisation.[11] For if the confessionals had entered a period of possibly terminal decline, it would have made little sense for their perennial minor partner on the centre-right to maintain an affection for the *status quo*.

From the mid-1970s, the commitments of an all-providing state began to be questioned almost throughout the political spectrum. The chief beneficiary of this tide of opinion was to be the VVD. By 1982, the party had increased its share of the vote to 24% and was able to deal with the CDA on almost equal terms. The rise of the Liberals, therefore, in the period of competitive politics compares in significance with the re-marshalling of the confessional forces. Indeed the two processes became fused from 1977 on as a pattern of two-party government, CDA–VVD, moved into centre stage as the most likely outcome of successive elections. The model was dented only briefly in 1981–2, when the combination failed by two seats to achieve a majority in the Second Chamber. But it was rapidly re-asserted after the 1982 election and re-affirmed in 1986, even though the distribution of seats had swung heavily in favour of the CDA. In 1989, however, the partnership was not resumed and the Liberals left the cabinet.

New-style governing

The post-1972 period in Dutch national politics was marked by more than a change in the party configuration and its effects upon parliamentary arithmetic. The formation of the 'progressive alliance' in 1971, by the PvdA and its smaller allies, projected on to the screen a new signal to the electorate. This was not merely the heightening of inter-party, or rather inter-bloc competition, nor simply the quest for a clearer polarisation of ideologies. It was additionally a bid to seek an entirely novel way of conferring authority in a hitherto accommodationist system; an attempt to acquire a specific mandate to govern.

Under the circumstances of *verzuiling* such an endeavour would have breached the understandings between the élites who headed the several pillars. It would also have been essentially futile. For given the logistics of party support, only carefully assembled cross-party coalitions could hope to command parliamentary assent. This was why neither the confessionals nor the major secular parties could commit themselves before an election to any precise formula for the composition of the succeeding cabinet, a feature which D'66 had focussed upon in its catalogue of the defects of the system. Once a cabinet had been formed, however, it could be reasonably assured of a parliamentary majority for its programme, which represented the final compromise between the election platforms of the governing parties. The process of cabinet-making was, traditionally, determined largely by the preferences of the parliamentary managers, who habitually saw ministers as delegates rather than policy-makers. Hence cabinet posts went often to second-rank party figures or even outsiders, while the group leaders in the Second Chamber retained their control of the political agenda.

The practice of staffing cabinets with ministers whose connections with their parliamentary party was often tenuous, was vividly illustrated by Lijphart in the mid 1960s. In a by now well-publicised passage he pointed out that 'Of the 334 ministers between 1848 and 1958 almost half never served in parliament . . . [and] only slightly more than a third had prior experience in parliament.'[12] His comment on this feature was that it was 'based not on constitutional provisions but on informal, but nonetheless deeply ingrained political practice'. For the past half-century, however, this 'semi-separation' of cabinet members from parliament has been constitutionalised. Since 1938 cabinet ministers have been debarred by law from taking up or retaining parliamentary seats, and since 1948 their deputies (State Secretaries) have also been excluded. Ministers may attend parliament and speak in debates; but they have no vote and cannot be members of either chamber.

The managerial dimension of old-style cabinet-making was explained to the author by an eminent former leader of a major parliamentary group.[13] A group leader for a decade (1952–62), and therefore closely involved in successive cabinet formations, he had never proposed himself for a cabinet post. His reasoning was that as a parliamentary figure he could speak on any topic and retain freedom of manoevre on any issue; whereas a cabinet post, in his view, 'removed' a person from the arena of politics.

The traditional habit of placing the cabinet at some distance from the parliamentary coming and going had a variety of consequences. One was that entering parliament was merely one form of political ambition, and by no means the sole route to public office. Another was that parties were able to 'survive' the performances of their ministers. Ineffective or unpopular ministers could be dropped without grave risks; even the collapse of a cabinet could leave the parliamentary forces unshaken. Thus new coalitions could be assembled without further recourse to the electorate, a facility which had become the target of widespread criticism by the latter 1960s.

In 1971 this approach to cabinet-making was departed from when four parliamentary leaders – Geertsema (VVD), Schmelzer (KVP), Udink (CHU) and Drees (DS'70) – entered the Biesheuvel cabinet. In 1973 there was a further development when the Labour leader, Joop den Uyl, took most of his first team into the cabinet with himself as Minister-President. By the 1970s, therefore, it could be said that a new style of government had been inaugurated. Of the many consequences, one was to re-instate the notion of continuity at prime-ministerial level. This, under very different circumstances, had been a feature of both the inter-war period and the 1950s. But from 1959–71, Minister-Presidents, none of them formerly party leaders, had each served only one term or less and been regarded as disposable by their party when a new cabinet came to be formed. Den Uyl's two successors, van Agt (1977–82) and Lubbers (1982 to date) both campaigned at elections from a prime-ministerial vantage point, appealing to voters explicitly on the basis of the advantages of continuity of leadership. On each occasion this approach was vindicated; they were empowered to continue in office.

Party competition in the 1980s

The amalgamation of the confessional trio and the rise of the Liberals as the embodiment of the secular right, converged after the 1977 election in the formation of the first two-party government of the modern period. The new streamlined coalition was, however, only assembled after prolonged negotiations between the CDA and Labour – who had made an unprecedented gain of ten seats after four years in office – failed to result in an agreement. Explanations for the failure have been offered by commentators in a variety of terms. Uneasy relations between the two party leaders, den Uyl and van Agt, may have played some part in the

Table 4.2
CABINET COMPOSITION, 1973–89

	Prime minister	Ministries			
1973–7	den Uyl	*PvdA(7)	KVP(4)	ARP(2)	D'66(1) PPR(1)
1977–81	van Agt	*CDA(10)	VVD(6)		
1981–2	van Agt	*CDA(6)	PvdA(6)	D'66(3)	
1982 (May–Nov.)	van Agt	*CDA(10)	D'66(5)		
1982–6	Lubbers	*CDA(8)	VVD(6)		
1986–9	Lubbers	*CDA(9)	VVD(5)		
1989–	Lubbers	*CDA(7)	PvdA(7)		

* Party of the Prime Minister.

debacle, since the logic of an alliance between the two forces seemed compelling.

A review of the apparent preferences of voters suggested over-whelming support for a centre-left coalition (60%), as against a CDA-VVD combination (34%).[14] But there were other elements at work. Since Labour had achieved what could be regarded as a landslide, its claims to office seemed irresistible. This very fact, however, seemed to produce a boomerang effect. Analysing the situation from the standpont of tensions within the PvdA between middle and top élites, van Mierlo concludes that the former used Labour's success 'as an argument to press political demands on the CDA.'[15] He sees this as a major factor in turning the CDA leadership away from a deal to its left, in favour of an ostensibly less threatening combination with the Liberals. The latter had also made striking gains in the election, from twenty-two to twenty-eight seats, hence the capacity for a majority centre-right coalition. But the VVD could still be treated as less than an equal partner by a Christian Democrat group with forty-nine seats.

Whatever the most apt exegesis, there can be no doubt that the alliance between the CDA and the Liberals proved a crucial turning point in the complexion of recent politics, for it shifted the balance manifestly to the right. It is in the context of that shift that the electoral contests of the 1980s must be viewed.

The 1981 election

Somewhat against the odds, given a formal majority of only four seats and the presence of dissenting MPs within the CDA parliamentary group, the centre-right cabinet assembled in 1977 managed to survive for a full parliamentary term. During its period of office, the government faced deteriorating economic conditions and the controversial issue of whether or not to accept the installation of Cruise missiles made its unwelcome appearance on the political agenda. In the latter stages of the administration, the government found itself relying on the support of the small religious parties.

Given all the circumstances, the 1981 election campaign might have been expected to generate considerable inter-party hostility.[16] But the leading opposition parties – Labour and D'66 – were reluctant to antagonise the CDA, since their return to office would depend upon successful negotiations with the pivotal cabinet-forming party. The one clear-cut divergence between the major party programmes was on the missile question. The PvdA rejected their installation outright, whereas the VVD committed itself to their acceptance – with a token caveat about Soviet arms reductions. But this was a permissible disagreement between parties which were unlikely to have to serve together. The crucial pre-poll question was whether the CDA-VVD coalition could retain its slender majority. This it failed, by two seats, to do. After the election, which saw Labour lose nine seats but D'66 soar from eight to seventeen MPs, the crucial question was which way the latter party would go. Would it augment the previous coalition, which would mean it moving to the right, or would it be the catalyst of a new combination involving Labour and the CDA? After 108 days of negotiation the second option was the outcome; and an uneasy tripartite cabinet took office in September 1981 with van Agt continuing as Prime Minister.

This precarious dénouement harked back in many ways to the instabilities of the early 1970s. The CDA, now fully amalgamated, was having difficulty holding its ground within the electorate, its vote nearly 100,000 down on 1977. The Liberals, after two highly successful contests, had slipped back two seats, while Labour had been shorn of almost all its 1977 gains. Only D'66 and three of the smaller parties (one, the RPF, newly formed) had made gains. It seemed an open question whether the party system was to plunge back into uncertainty, or whether the 1981 election was aberrant in terms of the evolution of medium-term stability.

The prospect of three-party government with a left of centre inflection failed to crystallise. A mere five weeks after taking office the Labour ministers quitted the cabinet in a dispute over fiscal policy. A nervous reconciliation brought them back for a while until, in May 1982, the Labour ministers refused to agree to certain cuts in public spending and the cabinet broke up. Two months earlier, in the provincial elections, Labour had returned a dismal performance losing second place overall to the Liberals. It was with some confidence, therefore, that Premier van Agt sought a dissolution of parliament (only the third since the war) and set new elections for September 1982.

The 1982 election

After a mere fifteen months since the previous contest, the issues faced by the parties had changed little, given that the three-party coalition had achieved virtually nothing in terms of policy initiatives. Resort to the verdict of the people as a way out of the governmental impasse seemed therefore something of a gamble upon greater volatility than was comfortable. Labour faced the voters with little to offer in terms of constructive cabinet-forming, since it had demonstrated beyond all possible doubt that it could not work with the CDA under its existing management. But it was D'66 who found itself in the dock, its ministers having chosen not to leave the cabinet with Labour but to stay with van Agt until the election. Only the Liberals had clean hands – for which, if the decisions of voters constitute any form of approval, they were richly rewarded.

In 1981, after a four year gap between elections, twenty-eight seats out of the complement of 150 in the Second Chamber were redistributed. Little more than a year later thirty seats were reapportioned. The outstanding beneficiary was the VVD, which increased its vote from 17 to 23% of the poll and gained ten seats – its highest score since 1918. Despite all prognostications Labour recovered three seats. The two losers were the CDA (three seats) and, more resoundingly, D'66 whose vote fell from 11% in 1981 to 4.3%. The new arithmetic pointed inexorably to a restoration of the former CDA-VVD coalition , and after a mere eight weeks of negotiation a new centre-right cabinet took office in November 1982. Both the governing parties were now under new management. Ruud Lubbers had succeeded van Agt as the CDA list-leader and now became Prime Minister. The new Liberal leader Ed Nijpels chose to stay in parliament as chairman of the *fractie*. The VVD's success at the polls had put the party on an almost equal footing with the CDA whose support had ebbed to less than 30% of the total vote. Six portfolios were filled by the Liberals and eight by the CDA, each party having eight state secretaries.

The formula of centre-right government, which had emerged so uneasily from the protracted negotiations after the 1977 election, had now been far more firmly re-instated. Labour, though the largest single party, took on an air of isolation within the system, and seemed condemned to a prolonged period out of office. Over the next three and a half years, the Lubbers cabinet made a resolute effort to take a grip on fiscal policy. A public sector deficit of 14% in 1982 was reduced 8% by 1986. Measures to lessen the cost of government included a 3% cut in civil service salaries in 1984, and the burgeoning bill for social security was contained by successive freezes of the rates of benefit. Endeavours were, however, made to protect the lower-paid, and income tax was made slightly more progressive. By March 1986, the generically pessimistic compilers of OECD reports were prepared to concede that 'in many respects the economy is now in a better position than four years ago.'[17]

By the end of the government's term, however, there remained perplexing problems. Despite cabinet undertakings to take steps to reduce unemployment, it had climbed to a rate of 15% of the potential workforce. A backlash was feared over the eventual decision to deploy Cruise missiles. Chernobyl had cast a cloud over proposals to expand the civil nuclear energy programme. The performance of several Liberal ministers had aroused criticism, and the government had been gravely embarrassed by a long-running scandal over grants to a private company, RSV of Rotterdam. So the centre-right coalition faced the 1986 election with a mixed record and uncertain expectations of the likely outcome, though the two governing parties were resolved to stay in office if they retained a joint majority.

The 1986 election

The two principal issues on which the election programmes of the major parties focussed were unemployment and nuclear matters.[18] The governing parties placed much emphasis on the evidence of economic recovery as a favourable prognosis for creating more jobs. Labour, as the leading party of opposition, but with ambitions to enter government, struck a cautious note on unemployment, supporting a reduced working week but avoiding a commitment to heavy public expenditure on job creation. The Cruise missile problem, though figuring prominently in party manifestos, had been settled on the eve of the election by a parliamentary vote in favour of deployment. This left the question of civil nuclear energy on which Labour took a hostile stand.

On the day before polling the leading sampling agencies gave the governing parties a slightly less than even chance of securing a majority, largely because of the Liberal showing in the polls.[19] Since the CDA's record in the preceding three elections had been one of gradual attrition, it seemed unlikely that it could offset any Liberal losses.

Twelve parties had been represented in the Second Chamber prior to the election, three of which, when the polls closed on 21 May 1986, failed to reach the threshold of 0.67% of the vote. These were the CPN, EVP and the Centre Party. The fate of the Communist Party, which lost all three former seats, was without precedent in post-war elections. Of the nine parties which now secured seats, the outstanding winners were the CDA, which raised its holding from forty-five to fifty-four seats, and the PvdA which rose from forty-seven seats to fifty-two. Labour had expected to make substantial gains, but the performance of the CDA exceeded all expectations and for the first time appeared, by attracting non-confessional voters, to vindicate the strategy of confessional amalgamation. D'66 was the only other party to improve on its 1982 score. The VVD, with a drop of nine seats, suffered a severe reverse which interrupted fifteen years of Liberal ascent in the polls.

The overall pattern of votes showed considerable switching between the CDA and the other major ·parties.[20] One-third of the CDA's increased vote came from electors who had voted Liberal in 1982. The CDA also attracted many new votes (23% of its gains) as did the PvdA (25% of its increase). Almost one quarter of Labour's increased vote came from former supporters of the smaller left parties, while D'66 took the highest proportion of its gains from Labour (32%). These movements can be distilled into a set of shifts – from the VVD to the CDA, from Labour to D'66, and from the further left to Labour – each of which represents a move towards a more centrist position.

In the broader terms of the rise and fall of electoral support over time, three features of the 1986 election are worth comment. The first is that Labour came within one seat of its best-ever result – in 1977. This was however overshadowed by the striking success of the CDA which represented the first significant advance of the Christian grouping since the 1960s, and made the CDA the largest party in the Second Chamber. The third feature was the Liberal setback.

The election outcome enabled the CDA and VVD to re-form their cabinet coalition with an unchanged majority of twelve seats over the other parties. The balance between the partners had however changed, and this was reflected in the 9–5 allocation of portfolios in favour of the CDA, as against 8–6 in the previous parliament. The process of cabinet formation was relatively swift and the new government took office on 14 July 1986.

Developments after 1986

The 1986 election appeared to consolidate a sequence of development which, over almost a decade, had created a bias towards centre-right government. Superficially this could be seen as analogous to the pattern of the 1960s, which also yielded confessional–Liberal cabinets. But the character of the components had changed profoundly. Instead of a trio of denominational parties, two of which were progressively losing their grip on their constituencies, a new supra-denominational entity, the CDA, had now recovered the centre ground. Also, instead of being a minor accessory to confessional government the Liberals had become a major party, able to impart a strong free market inflection to public policy.

The confessionals, with their deep communitarian instincts, had been a vital element in the establishment of a comprehensive welfare state in the Netherlands. As a generalised Christian Democrat force, shorn of much of the associational baggage of *verzuiling*, the erstwhile confessionals were now prepared to countenance a less collectivist approach to socio-economic problems. This left the Labour Party, as in Britain, in a more vulnerable position as the political tide turned against social-democratic solutions.

But Dutch cabinets still remained coalitions, with at times somewhat uneasy relations between the governing parties so that parliamentary groups did not always feel obliged to adhere rigidly to the coalition geometry. In September 1986 a proposal of the CDA Minister for Education to raise the age at which elementary schooling should begin was defeated in the Second Chamber. And in May 1987 the Liberal parliamentary group voted with Labour in support of a motion calling for the publication of the forecasts of the Central Planning Bureau. Tensions were evident within the second Lubbers cabinet, and between the cabinet and its respective parliamentary groups. At the VVD party Congress at Leeuwarden in May 1987, the Liberal parliamentary leader, Voorhoeve, spoke openly of rifts in the coalition. The CDA parliamentary leader, de Vries, recurrently expressed, during 1987, his dissatisfaction with government policies *vis-à-vis* the economy and called for more energetic action to reduce unemployment.[21] Also there were various administrative scandals involving, *inter alia*, the issue of a new-type passport and housing subsidies.

These examples symptomatize the generic relations between government and parliament in the Netherlands. The semi-separation between the two, which Lijphart characterised in the late 1960s,[22] has survived the multiple changes over the past generation just as the centripetal geometry of the party spectrum continues to mitigate against the emergence of an adversarial system. What has not changed at all is the scale of operations; for within a relatively small legislature there is equal scope for close personal relations regardless of party, and for highly personal rivalry and discord. Such features help to maintain flexibility and uncertainty, and thus keep open the propects of fresh alignments in both the short and long term.

The 1989 election

As the last section has illustrated, strains in the CDA-VVD coalition had been evident at various points since its re-instatement in 1986. But such tensions are rarely absent from cabinet coalitions and seemed unlikely to unseat the government before the end of the term in 1990. On 2 May 1989 however, the Liberal parliamentary leader, Joris Voorhoeve, raised objections to an item in a major long-term plan for environmental improvement. The plan had been agreed in cabinet and endorsed by the Environment Minister, Ed Nijpels, himself a former VVD *fractie* chairman. The matter might well have been dealt with as a minor disagreement. Instead the Prime Minister used the occasion to dissolve parliament and call fresh elections for September.

The strategies of the protagonists – Voorhoeve and Lubbers – seemed unclear, even to their supporters. The Liberals stood to gain little electoral advantage from a narrow dispute – essentially over the removal of tax relief from cars used on journeys to work. At the same time, the CDA premier appeared to show little inclination for a change of coalition partner. There was also the probability that a premature election in late summer would not arouse great enthusiasm on the part of voters. This was compounded by the reluctance of the major parties to offer controversial manifestos. Only on the environment front was there a significant divergence, with the Liberals opting for passing pollution costs on to the consumer, while the other formations proposed that the polluter should pay.

Apart from the voters' reactions to the government's record, the only interesting question was whether the election would trigger a change in the make-up of the next cabinet. It was generally thought by the pollsters that the CDA would remain the largest party, which would give Lubbers the key voice in determing its coalition partner or partners[23] One scenario canvassed by press and television pundits was a grand coalition of the CDA, PvdA and D'66; but the auspices for this were unimpressive given the experience of 1981–2.

On election day doubts about the turnout were confirmed; at 80.1% it was the second-lowest since the war.[24] All three major parties collected fewer votes than in 1986. The CDA was down by a mere 1% and its share of the poll was slightly up, enabling it to maintain its holding of fifty-four seats. Labour's vote fell by 7%, reducing its seats in the Second Chamber from fifty-two to forty-nine. But the biggest loser, as in 1986, was the VVD, which lost 13% of its previous support and dropped to

twenty-two seats – its poorest result since 1972. The eight seats shed by
the Liberals and the PvdA went to D'66 (up by three seats to twelve), the
Green Left alliance (up by three seats to six) the GPV (up from one seat to
two) and *Janmaat*, which won one seat.[25]

Altogether sixteen seats were redistributed (see Table 4.3), compared
with a total of thirty-four seats in 1986. The resulting arithmetic allowed
for two principal alternative outcomes: a CDA-PvdA coalition (always
available at previous elections, though not attempted since the CDA's
inauguration); or a restoration of the previous CDA-VVD cabinet with
a bare majority in the Chamber of seventy-six seats to seventy-four. The
complex pattern of voter movement between the parties showed D'66 to
be the chief beneficiary of Labour's losses while, as in 1986, the CDA
picked up a majority of Liberal defectors.[26] But the spread of gains within
the party spectrum was, to say the least, bewildering from the standpoint
of whether the election had benefited the left or the right.

Yet again the evidence underlines the fact that the Dutch party system
is not a linear progression from left to right. Instead it has two main
axes – secular and confessional – with a lesser third dimension of
sectarian fragmentation.[27] These divisions still retain a significant
regional expression. The CDA, in 1989, drew proportionately more
support from its traditional Catholic heartland of Limburg and North
Brabant, in the south, and from the Calvinist concentration in
Overijssel. Labour, similarly, gained its best results in its long-time
northern stronghold of Groningen, Drenthe and Friesland. The Liberals
were most successful in North and South Holland and Utrecht, a pattern
closely paralleled by D'66.[28]

The task of government formation was begun with the appointment
of Lubbers as *informateur*. The main discussions took place between the
CDA and Labour, and the prospects of either VVD or D'66 participation were successively eliminated. By the third week of October, a
draft coalition agreement had been drawn up. The new cabinet would
consist of an equal number of CDA and PvdA ministers, under the

Table 4.3
SEATS GAINED AND LOST ACROSS PARTY SPECTRUM, 1989

Green Left	PvdA	D'66	CDA	VVD	Calvinist Sectarian	Far Right
+ 3	– 3	+ 3	0	– 5	+ 1	+ 1

premiership of Mr Lubbers, with Wim Kok, the Labour parliamentary leader, as Minister of Finance. The new government was installed on 7 November 1989.

It represented a fresh stage in the sequence of governing coalitions since the war, and brought to an end the long period (effectively twelve years, setting aside the fiasco of 1981–2) in which Labour had been out of office. It signified less a lively accord between the Christian Democrats and the PvdA than a conviotion on the part of the former than the partnership with the Liberals had ceased to be fruitful. The new coalition also signified a re-balancing of centre-dominated government, demonstrating that the traditional flexibility of the Christian centre had not been abandoned in the prolonged era of centre-right rule.

NOTES

1. Extract from the English version of the D'66 Appeal.
2. See Gladdish (1972).
3. The most celebrated of these publications was *Tien Over Rood* (1966), compiled by a young economist, van den Doel. Its literal meaning is Ten over Red, a term in billiards.
4. In Paterson and Thomas (1979).
5. Interviews by the author with van den Doel and van der Louw (PvdA Chairman), June 1971.
6. See Gladdish (1987).
7. Interviews by the author with Vondeling (former PvdA Chairman) and van Lier (Secretary PvdA parliamentary group), June 1971.
8. Andeweg *et al.* (1980), pp. 237–8.
9. This was attested in interviews by the author with KVP leaders, including Schmelzer (Parliamentary Party Chairman) in April 1971. But it was already a matter of open discourse.
10. There is little in English about the confessional amalgamation, except for conference papers. See papers given at the ECPR Salzburg Workshops 1984 by van Mierlo, Pijnenberg and de Jong.
11. Interview by the author with Geertsema (VVD Parliamentary Party Chairman) April 1971.
12. Lijphart (1968, 1975), p. 135.
13. Interview by the author with J. Burger (former PvdA Parliamentary Party Chairman) April 1971.
14. Foppen (1983) reported by van Mierlo (1986).
15. Van Mierlo (1986).
16. See van Mierlo (1981).

17. *OECD Economic Survey of the Netherlands*, 1986, p. 55.
18. Gladdish (1987a).
19. De Hond (1986), TROS/NSS and NIPO. See *Algemeen Dagblad* 20 May 1986.
20. Intromart Exit Poll analysed by Andeweg and Irwin in *De Volkskrant*, 22 May 1986.
21. These instances have been culled from the Dutch press, 1986–7.
22. Lijphart (1968, 1975).
23. The *NRC Handelsblad* of September 6 reported a late opinion poll which gave the CDA a maximum of 56 seats, as against 52 for Labour.
24. The lowest (79%) was in 1971 at the first election after the abolition of compulsory voting, in 1970.
25. Formerly the Centre Party, now regrouped under the eponymous banner of its leader.
26. See Rudy Andeweg and Galen Irwin's exit poll analysis, *De Volkskrant*, 7 September 1989.
27. See Gladdish (1987), p. 223.
28. Ibid.

5

THE PARTY DOMAIN

The geometry of competition

The emergence and development of political parties in the Netherlands is, as one would expect, one of the dimensions of the evolution of parliamentary representation. This evolution begins with the introduction of direct elections for the Second Chamber after 1848, and it proceeds through extensions of the franchise and revisions of the electoral machinery, culminating in the conferment of adult suffrage following the constitutional settlement of 1915-17.

Although progress towards full democratisation was relatively smooth in the sense that there were no reversals, the emergence of national mass parties was spread over many decades. From a start in the late 1870s, its final phase was prolonged until the aftermath of the Second World War. One feature of the process is that each of the main formations of the party system mobilised at its own pace and in its own way. Thus if one reviews the principal stages along the road to universal suffrage, the big jumps in the size of the electorate do not particularly coincide with accelerations of party development. In 1888 the electorate doubled in size from 14% to 27% of the adult male population, and doubled again in 1897 to 52%.[1] But this did not immediately result in dramatic manifestations of increased party activity. The most obvious explanation for this apparent lack of synchronisation is that each political sub-culture had its own ethos and therefore organised its followers with a marked degree of autonomy .

During the first phase of direct parliamentary representation, from 1850 to 1880, competition for membership of the Lower House was organised by local committees whose complexion was a matter of broad sentiments - whether Liberal, Conservative, Calvinist or, by the end of the period, Catholic - without much programmatic definition.[2] The formation of the Anti-Revolutionary Party in 1879 by a meeting of representatives from a group of local electoral committees,[3] heralds the beginning of national mass parties. Thereafter it is possible to trace most of the subsequent unfolding of the party system in terms of the genealogy of major groupings.[4]

The formation of the ARP was followed by the first attempt to mobilise socialist support – the Social Democratic League (SDB) – in 1882, and to organise liberal opinion – the Liberal Union – in 1885. Both attempts were partial and provisional. The SDB was superseded by the formation of the Social Democratic Workers Party (SDAP) in 1894, which up till 1946 was the mainstream agency of social democracy. Liberal organisation, however, remained fragmented both up to the pacification and during the inter-war period when it divided between an originally radical association – the VDB (formed in 1901) and a more conservative grouping, the Freedom League (1921), later the LSP. Unlike the socialists, the various liberal formations retained something of the earlier character of electoral committees even after the establishment of the People's Party for Freedom and Democracy, the VVD, in 1948.

The Catholics were the last of the major formations to organise on a national basis. A common political programme had been issued as early as 1897, and a group of local Catholic associations had formed a General League, the AB, in 1904.[5] But a concerted national movement was not forthcoming until the launching of the Roman Catholic State Party (RKSP) in 1926.[6]

From these basic genera innumerable offspring were to emerge at successive stages. The Anti-Revolutionaries were thus parents of a major offshoot which in 1908 became the Christian Historical Union, the second most important Calvinist party. They were also the source of breakaways by fervent smaller groups such as the Political Reformed Party (SGP) in 1918, and the Reformed Political Union (GPV) in 1948. The socialist movement was also to create progeny, notably the Social Democratic Party in 1909 which became the Dutch Communist Party in 1918, the Pacifist Socialist Party in 1957, and, in a rightward split, the Democratic Socialists in 1970. The Catholics, despite periodic problems in maintaining unity, were less prone to splinter groups, though there were periodic dissents by individual MPs, which in 1968 produced a radical ecumenical formation, the PPR.

Outside the frame of the major formations, ephemeral parties have frequently appeared, in some profusion after the introduction of proportional representation in 1918. During the inter-war period, the most notorious was the Dutch Nazi Party, the NSB, although its support in parliamentary elections remained small.[7] Post-war, and most conspicuously in the 1960s, single-issue and protest groups were to become fashionable. The poujadist Farmers Party, BP, formed in the late 1950s and winning seven seats in the Second Chamber in 1967, was an important example of the latter. More significant was the constitutional reform movement, Democrats '66, which survives as the fourth largest party in the post 1989 legislature, having twice formed part of governing coalitions (1973–7 and 1981–2). The current party system is therefore a palimpsest of formation, re-formations, splits and amalgamations over several generations. The most outstanding recent example of this process has been the merger of the three major confessional parties to form an interdenominational front, the Christian Democratic Appeal, in 1977.

For more than half a century after the introduction of universal suffrage, five major groupings – the Catholics, the two major Calvinist parties, Labour and the Liberals – dominated the national scene. But the party universe was always open to the entry of minor groups at both national and local levels. The absence of other than an arithmetical threshold for parliamentary and local representation invited the cultivation of expressive, as against instrumental politics. At the first PR elections to the Second Chamber in 1918, thirty-two party lists were presented. In 1922 the total rose to forty-eight and reached a peak of fifty-four lists at the election of 1933.[8] In the inter-war period this was often the subject of criticism.[9] But post-war it continued to be thought appropriate that a proportional system should be open to all contenders. In fact the number of lists filed from 1946–59 ranged from a mere ten to thirteen; but the figure rose to eighteen in 1963 and resumed pre-war proportions in 1971 when twenty-eight lists were fielded.[10] This openness was augmented in 1956 when the size of the Second Chamber was increased from 100 to 150 members, which reduced the target for a parliamentary seat to 0.67% of the total national vote. Small group participation in elections was further encouraged by the modest procedural requirements for the submission of lists of candidates. A list of up to thirty candidates could be presented in each polling district if signed by twenty-five voters and accompanied by a deposit of 1,000 guilders.[11]

The overall picture of party activity nationally is therefore that of a vast array of groups, only a small fraction of which achieve representation in parliament. In the 1986 election for the Second Chamber a total of twenty-seven groups submitted lists of candidates in one or more of the country's nineteen polling districts.[12] Of this number perhaps half could be regarded as serious contenders for seats given that only twelve parties succeeded in gaining representation at the previous election in 1982. Of the half which had little expectation of success, several, such as the Green

Federation and the Socialist Party, had some form of national organisation, while others, such as *God Met Uns* (God with us) and *Loesje* (Lucy)
were purely expressive.

The ensuing pattern of representation in the chamber, from 1986-9,
was stratified according to the size of parliamentary groups. The two
largest, the CDA and PvdA, having each amassed more than 3 million
votes, had groups of more than fifty members. Next in size came the
VVD, with twenty-seven seats representing 1.5 million voters, and then
D'66 with nine seats representing 0.5 million voters. The remaining five
parliamentary groups, each with between one and three seats, fell into
two camps: minor Calvinist and minor left-wing parties. The latter had a
spread of electoral support in all regions, whereas the former were more
concentrated geographically, in a 'Bible Belt', stretching from the north-
east to the south-west.

The election of September 1989 resulted in relatively little change of
the 1986 pattern. There were slightly fewer groups submitting
lists – twenty-three as against twenty-seven – and only sixteen parties
presented lists of candidates in all districts. Four left-wing parties, PSP,
·CPN, PPR, and EVP, combined, as in the preceding European election,
to submit a joint list under the banner of Green Left. Once again there
was a fringe of expressive formations, such as 'Netherlands Realists',
'The Political Party for the Elderly', and, conceivably more seriously, a
'Women's Party'.

Only nine lists, as in 1986, achieved seats in the Second Chamber (see
Table 4.1). The CDA remained the largest *fractie* with fifty-four seats,
and Labour the second largest with forty-nine seats. Parties other than
the CDA, Labour, VVD and D'66, accounted for only 10% of the
national vote and acquired a mere thirteen MPs out of the 150 in the
Second Chamber. So despite the openness of the electoral system, significant mobilisation remained concentrated in a small group of well-
established formations.

In the ratifying First Chamber of Parliament, which has seventy-five
seats elected by the members of the Provincial Councils, a total of ten
parties gained representation following the provincial elections in June
1987. The extra party was the CPN which in 1986 had unprecedentedly
failed to secure a seat in the Second Chamber.

Finally at the level of the European Parliament, where the Netherlands has a quota of twenty-five seats, only the three largest parties are
assured of representation. This has induced the minor parties to

Table 5.1
DISTRIBUTION OF SEATS IN THE FIRST CHAMBER, 1987[13]

CDA	26
PvdA	26
VVD	12
D'66	5
GPV	1
SGP	1
RPF	1
PPR	1
PSP	1
CPN	1
Total	75

present combined party lists, so that the small Calvinist groups and the further left have each been able to win representation.

Table 5.2
DISTRIBUTION OF DUTCH SEATS IN THE
EUROPEAN PARLIAMENT

	1979		1984		1989	
	%votes	*Seats*	*% votes*	*Seats*	*% votes*	*Seats*
PvdA	30.4	9	33.7	9	30.7	8
CDA	35.6	10	30.0	8	34.6	10
VVD	16.1	4	18.9	5	13.6	3
CPN/EVP/PPR/PSP	5.1*	0	5.6	2	7.0†	2
GPV/RPF/SGP	3.3*	0	5.2	1	5.9	1
D'66	9.0	2	2.3	0	5.9	1

* Lists not combined.
† The parties stood as the 'rainbow' coalition.

Party organisation

Political parties in the Netherlands are voluntary and self-determining, there being no legislative provision for the way they should be organised. The sole control is that parties may be proscribed if they are deemed to infringe the security of the realm.[14] The form and extent of party organisation has varied greatly during their prolonged evolution. Until the Second World War, only the Social Democrats and

Anti-Revolutionaries constituted major parties with well articulated structures and a professional apparatus for electoral mobilisation. The Catholics, although the most numerous and influential of all the political groups, relied heavily on the church for mobilising support, and on the multiple associations which formed the Catholic pillar of the *verzuiling* network.[15]

Given that each party has its own history, purposes and constitution, it would seem unlikely that any overall model of party organisation could be convincingly assembled. Nevertheless a general model has been compiled which demonstrates that at least the major parties do tend to conform to a common pattern.[16] In the first place all parties are organised upon a foundation of individual membership in local branches. From this base three lines of ascent lead to the higher party organs. The most direct of these lines is to the annual party congress, delegates to which are elected by party members at local level.[17] The party congress elects or re-elects both the party executive and a smaller administrative bureau. The second line of ascent is from local to regional level which is where provincial party organisation and the administration of polling districts converge. The third line is from local sections for youth and women to their respective national sections. At national party level, all parties have institutes for education and research. At parliamentary level, parties with seats in either chamber have their own MP groupings or *fracties*.

Within each network of party organisation, four bodies stand out as being most influential in the formation and transmission of objectives. There is, firstly, the party executive which presides over the party nationally. Secondly, there is the party congress where party policy is debated and the national executive apprised of delegates' views. The outcome of congress debates are supposedly mandatory on the executive, and strongly supported measures will be taken seriously. Thirdly, there is the parliamentary group which determines the response of the party in the legislature to the governmental agenda. And finally, there is the regional level which manages the provincial elections and usually plays a key role in the selection of parliamentary candidates.

A schematic view of party organisation, whether in general or in terms of each party, does not in itself provide much information about how they actually operate. It is perhaps for this reason that organisational details tend to receive little coverage in the literature. For insights into party management, the best sources are the interpretations of party notables. One central feature of Dutch practice, certainly compared with Britain, is that there is a marked degree of diffusion in the allocation of decision-making. This reflects both historical circumstances and continuing dynamics within the system. Under the conditions of *verzuiling* there were a number of points of influence within each of the pillars. In the confessional *zuilen* especially, political figures were flanked by other articulators of the communal voice. At national level, the whole process of coalition formation has meant that party leadership and party presence in cabinets have tended to diverge.

Sometimes dominating personalities have bridged this gap, as with Willem Drees in the PvdA during the 1950s, or Colijn in the ARP during the 1930s. But often cabinet membership has cross-cut lines of command within parties, exacerbated by the formal separation between government and parliament. To the public at large, party policy is normally regarded as what the parliamentary groups determine in their response to the kaleidoscope of items on the national agenda. These somewhat negative relationships have been well-summarised in a recent study:

> The parliamentary groups are in all parties autonomous organisations, on which the extra-parliamentary party can exercise no direct control. Parliamentary parties choose their own leaders and determine their own political stand. The Parliamentary leader . . . is not the party chairman, and if a party is in government, political leadership tends to be effectively divided between the more prominent minister(s), the chairman and possibly other leaders of the parliamentary group, and the party chairman and other members of the party executive.[18]

Daalder goes on to point to recent efforts by the party organs of the PvdA to control the parliamentary group, but concludes that

> . . . the principle of parliamentary sovereignty and the practice of extensive inter-party negotiations leave Socialist deputies a clear measure of discretion.[19]

Members of parliament, in the Netherlands as elsewhere, do not of course either select or re-select themselves; that is a matter for party members to determine. It is at this interface that the behaviour of party legislators can, to an extent, be either censured or rewarded.

Candidate selection

The selection of political personnel remains the most important function that political parties fulfil in Dutch society.[20]

In a list system of national PR, the presentation of party candidates has a very different character from the choice of MPs in a constituency system. For in the former it is the greater truth that 'the actual competition for a parliamentary seat takes place within the party, not on election day.'[21] The actual mechanics of selection in the Dutch case have two crucial dimensions. One is the fact that votes, wherever cast, accrue to parties nationally in the share-out of seats. The other is that the way elections are orchestrated sub-divides the nation into nineteen polling districts (*krieskringen*) for the process of voting. The latter circumstance means that candidate lists have to be compiled with regard to the expected support for each party in each of the polling districts; because the determination of who has been elected, itself a complex mathematical operation, has regard to the number of votes accumulated in each district.

Accounts of the process of candidate selection within each party are understandably hard to come by, since there is some reluctance to divulge the subtleties of the internal 'tugging between central party organs and district organisations'.[22] In the recent anthology of cross-national practice, aptly subtitled 'The Secret Garden of Politics', Koole and Leijenaar make the general observation that in the Netherlands selection has slowly swung from highly centralised to more regionally determined selection.[23] In the case of the larger parties this move has a clear logistical basis, since the electoral law limits the number of names per party list to thirty. Some variation between lists is therefore essential if parties expect to secure more than thirty seats nationally. But there is also pressure to make lists more localised in order to appeal to voters regionally. This pressure has mounted as dissatisfaction with the absence of locality representation has become more evident.[24]

Koole and Leijenaar have considered the available evidence in respect of candidate selection in the three major parties – CDA, PvdA and VVD. The CDA is something of a special case for it has only operated a fully-fledged system of 'democratic' selection since the election of 1986. Before that, lists were assembled according to a fixed allocation between the former components of the Appeal. The new approach attempts to give weight to local initiative by means of a complex process of consultation. This has tended to work against the production of 'balanced' lists which both reflect the needs for various kinds of expertise within the parliamentary group, and also allow space for young and female candidates. There is also the persistent fact that religious affiliation within the CDA still has a regional character.

The PvdA has a much longer record of endeavour to harmonise local interests with the requirements of an effective parliamentary group. Before 1966, all party members had an opportunity to vet the candidate lists. The removal of this provision only slightly preceded demands for greater democratisation within the party.[25] In 1981 a special commission was formed to lay down guidelines for local branches and regional organisations, but the debate continues within the party on how best to reconcile the various imperatives. The complexity of the problem can be instanced from informal accounts by party notables.[26] As already observed, lists must take account of the likely support in each polling district. Taking the example of the Leiden list in 1986, the expectation was that Labour would collect rather more than 400,000 votes in the *krieskring*, which on a national denominator of about 60,000 would yield seven seats. Clearly the order of names had to refer to that probability. The first name, that of the party leader, would end up with the last seat allocated to the PvdA nationally and could therefore be discounted. Thereafter names 2 to 8 could be regarded as safe seats, but names from 9 onwards might still become MPs. There was first the possibility that Labour might enter government, which could mean perhaps a dozen party seats would need to be refilled. There was also the fact that if MPs retired, vacancies would be dealt with by elevating the highest ranked of the unsuccessful candidates at the previous election. A further variable was the accuracy of the forecast of support. Lists have to be filed eight weeks before polling. Before each list is finalised all possible evidence of support in each district has to be scrutinised, from the results of local elections to opinion polls and canvass returns. It seems fair to note that this combination of ticket-balancing and clairvoyance would test to the limit political managers in simpler systems.

In the Liberal party, selection has recently become more co-ordinated though the tradition was long that of influential local associations. The final order of candidates in each polling district is now determined by a special election council presided over by the party chairman: the regional party organisations are represented in the council and now exert ultimate power.

Viewed overall there would seem to be three sources of 'legitimacy', all potentially conflicting, in the elaborate business of candidate selection in the Netherlands. There is first the notion of 'meritocratic' team-building in terms of the needs of an effective parliamentary group with experts in all the key areas of public policy. This imperative is clearly the principal concern of the national party managers. Secondly, there is the realm of regional and local affinity, which may have considerable importance to voters. Thirdly there is what might be called the intra-party democratic domain of selectoral concern, which refers to individual party members who may not wish the entire process to be the preserve of either regional oligarchs or national managers. At the root of the puzzle is of course the absence of formal locality representation. Regionalism and localism must therefore operate as informal controls upon an otherwise impersonal system of relations between MPs and the citizens.[27]

Party resources

Two circumstances are central to an account of the resources available to Dutch political parties. The first is that all are associations of individual members; indirect or corporate membership does not exist, and corporate contributions to party treasuries are not normally part of the resource picture. The second fact is that the state does make modest contributions to party expenditure, but they are confined to a limited set of activities, essentially those of research, education and youth programmes. It follows that dues from individual members form the bulk of party finances, so the size of the membership and the amount each member can be expected to contribute largely determine party budgets. Available figures show that, on average, four-fifths of the income of the major parties' national bureaux accrues from membership dues: 84% in the case of the VVD, 82% for the CDA and 79% for the PvdA.[28]

Over all parties, the annual fees levied upon members in the early 1980s ranged from 30 to 95 guilders, both extremes applying to small parties – the SGP and PSP respectively. Of the major parties, the CDA exacted on average Fl38, the VVD Fl52 and the PvdA Fl80, in all three cases according to a sliding scale relating to individual income.[29] Since 1960, there has been a dramatic decline in membership figures for the major parties, from a total of over 700,000 in 1960[30] to a little more than 300,000 in 1987.[31] The decline has been most precipitate on the part of the CDA compared with the joint membership of its three antecedent parties. In 1960 the KVP recorded 385,000 members, the ARP 98,000 and the CHU 48,000. These numbers of course supported three separate party organisations but, that apart, the scale of formal participation by Christian party supporters has shrunk to almost a quarter of its former extent. Labour has also suffered a loss of membership though in less drastic terms, from 143,000 in 1960 to 103,000 in 1987. Only the Liberals have reversed this trend, which marks their ascent from a middling to a major party over the last fifteeen years. In 1970 they claimed a mere 38,000 members; by 1987 this had risen to 85,000, though the party has since sustained considerable losses.

Of the major parties, Labour had in 1986 the lowest ratio of members to party voters, at 3.4%. The CDA ratio at this point was slightly above 4%, while the VVD ratio stood at approximately 6%. Ratios tended to be higher for the smaller parties, especially the minor Calvinist groupings, rising to nearly 15% in the case of the GPV. In the most general terms, the habit of party membership has declined alongside the disintegration of the *verzuiling* networks, and parties now have to work with considerably slimmed-down budgets from which to finance both party organisation and election campaigns. In 1980, the total income of the most affluent party, the PvdA, was a mere 940,000 guilders.[32] It follows that election campaigns are low cost affairs with very limited provision for close coverage of voters. Broadcasting time, on television and radio, is therefore of enormous value in affording access to the electorate, especially for the smaller parties. Representation in the Second Chamber carries the right to free time on radio and television which is allocated fairly evenly regardless of party strength.

Given the straitened financial circumstances of Dutch parties, and the fact that there is no legal bar to corporate donations, one might ask why has this not become a feature of party financing? The answer appears to be that the climate of opinion does not favour such transactions. Where they have occurred in the past this has attracted criticism; so the quest for individual members remains the principal means of fulfilling party commitments and avoiding insolvency.

Party profiles

Traditionally Dutch parties constituted a somewhat hybrid universe, within which religious or confessional parties of 'principle' confronted secular parties with more programmatic profiles. The confessional parties, major and minor, mobilised in the main those who adhered to their particular religious denomination. After 1945 the confessionals came to compete with secular parties in the production of election manifestos, but this did not convert them into programmatic parties. Such a conversion has however been what the CDA, since 1977, has aspired to achieve.[33]

Clearly, although parties of 'principle', the confessionals mainly mobilised 'interests', i.e. those of their co-religionists. For the main secular parties there was also a convergence of 'principle' and 'interests', though the latter were wooed, or thought to be, more in terms of programmes than of existential commitment. In fact Labour, the most overtly ideological of the leading secular parties, having dropped Marxism from its platform back in 1937, has always been prepared to adapt its message to the actual agenda; and its internal debates, which from time to time shed dissidents, were normally predicated upon practical assessments of electoral advantage. Labour's *raison d'être* however – the incremental improvement of the lot of its prime constituency, the urban and rural working class – remained clear enough. The Liberal combination of principle, interest and programme was perhaps less clear-cut, but they have traditionally offered a distinctive rationale – that of social and economic individualism, in the face of the communalism, or collectivism, of the other major contenders. Democrats '66, coming late into the field, have had less of an obvious interest orientation, although their support is marked in the upper social echelons. Constitutional reform has been their prime concern, and their programmes have been pitched somewhat obliquely in terms of socio-economic issues.

One point of access to the character of the principal parties is the political complexion of their activists. Here interesting data are available on members who attended party congresses during 1978–9.[34] The predominant occupations of congress delegates were, in the cases of the PvdA, CDA and D'66, the public services (roughly one quarter) and in the case of the VVD, commerce and transport (also one quarter). In respect of the self-ascription of social class, D'66 had the highest percentage (35%) who regarded themselves as upper class. Two-thirds of all delegates considered themselves to be of the middle class, with only the PvdA registering a significant fraction (10%) labelling themselves lower-class. D'66 also contained the largest proportion which had received higher education (50%), whilst the PvdA and CDA congresses had the highest percentages of delegates whose education had been sub-secondary, 27% and 20% respectively. Among the representatives of the secular parties, the VVD disclosed the biggest fraction of regular church-goers (21%) and the PvdA the smallest (7%).

It would be difficult to distill from these findings a matrix which would clearly differentiate party delegates in terms of their social 'interests', however broadly defined. When one turns to issues the picture remains strangely indistinct. On matters such as unemployment, inflation, the environment and European integration, there was a remarkable degree of consensus among delegates of all four parties, though their perceived salience differed somewhat. Issues which divided the parties most visibly were policies towards income differentials and the multinationals, though even these were qualified by unequal perceptions of their importance. Asked to place themselves within a 10-point left-right scale, delegates did diverge more predictably. PvdA respondents averaged 2.7, compared with 6.4 for the VVD, D'66 occupying a middle position at 4.0 (CDA delegates were not sounded on this). In their attitudes towards a range of pressure groups, PvdA and D'66 delegates shared certain sympathies, as did CDA and VVD delegates.

The same data, which were compiled in the course of an international project on the characteristics of party delegates within the EEC, were further analysed by M. de Vries in terms of a cross-national comparison.[35] Table 5.3 presents a select comparison of the attitudes of Dutch party élites, alongside those of their counterparts in the British Labour and Conservative parties.[36]

Of the various insights which the table below appears to offer, perhaps the most vivid is that the addition of the British Conservative party to

Table 5.3
ATTITUDES OF DUTCH AND BRITISH PARTY ACTIVISTS

% in favour of:	Con.	Lab.	VVD	CDA	D'66	PvdA
Implementation of sex equality	57	97	95	90	98	99
Increase of military spending	96	10	71	35	7	1
More control of multinationals	47	99	33	71	83	99
Less control of private firms	96	8	86	48	27	8
Reduction of income differences	17	92	23	72	82	99
Development of nuclear energy	92	53	87	68	37	17

the Dutch political spectrum would extend its ideological scale palpably to the right. For with the exception of their stance on multinationals, the Conservatives robustly out-perform the VVD in a rightward direction, most spectacularly in the matter of sex equality. At the other end of the spectrum, British Labour party delegates come out slightly to the right of the PvdA over military expenditure and nuclear energy (though the latter has a less clear ideological status). But in socio-economic affairs the two are extremely closely aligned.

The second reflection is that, presented in terms of straight preferences regardless of perceived salience, the differences between Dutch party activists assume a much sharper edge. Sex equality clearly commands assent in all parties. But on the other items the VVD and PvdA are clearly at opposite poles of conviction. Equally clearly the CDA and D'66 are uniformly positioned *vis-à-vis* the five controversial issues. In each case the CDA is next to the VVD whilst D'66 is next to the PvdA. So the evidence does point to a sustained relationship between parties and positions on key questions. There is, furthermore, evidence that the spectrum is not evenly divided. For although in all examples the CDA falls between the VVD and D'66, it is markedly closer to the latter on items which are at the core of socio-economic policy. Overall there is seemingly a significant gap between the VVD and CDA, a smaller gap between the latter and D'66, and a still smaller gap between D'66 and Labour.

Aims and programmes

There are commonly three strata in the geology of party self-definition in the Netherlands: the statutes which embody the party, periodic statements of principle, and election programmes or manifestos. Each stratum has a distinct purpose and a different level of specificity. The statutes contain the most general description of a party's rationale. Statements of principle are variously updates of party thinking, responses to internal debates and announcements of new directions. Most specific, but also most ephemeral, are the programmes compiled for each election campaign. Over recent years, election manifestos have become lengthy inventories setting out the party's position on every conceivable issue, with much space devoted to matters on which the party is likely to have little impact, such as international affairs. There is therefore a plethora of information, at any given time, on each party's perceived stance and aspirations – which makes the task of summarisation rather difficult.

The Christian Democratic Appeal highlights this problem. Formed from three previously independent confessional parties, its religious character, now inter-denominational, is clearly a central element in its being. Article 2 of its statutes firmly declares that 'the CDA regards Holy Scripture as the guide for political actions'.[37] But this guiding principle obviously requires continual conversion into the language of everyday politics. This translation is made both in long-term policy statements and in successive election programmes. In the broadest terms, the party, like its predecessors, has tended to adopt an intermediate or centrist position in socio-economic matters, balancing a belief in personal responsibility with a communitarian outlook which reflects its components' former *verzuiling* operations. On so-called 'ethical questions' the party's stance has been one of religious conservatism, hostile to wide-scale abortion, a too libertarian interpretation of sexual freedom, and of course euthanasia.

For most of the period since its formation, the CDA has been in coalition governments with the Liberals, which has undoubtedly affected its policies. Increasingly it has become perceived as a party to the right of centre, even though many of its activists disclose a substantial distance from the views of their counterparts in the VVD (see previous section). It would be nearest the truth to point to a range of opinion within the Appeal, which after all is very much a *rassemblement* rather than a single movement. Two of its components, the former Anti-Revolutionary and Catholic People's Parties, contained left wings which came close to Labour in their social and economic outlook, and these strands have not been eliminated. Given the potential for flexible strategies in a movement which is pivotal so far as government is concerned, it is likely that the latest coalition with Labour will amend the party's recent gravitation towards the centre-right.

From an external perspective, the Dutch Labour Party may seem logistically one of the weaker of the West European Social Democratic formations. For unlike its counterparts in Britain, Scandinavia, the German Federal Republic and, more recently, France and Spain, it has never attracted more than a third of the poll in national elections. Also, out of the past thirty years, it has been in office, in coalitions, for a mere seven. Nevertheless it has frequently been the leading party in the legislature (after the elections of 1956, 1971, 1972, 1977 and 1982) and has played a vital role in the shaping of Dutch society since the Second World War.

Wolinetz, writing in the late 1970s, included the following items in his characterisation of the party's fundamental aims:[38]

1. 'priority for the needs of lower income groups';
2. 'redistribution . . . and greater public control over private investment and financial institutions';
3. 'extensive participation in and popular control over political, social and economic institutions';
4. 'extensive co-determination in industry';
5. 'a desire to reduce defence expenditure and increase aid to developing countries'.

These commitments place the party squarely in the line of traditional European Labour parties. Although clearly grounded in the philosophy of protecting wage-earners, the party's programme is independent of that of organised labour, since there are no direct institutional links between the party's organs and the trade union federations. Translated into recent electoral politics, the core concerns of the PvdA mainstream have been tempered, not merely to appeal to the widest wave-band of support, but also to enhance the party's eligibility for inclusion in government. Thus the 1986 election manifesto proposed no massive programme of public expenditure to deal with an unemployment rate of 12%. Instead, the main emphasis was put upon work-sharing through a reduction of the working week. The ability to approach problems pragmatically is facilitated by the presence of small parties to the left of the PvdA, with representation in the legislature. These serve to tap off more extreme views which might otherwise cause internal discomfort. It was noticeable that in 1986, a number of former supporters of small left parties took refuge in Labour in a climate where the centre of gravity had moved to the right.

Article 1 of the VVD's Clarification of Principles, 1980, sets out the party's beliefs in freedom, responsibility, tolerance, social justice and equality.[39] This last conviction is to be interpreted as a commitment to equal political rights and not to a society of equal rewards. In the original crucible of party formation in the Netherlands, the Liberals were not regarded as a movement of the right. This was partly because of their support for 'progressive causes' such as wider suffrage, public welfare and religious equality, and partly because the defence of 'conservative' values was thought to be the prerogative of the confessional parties.[40] In recent years however the party has come to occupy the position of the contemporary European right, embodying a belief in economic freedom together with a pro-employer view of economic decision-making. As it has risen from the status of a medium-sized formation to that of a major party, its right of centre complexion has solidified. Thus on most indicators, from income differentials to lower government expenditure (except in the realm of defence), and a tough-minded attitude towards welfare payments and law and order, it now offers the electorate a recognisable alternative to social democratic or centrist recipes. It remains however dedicatedly libertarian in matters of personal freedom such as abortion.

The fourth party in the parliament, Democrats '66, was formed in the mid-1960s, as its title reveals, to win support for a radical reform of the machinery of democracy. Its original activists sought to confront the traditional five party ruling élite with a campaign to open up the system to greater popular participation. In the subsequent turbulence which attended the collapse of *verzuiling*, the party found its strongest affinity with the modernisers in the Labour Party, although some of its founders had former Liberal connections. The present role of D'66 in the political system might not unfairly be described as that of an intellectual junction, or cross-over, available for those in transit between a secular centre (which no party actually embodies) and the mild left. Its survival over more than twenty years, which has included membership of two governing coalitions, suggests that in a multi-party system where the centre remains residually religious, such a junction has both value and continuing viability.

The remaining parties of any significance within the spectrum, since 1986 somewhat reduced in parliamentary strength, are divided between small left-wing movements and small sectarian Calvinist groups. The former were formerly represented in parliament by the Radical Party (PPR), the Pacifist Socialist Party (PSP) and the Communist Party (CPN – First Chamber only). Since the 1989 election they have combined as Green Left. The Calvinist groups comprise the Political Reformed Party (SGP), the Reformed Political Union (GPV) and the Reformed Political Federation (RPF). The entire phalanx of small parties has, since 1986, reflected the support of 7–10% of the voters for the Second Chamber.

Party support

Any analysis of the character of political parties within a system must extend to their impact upon the electorate, not only in terms of their relative numerical success in attracting votes, but also in respect of what kinds of voter they habitually persuade. Indeed once their aims, programmes and organisation have been surveyed, the delineation of what parties stand for has to be completed by reference to the complexion of their supporters. To construe this usefully means first deciding what are the significant divisions and distinctions within a mass electorate. From a British perspective, probably the most salient index will be that of the class basis of party support, although the very notion of class may have subtly different meanings within each polity. A second and different form of diagnosis will be the extent to which party support has any geographical significance, in terms of regional patterns which may themselves embody broad economic, historic or sub-cultural divisions within the state. Knowledge of support in terms of age, in particular how far the various parties appeal to younger voters, may convey something of the dynamic character of party appeal. Information about educational levels may also contribute to an assessment of the parties' natural constituencies; and finally there may be certain indicators which relate party support to other forms of behaviour, notably, in the case of the Netherlands, religious affiliation and the intensity of denominational allegiance.

A modicum of evidence regarding the class basis of party support has been available in various forms since the 1970s, from surveys, national election studies and most recently exit polls. Irwin, for example, derived the following table (5.4), showing party support by manual and non-manual workers, from the 1977 National Election Study.[41] He points out that although Labour attracted the highest percentage of manual workers, this was still less than 50% of the category, largely because of the continuing capacity of the confessionals to mobilise the near 40% of blue-collar voters with strong religious affiliations.

Table 5.4
DISTRIBUTION OF BLUE- AND WHITE-COLLAR VOTES, 1977

Support for:	CDA	Labour	Liberal	D'66	Minor religious parties	Other
Manual workers %	34	48	6	3	4	5
Non-manual %	36	28	22	8	2	4

More recent data have been assembled by Daalder, working from the National Election Studies of 1982 and 1986.[42] Here, as in Table 5.5, the electorate is divided into four social categories. The distribution of party support relates to a sample of about 1,200 voters at each election.

Table 5.5
PARTY VOTING IN TERMS OF SOCIAL CLASS (self-ascribed)

	Overall '82 '86	CDA '82 '86	Labour '82 '86	Liberal '82 '86	D'66 '82 '86
Upper middle %	15 19	11 15	8 10	26 41	22 29
Middle %	49 46	56 53	39 39	57 48	58 45
Upper working %	10 11	9 10	13 15	8 7	7 9
Working %	25 24	24 23	40 37	9 4	13 17

Figures have been rounded off to the nearest unit.

Much interpretation could be lavished on these figures, but there are obvious cautions given that they relate to self-ascriptions of class. The first point to note is that nearly two-thirds of each sample regarded themselves as middle class or above – which is perhaps now a norm for European post-industrial societies. Of those below middle class, although Labour drew more than 50% of its votes from this section, the CDA also relied significantly on their support. So substantial was working-class support for the CDA, that it might be thought to have repercussions on party policy. Certainly this contrasts markedly with the lack of worker support for the CDA's former coalition partner, the VVD. There is also the fact that the distribution of CDA votes overall matches closely the distribution of voters through the social structure.

Age, as a demarcator of party support, has less apparent salience than class. Nevertheless the distribution of support in terms of the age of voters is suggestive of the continuity of party appeal, especially where there is a marked disparity between the choices of the youngest and the oldest age groups. Table 5.6 shows the relationship between age and party choice, according to data assembled from the 1986 National Election Study.[43]

If the distribution of CDA support corresponds most closely to the overall class structure, then support for the PvdA, on this evidence, conforms most neatly to the overall age structure. The D'66 vote included a higher than average proportion of electors aged forty and below, while the CDA was backed by the lowest proportion of the youngest voters and the highest proportion of voters over the age of sixty.

Interesting evidence of the changing appeal of parties to the youngest cohort of voters is provided by Daalder, from a variety of sources over

Table 5.6
AGE AND PARTY CHOICE, 1986

Age groups:	Overall	CDA	Labour	Liberal	D'66
18–30	25	18	25	24	29
31–40	26	22	29	28	32
41–50	15	17	13	20	17
51–60	12	12	12	13	13
Over 60	22	31	22	15	9
	100	100	100	100	100

Table 5.7
PARTY CHOICE OF THE YOUNGEST AGE COHORTS (%)

	CDA*	Liberal	Other non-left	Labour	D'66	Minor left
1961 (ages 18-25)	59	11	1	26	-	3
1972 (ages 18-22)	18	17	7	24	7	27
1986 (ages 18-24)	30	21	5	30	8	5

*Combined major confessional parties 1961 and 1972.

the period 1961–86."Table 5.7 selects three reference points (1961, 1972 and 1986) from the data he presents. From these figures may be discerned evidence of substantial swings of opinion among the youngest voters – which could be regarded as a mirror of attitudinal changes within Dutch society over the past quarter-century. Viewed in broad terms, the confessional centre, which in 1961 was the dominant choice of young voters, appealed to less than 20% in 1972, to recover somewhat, under new management, by 1986. To its right, the VVD gained ground over the period, but the most dramatic changes were registered in support for the minor parties of the left, peaking at more than a quarter of the youngest voters in 1972, but falling back by 1986 almost to the miniscule level of 1961.

During the prolonged era of *verzuiling*, religious adherence was a key determinant of party support, since half the electors were regularly mobilised by the major confessional parties. From the late 1960s on, the salience of religion has become much weaker in relation to voting behaviour. Nevertheless, a high correlation between church affiliation and party preference still marks the voting pattern. In the 1977 National Election Study, figures for weekly church attendance, as reported by Irwin,[45] showed that over 70% of regular churchgoers cast their vote for the CDA, and a further 11% backed the minor Calvinist parties. Only 8% of this group opted for Labour, 6% chose the VVD and a mere 2% supported D'66.

The simplest inference from this evidence is that, in 1977, the secular parties were restricted to competing for the favour of less than 20% of practising Christians, although the number of electors who disclaimed any compelling religious adherence was growing steadily. Daalder has brought this picture up to date in terms of expressed religious affiliation in the 1982 and 1986 elections (see Table 5.8).[46]

The most significant change between the elections of 1982 and 1986 is the overall increase of voters acknowledging no religious affiliation, up from 37% to 43%. This has increased the proportion of secular voters supporting all major parties, including the CDA. Thus by 1986, 60% of Labour and D'66 voters and 51% of Liberal voters recorded no church connections. Of these three major parties, Labour alone showed a slight increase in support by religious voters, and that was in respect of Catholics only.

Educational levels and their distribution in terms of party support to an extent supplements the available information about the pattern of class voting. The correlation between the two indicators is clearly less than perfect, but sample evidence of education is inherently more concrete than self-ascriptions of social class. From the 1986 Election Study the data in Table 5.9 on educational levels and party choice have been derived.[47] In this table, the secondary category combines a variety of schools which continue education up to the ages 17–19. In the

Table 5.8
RELIGIOUS AFFILIATION AND PARTY VOTING, 1982-86

Religious denomination	Overall '82 '86	CDA '82 '86	Labour '82 '86	Liberal '82 '86	D'66 '82 '86
Catholic	33 32	58 51	21 23	33 29	23 23
Dutch Reformed	17 15	18 20	16 12	19 12	18 14
Gereformeerd	9 6	17 11	2 1	4 2	4 4
Other	5 4	1 3	5 4	5 5	9 0
No church	37 43	6 16	56 60	40 51	47 60
Totals ca. 100%					

Figures have been rounded off to the nearest unit.

Table 5.9
PARTY CHOICE AND EDUCATIONAL LEVELS, 1986 ELECTION

% voters completing:	Overall	CDA	Labour	Liberal	D'66
Primary	16	17	23	3	2
Secondary	65	73	59	66	61
Higher	19	10	18	31	37

case of voters whose education ceased at primary level (now less than a sixth of the electorate) the CDA conforms best with the national proportion, while Labour exceeds it. But this category in 1986 contained fewer voters than the number who had experienced higher education. Within this latter contingent, differences in the proportion each party mobilised in 1986 are striking. The share of the higher-educated attracted by Labour matches the proportion of these voters within the electorate. Both the VVD and D'66 have a very high percentage of support from this 'class', but the CDA draws only 10% of its following from the clerisy of graduates.

The question of what constitutes regionality in a state as compact as the Netherlands is somewhat problematic. Under the conditions of *verzuiling* from, say, 1922 to 1967, the religious sub-cultures could to some extent be given a territorial focus.[48] Thus the Catholic party (RKSP up to 1940, KVP from 1946) originally drew much of its strength from North Brabant and Limburg in the south, with less support from the central provinces. In the north – Friesland, Groningen and Drenthe – it attracted relatively little backing, given the absence of an indigenous Catholic population. By contrast, the three northern provinces were *inter alia* a bastion of the Anti-Revolutionary Party, and also provided considerable support for the Christian Historicals, together with Zeeland, Overijssel and Guelderland. This basic pattern was, however, subjected to extensive mobility and substantial population increase. Thus by 1967, the south was less important as a source of Catholic strength, though the north had become even more crucial to the ARP and CHU.

Of the major secular parties, the SDAP in the 1920s was proportionately strongest in Groningen, Friesland and North Holland. In the central provinces its support was fairly evenly spread, but it was relatively weak in Zeeland and the Catholic south. By 1982, however, the PvdA had made great strides in the south and had achieved an impres-

Table 5.10
GEOGRAPHICAL PATTERN OF PARTY SUPPORT,
1986 ELECTION

	% Overall	CDA	Labour	Liberal	D'66
North	12	11	14	14	9
East	19	21	18	19	17
West	47	38	46	51	54
South	22	29	22	17	20

Legend: North = Groningen, Friesland, Drenthe.
East = Overijssel, Guelderland, Flevoland.
West = Utrecht, Zeeland, North and South Holland.
South = Limburg, North Brabant.

sively uniform basis nationally. Liberal support, in its various forms, was in the inter-war years most marked in Guelderland and South Holland, and least visible in the south. By 1967 however, before the VVD's climb to major party status, it had much improved its position in the south, and had acquired a reasonable following in Drenthe, Utrecht and Groningen. Over the next fifteen years, the Liberal share of the national vote rose from 11 to 23%. In the process its spread of support became more even across the provinces, with the south now registering slightly higher proportionate strength than the north.

To complete the picture, the confessional merger which resulted in the CDA brought together the residual strengths of the three components, yielding a support pattern with weak links only in Groningen, and North and South Holland. The outcome of these various flows of support was, in the latter 1980s, an overwhelmingly national party universe, with the few cases of markedly regional activity confined to the small sectarian movements. For statistical proof of this conclusion, a quadripartite division of the country yields the distribution of major party support in respect of the 1986 election shown in Table 5.10.[49]

NOTES

1. Verhoef (1974), Table 1, p. 209.
2. Van Tijn (1971).
3. Verhoef (1974), p. 210.
4. Koole (1987), Compendium A 1100–37, Fig. 1.
5. Koole (1987), ibid.
6. See Koole in *DNPP Yearbook* 1987, pp. 99–117.
7. See Smit and van der Wusten (1980).

8. Daalder (1975), p. 230.
9. In the literature, this feature has given rise to differing views. See Lijphart (1975), pp. 162–77.
10. Daalder (1975), p. 230.
11. Higher financial and attestation provisions have been proposed for subsequent elections.
12. Supplement to the official gazette (*Nederlandse Staatscourant*), 3 June 1986.
13. *DNPP Yearbook* 1987, p. 19.
14. See Koole (1987), Compendium A 1100–104/5.
15. See Bakvis (1981).
16. Koole (1987), Compendium A 1100–62.
17. Except D'66, whose constitution allows any member to attend the party congress.
18. Daalder (1987), p. 236.
19. Ibid., p. 237.
20. Koole and Leijenaar (1988), p. 207.
21. Ibid., p. 192.
22. Daalder (1975), p. 232.
23. Koole and Leijenaar (1988).
24. See Gladdish (1972).
25. See Chapter 4, 'Labour's Response to the Crisis' (pp. 52–4).
26. In particular an interview by the author with the Director of the Wiardi Beckman Stichting (Labour Party Research Foundation), May 1986.
27. See Gladdish (1985).
28. Koole (1987), Compendium A 1100–123.
29. Koole (1989) 'The Modesty of Dutch Party Finance' in H.E. Alexander (ed.), *Comparative Political Finance in the 1980s*, Cambridge, 1989.
30. Daalder (1987), p. 234.
31. *DNPP Yearbook*, 1987, p. 20.
32. Koole (1989), op. cit.
33. In a detailed analysis of CDA electoral strategy in 1986, van Holsteyn and Irwin show that whereas in 1977 36% of CDA voters cited religion as a motive for supporting the party, only 13% did so in 1986. *DNPP Yearbook*, 1987, p. 85.
34. Assembled by Middel and van Schuur, *DNPP Yearbook*, 1980, pp. 61–85.
35. *DNPP Yearbook*, 1982, pp. 129–60.
36. Sampled at the British Labour Party Conference in 1978 and the Conservative Party Conference in 1979.
37. Author's translation. Original in Compendium A 1100–40.
38. In Paterson and Thomas (1977).
39. Author's translation. Original in Compendium A 1100–52.
40. See Daalder and van der Berg (1982).
41. In Merkl (1980), p. 182.
42. Daalder (1987), p. 227.
43. Zielonka-Goei and Hillebrand, *DNPP Yearbook*, 1987, Table 1, p. 118.
44. Daalder (1987), p. 218.
45. In Merkl (1980), p. 181.
46. Daalder (1987), p. 227.
47. Zielonka-Goei and Hillebrand, op. cit., Table 7, p. 122.
48. De Hond (1986).
49. Zielonka-Goei and Hillebrand, op. cit., Table 18, p. 130.

6
REPRESENTATION

And would you represent our queen aright, it were convenient you had such a devil.

— Shakespeare, *Titus Andronicus*, Act 5, Scene 2

To devote a chapter to representation, in addition to accounts of both the party and parliamentary domains, requires some explanation. For in many systems the electoral provisions and their consequences could be subsumed either in an analysis of party competition or in an account of the legislature. In the Netherlands, however, the formal structure of representation is both distinctive in itself and the object of extended reflection by commentators and politicians. Indeed, much of the constitutional debate during the years from the mid-1960s to the revision of 1983 was either directly or indirectly predicated upon the aptness, adequacy and congruity of the electoral system in relation to the changing political landscape.

This preoccupation with the modalities of representation signals a dilemma. For the Dutch electoral system can be regarded both as a striking response to a particular process of development, and as a possible obstacle to further evolution. To evidence this requires some reference to the origins of the current system and of the provisions it replaced.

The evolution of proportional representation

From the introduction of direct elections to the Second Chamber in 1849, up to 1918, a system of locality representation obtained.[1] Initially divided into two-member constituencies on the basis of one MP for approximately 45,000 citizens (some 1,000 voters), the pattern was modified in 1888 when the electorate doubled in size and the Chamber's composition was fixed at 100 members. Single-member constituencies were then introduced, a process completed by 1896, on a majoritarian footing with provision for subsequent run-offs if necessary. By this stage inter-party competition was acquiring its modern shape, as four groupings – Calvinist, Catholic, Liberal and Socialist – were presenting candidates in contests with only one possible winner. Inter-confessional pacts helped to settle the distribution of Calvinist and Catholic candidates; but Liberals and Socialists found it more difficult to

95

apportion outcomes. The need for a more congruent electoral system in a multi-party universe became therefore a key item on the agenda of the grand 'pacification', which by 1918 brought about universal male suffrage.

Accounts of the decision to adopt nationwide proportional representation are surprisingly sparse, as Daalder notes when providing his own summary of party positions on the issue.[2] His conclusion was that all the major parties saw advantages in a meticulously proportional system, though their assumptions about its likely effects differed. In a recent assessment, Andeweg[3] observes that the Liberals, who controlled the cabinet at the time, regarded PR as a survival mechanism, while the Catholics – the largest single bloc – foresaw an increase in their parliamentary strength, since it would realise their previously surplus votes in the southern provinces. The Social Democrats looked forward to a rising curve of national support which PR would translate into seats, whereas the Calvinists believed they could maintain their position. In the event it was the Liberals who lost ground after 1918, and the Catholics and Social Democrats who improved their positions, though demographic changes and the introduction of female suffrage complicated the question of what was attributable to PR.

Higher motives were of course invoked in support of the adoption of the new electoral system. First suggested in the mid-nineteenth century,[4] PR had always imparted the flavour of an enlightened formula which offered the greatest fairness in the measurement and instrumentation of opinion. The emergence of modern inter-party competition made it even more persuasive, when it was realised that what counted nationally were party votes, so that the random results of locality contests could be thought increasingly incongruous. Various forms of PR therefore became a widespread response in Western Europe to the introduction of universal suffrage.

The modus operandi

The method of proprotional representation adopted in the Netherlands took the case for mathematical accuracy in the translation of party strengths to its ultimate limit. The whole country was regarded as a single constituency without geographical sub-divisions. This was the basic premise, though the actual arrangements were inevitably more complex.[5] A number of electoral districts were created, nineteen at the time of writing, in each of which parties were able to present lists of candidates. Each list was limited to thirty candidates, and electors were allowed a single vote. Mostly this resulted in voters simply endorsing the first named candidate on the list of their choice, though any name on the chosen list could be opted for. This latter possibility was termed 'preference voting', and could, albeit very rarely, result in the election of a candidate other than by the normal allocation of seats according to the totals of party votes.

On the completion of the count, the Central Polling Office in The Hague was required to determine an electoral quota by dividing the entire national vote by the number of seats in the Second Chamber. This quota was then applied to the distribution of votes among parties in each electoral district, which produced an initial distribution of seats according to the rank order on each list. But names could be entered on more than one list, so the leading figures in each party might well appear on the lists in all districts. Such figures, if successful in more than one district, could then choose the district in which they wished to be elected. This would necessitate a further round in the distribution of seats. Since the linking of party lists is now permitted, a tactic attractive to small parties as a way of enhancing their chances of achieving the quota, this also requires a further computation. Finally the residue of votes which cannot be allocated by the straight application of the quota, is apportioned nationally according to the de Hondt method of the highest average.[6]

This ultimate stage will tend to favour the larger parties. But this is the sole inhibition on the ability of small parties to gain representation, since the threshold for entry to the Second Chamber is purely arithmetical. When the Chamber consisted of 100 members, approximately one percent of the total national vote could secure a seat. Since 1956, when the size of the Lower House was increased to 150 members, this hurdle has decreased to 0.67%. In the 1986 election the total poll was 9,172,159 valid votes,[7] which produced a quota of 61,147. This meant that the Calvinist Reformed Political Federation, though it collected only a few thousand votes in each of several districts, by mustering a total of 83,582 votes overall was able to obtain a seat. This miniscule barrier has been challenged from time to time on the grounds that it encourages a fragmented pattern of representation. But the presence of very small parties in the House can provide room for legislative manoeuvre, and has been utilised by governments of varying stripe to achieve majorities where the balance was tight. Also the facility of entry to parliament has been upheld as a democratic safety valve, since

new groups can readily acquire a voice in national affairs, and those with a small but faithful following can retain a foothold in the national arena.
   The fundamental revision of the electoral rules in 1917 gave the vote in elections to the Second Chamber to male citizens aged twenty-five and above.[8] Since some 70% of males in this age group had previously been enfranchised, the increase in the size of the electorate – from 1 to 1.5 million – was less dramatic than the outcome of the conferment of female adult suffrage in 1922. This resulted in a potential electorate of around 3.5 million by 1925. After 1945 the electorate expanded more rapidly as population growth (see Table 3.2) was compounded by reductions in the voting age. The age qualification was lowered to twenty-three in 1946, to twenty-one in 1967, and to eighteen in 1972. By 1986 the number of citizens entitled to vote in Second Chamber elections had risen to 10.7 million.

The effects of PR

One obvious consequence of the Dutch electoral system is that it makes no overt provision for locality representation, which has profound repercussions upon the relationship between voters and MPs.[9] The decision to move from a constituency-based parliament to one compiled according to the volume of party support nationally, recognised, *inter alia*, the emergence of a pattern of mass mobilisation which was intimately related to the consolidation of the *verzuiling* network. The kind of politics associated with *verzuiling*, certainly as articulated by Lijphart and others in the 1960s,[10] reflected a dichotomy between hermetic party followings at mass level and co-operation, or at least accommodation, at élite levels. Therefore élites at national level might be expected to be well satisfied with an electoral system which delivered the votes of each phalanx, without the complications and distortions of a set of contests between individual candidates in localities.
   But how far the dimension of local identity was thought effectively obsolete when nationwide PR was installed is hard to assess. The Dutch historical experience was one of hyper-particularism until the impact of the French model at the end of the eighteenth century, which was followed by that of monarchical centralisation. From 1814 onwards the formerly quasi-autonomous provinces were steadily divested of importance as a national bureaucracy extended its web. Andeweg, commenting on this process, contends that 'it is symbolic of Dutch centralism that in no other democracy are provincial governors and municipal mayors

still appointed by the central government rather than elected locally'.[11] He might have excepted the French prefectoral system, but the observation remains striking.

The adoption of national PR therefore engrossed a century of increasing centralisation. But local and regional features still characterised political organisation and behaviour in the second decade of the twentieth century. Sectarian movements which had resisted the major Calvinist groupings tended to have a strong regional flavour. Radical left-wing formations had in certain cases a marked local character, and in areas like Friesland there was still some cultural, even linguistic distinctiveness. Nevertheless in a country as compact as the Netherlands the idea of a parliament compiled as a national assembly, with national perspectives, was not only conceptually persuasive; it could be viewed as an indispensable roof to the potentially divisive *verzuiling* edifice.

The implementation of nationwide PR was also accompanied by the introduction of compulsory voting. In practice this meant obligatory attendance at the appropriate polling station, since electors could not be · compelled to endorse any of the party lists. This provision was abolished in 1970, but during the half-century of its application it had palpable effects upon elections, and not merely in terms of turnouts. Given that the population was largely mobilised into *zuilen*, compulsory voting enabled party managers to conduct operations from their headquarters. Writing in the 1950s, van Raalte could report that 'canvassing at elections is unknown'.[12] Even today, election campaigns are unelaborate and party finances neither permit nor provide for lavish importuning of the citizens (see Chapter 5).

The use of list systems has further consequences. The lists are available as reservoirs of replacement if MPs decline to take up their seats, join the government, retire, or suffer untimely demise. This eliminates the need for by-elections and means that there is no resort to the electorate in the course of a parliament. This serves to insulate the Second Chamber from oscillations of public opinion and furthers the impression of a detached legislative élite.

The affirmation, through the medium of nationwide PR, that the States-General was a national assembly whose members spoke for the nation as a whole, did not of course dispense with provisions for local or regional politics. Provincial Councils, also after 1922 elected by a list system of PR, afforded participation at provincial level; while municipalities, whose operations account for a sizeable share of public resources,[13] offered scope for citizen involvement at local level. Since the members of Provincial Councils elect the First Chamber of Parliament, there is a somewhat tenuous strand between the regions and the national legislature. But there are no links between either localities or regions and the directly elected Lower House.[14] How then do voters behave in relation to MPs, and how are MPs affected by the fact that they have no constituents?

MP–voter relations

In a recent survey of the British House of Commons of 1983–7, MPs were invited to state what value they ascribed to various properties commonly attributed to the electoral system.[15] 95% of respondents, from all parties, gave the highest value to the relationship between MPs and their constituents. The precise character of that relationship has since been the subject of further enquiry.[16] But there is much to suggest that both representatives and constituents believe that this feature of a locality system is of great importance.

Studies of political participation in the Netherlands have to deal with the opposite circumstance – that there are no direct links between members of the effective chamber of parliament and the voter. A study was carried out in 1970–1 at the University of Leiden; in it, various forms of participation at both local and national levels were surveyed.[17] In matters of local concern, MPs were entirely absent from the gallery of public figures to whom citizens resorted. This may be contrasted with the British case, where MPs' post-bags are as likely to contain complaints about local matters as objurgations on issues of national policy.

On questions of wide public concern, the Leiden survey found that Dutch MPs did have a place among the targets selected by the curious or disaffected populace. But their place was a surprisingly humble one, nearly at the bottom of a list below national labour leaders, ministers, high civil servants and provincial officials. Criticism or commendation was almost as often addressed to national party leaders as to individual MPs; a fact which the authors of the survey report found worthy of particular comment.

In 1972–3 a more extensive survey was undertaken at the University of Nijmegen, which examined citizen attitudes towards the political system as a whole.[18] In respect of the operations of parliament, opinion was divided equally between respondents who expressed confidence in the legislature, and those who expressed the opposite. Less even was the distribution of approval for the activities of the political parties, with

47% of the sample registering little or no satisfaction and the remainder spread between moderate and reasonable contentment. On the aptness and utility of the electoral system, 51% of those canvassed were prepared to support the view that MPs should be elected on a constituency basis. More cogently from the standpoint of MP–voter relations, those sampled were asked about their experience of contacting national representatives, and their judgement was sought about how effective this had been. Over 70% regarded contacting MPs, on either local or national matters, to be an ineffective way of airing problems. Representatives at municipal level were thought to respond most effectively to approaches about local issues. At national level, members of the Royal Family turned out to be the object of slightly more frequent contacts than individual MPs.

This evidence serves to confirm that in the absence of local constituencies, voters will be unlikely to refer to members of parliament, since they cannot identify which MP it might be worth addressing. This does not signify an absolute lack of channels of communication between the voting mass and the presiding élite. But it does reveal something about perceptions of the role of parliamentarians. The role of MPs has received much systematic attention from Dutch political scientists. The most comprehensive study of the parliamentary universe was reported upon by van Schendelen in 1981.[19] In this survey an encyclopaedic range of questions was put to members of the Second Chamber about every conceivable aspect of their duties. One of its more general findings was that the indifference of voters towards MPs as fertile objects of personal communication was paralleled by the extremely poor opinion legislators held about the level of awareness of the citizens.

This overwhelmingly negative relationship was elaborated by van Schendelen in an article of the same period, in which he examines this central dimension of representative politics.[20] He conceded that 'strong negative orientations towards the main elements of representation-in-action' are widespread in Western democracies. Of the case of the Netherlands he has this to say:

> Only 4% of the citizens have ever had any contact with an MP and less than 10% of MPs consider individual citizens to be an important source of information for their own legislative activities. The direct linkage between Dutch electors and elected is, indeed, quite weak.

That this mutual isolation may be deepening is suggested by evidence from the 1979 survey[21] which reveals that members of the Second

Chamber placed even less emphasis upon dealing with citizens' complaints than members of the 1972 Chamber. A further detail was that MPs from the major centre and right of centre parties, CDA and VVD, were somewhat less impressed with the cognitive abilities of voters than their colleagues from Labour and D'66.

It is difficult to determine, without extensive cross-national comparisons, whether or not the Netherlands is exceptional in the apparent distance disclosed between legislators and the public. Some further illumination is however available from the findings of a study of role-perceptions on the part of Dutch, German and British parliamentarians.[22] All three contingents shared a high view of their role as policy-makers. As advocates of ideologies, however, Dutch MPs were much less enthusiastic than their counterparts, preferring to regard themselves as 'technicians'. But the most revealing disclosure, in the context of representation, was that the task of mediation between groups and individuals, an activity scored highly by British and even more highly by German MPs, was virtually ignored by the Dutch.

How far the electoral system contributes directly to these phenomena is difficult to assess. But there are certainly features of the representational process which tend to distance members of parliament from the people, and thereby to augment attitudes on the part of national legislators that their responsibilities are best fulfilled sealed off from the pressures of public sentiment.

The assault on 'Extreme PR'

Until the 1960s, apart from occasional attempts to raise the threshold for entry to parliament,[23] all of which proved unsuccessful, the system adopted in 1918 appeared to command broad acceptance. But with the sea-changes of depillarisation came a mood of challenge to long-established customs which extended to the practice of PR. Questions about its aptness and efficacy were interwoven with disquiets about the entire nexus between populace and government.

The Appeal drawn up by Democrats '66 set out many of the criticisms and proposed certain remedies.[24] The two central strands of the critique concerned firstly the outcome of elections in terms of the complexion of cabinets, and secondly the relationship – or lack of it – between parliament and the voters. The behaviour of parties and party leaders was common to both concerns. The major items of unease were summarised by this author in an article published in Amsterdam in 1972.[25] The initial item – the inconclusiveness of elections – addressed the architecture of representation. PR had been the concerted response of the political élite to the facts of multi-party competition. By faithfully reflecting the entrenched position of the major parties, the electoral system virtually ensured, firstly, that there would be little change in their volume of support at successive elections and, secondly, that there would be no clear-cut majorities in the Second Chamber. What followed each election therefore would be an elaborate game of inter-party bargaining, which might well override any gains and losses which might have been registered.

Prolonged delays in cabinet formation, and the possibility of subsequent manoeuvres which could change the composition of cabinets without recourse to the voters (as in 1958, 1965 and 1966) were further concomitants of the system. There was also the persistent fact that the perennial alliance between the three major confessional parties controlled the composition of all governments. This stranglehold was a product of two circumstances. One was the regular amassing by the confessional trio of around half the total national vote, so that no government could omit the Catholic party and one or both of the main Calvinist formations. The other feature was that since the confessionals held the centre of the political spectrum, no concerted opposition could be mounted against them.

Any build-up of frustration with the operation of national politics was thus bound to confront the intractability of confessional dominance. Most nostrums had this issue at their core, including proposals to restore some form of constituency system which would bring MPs into a direct relationship with the voters. If such a change would make representatives more accountable to the electors, what could ensure that *governments* reflected the wishes of the people? The most widely canvassed recipe for that became the notion that the Prime Minister should be chosen, in a quasi-presidential manner, by direct election, alongside the elections for the Second Chamber.

Credit for originating this idea is generally attributed to Professor Glastra van Loon, who first advanced it in an article of 1964.[26] The suggestion was taken up in the programme put forward by Democrats '66 and in 1967 a committee was set up by the Second Chamber to study proposals for constitutional reform.[27] The argument for a directly-elected Minister-President rested upon the belief that the formation of the cabinet by someone who commanded majority support among all voters would somehow result in a ministry which would reflect that majority.

How precisely an elected premier could tailor the parliamentary cloth so as to achieve that outcome was not however very clear. The construction of a cabinet with legislative support would still confront the stubborn geometry of a centre-based system, unless of course, as many advocates hoped, a presidential leader would so magnetise the party universe that a new configuration would ensue. This hope was bound up with the slightly later view that if the party system could be so polarised as to make elections into a contest between two major alternative strategies, then national politics could be rescued from inertia and cynicism.

The sense of malaise which afflicted critics of the system was captured by van Loon in a subsequent essay which spelled out his objections to the post-war record:[28] middle of the road government; the bowdlerisation of long-term issues to serve tactical compromise; and the dilution of policy-making by technicians. In the cause of attaining sharper and clearer outcomes, he proposed a constituency system with two-round parliamentary elections designed to produce majority alliances. The supposed defects of nationwide PR were now at the centre of debates about the whole structure of the political process.

To some commentators however the quest for a procedural answer to the deficiences of the system seemed vain. One recorded that 'such a reform of the electoral system would not cause the number of parties in parliament to diminish, the numerical relations between the main parties would hardly change, cabinet formation would be equally difficult and the proposed reform would not lead to a two-party system.'[29] To this pessimism, another academic countered with the conviction that a constituency system '*would* facilitate the formation of two large political groups which could offer real alternatives to the voters at the polls'.[30] Indeed, he went on to claim that given such a reform 'there would be no need for a directly-elected Prime Minister as proposed by D'66'.

As the debate proceeded, there were signs that the voters themselves, without the aid of new devices, were beginning to change the long-established mathematics of the party system, at least in terms of the volume of support for the big formations. In the 1967 election, the combined holding of the confessional trio fell from seventy-six seats (a majority in the Second Chamber) to sixty-nine. By the time the third report of the Cals-Donner committee appeared, in 1971, this figure had dropped to fifty-eight, and by the following year to forty-eight seats. So the grip of the confessional centre had, it seemed, been loosened.

In its third report, the committee opted for two principal reforms.

The first was that there should be provision for the direct election of a cabinet-maker, or *formateur*, but without stipulating that such a figure would automatically become Prime Minister. The second proposal was that the electoral system should be changed from nationwide PR. Instead, a partition of the single national constituency into twelve districts was recommended, thus instituting a regional list system, with each district returning a dozen or so MPs. The report was endorsed by the Labour Party, and in 1974, when Labour was the dominant voice in cabinet, the proposals were submitted to parliament. Following lengthy debate, however, they were eventually rejected, in January 1975, after prolonged opposition by the confessionals and the Liberals.[31] Thus ended a decade of controversy over the retention of extreme PR. Despite all efforts at reform, the *status quo* had been reaffirmed.

In retrospect it may seem that a great deal of time and energy had been expended in a cause which was somewhat peripheral to the issues as perceived in the late 1960s and early 1970s. For it is difficult to believe that a change from national PR to what would be relatively large multi-member constituencies, would have engineered significant changes in the political balance beyond those which took place as a result of voter behaviour. What such a revision might, however, have achieved is a recalibration of the distance between individual MPs and their electors. Under a district system most voters could identify with party representatives who would no longer be anonymous and who would have some linkage with a locality.

Since the mid-1970s the party system has consolidated in a way which now makes two-party government almost the norm. The heat has gone out of some of the earlier passions for inducing a more adversarial system, because the system has proved more viable than many forecast in the early 1970s. Locality representation has likewise gone off the agenda. During the 1980s parties have paid increasing attention to the regional dimension in both policy concerns and the process of candidate selection. But sensitivity in regional matters, although it may compensate for the absence of geography in formal representation, does not replace it. A further period of political turbulence will doubtless be necessary before this feature is re-examined.

NOTES

1. See Daalder's excellent summary of the history of Dutch electoral arrangements, (1975), pp. 223–6. Also Dittrich and Gosman, the Compendium A1200–6/8 (1986).
2. Ibid. (1975), p. 227.
3. 'Institutional Conservatism in the Netherlands', *West European Politics*, 12/1 (1989).
4. Credited by Lakeman and Lambert, *Voting in Democracies*, London 1945, to Thomas Gilpin (Philadelphia, 1844) and Victor Considerant (Geneva, 1846).
5. See Summary of the Franchise Act, in *The Kingdom of the Netherlands*, Ministry of Foreign Affairs 1984.
6. A formula adopted in 1933 at the instigation of the Catholic and Social Democratic parties. Daalder (1975), p. 228.
7. Supplement to the *Staatscourant* (official gazette), 3 June 1986.
8. Details of voting ages and the size of the electorate derived from Dittrich and Gosman, The Compendium A 1200–24/32.
9. See Gladdish (1985).
10. Lijphart (1968, 75).
11. Andeweg (1989).
12. Van Raalte (1959), p. 81.
13. Approximately one-third of total current public expenditure.
14. Israel seems the only other example of a complete absence of locality representation.
15. K. Gladdish, A. Liddell and P. Giddings, 'MPs' perceptions of the British electoral system'. Reading Politics Research Group Paper no. 1, 1984.
16. Ivor Crewe, 'British MP's and their constituents: How strong are the Links?' Essex Paper in Politics, 1987.
17. G. Irwin and H. Molleman, 'Political participation in The Netherlands', Leiden, 1971.
18. L. de Bruyn and J. Foppen, '*The Dutch Voter 1972-3*', 2 vols, Nijmegen, 1974.
19. M.P.C.M. van Schendelen, '*The Dutch Member of Parliament, 1979-80*', Rotterdam, 1981.
20. M.P.C.M. van Schendelen, 'Disaffected Representation in The Netherlands', *Acta Politica*, XVI (April 1981).
21. See Note 19.
22. S. Eldersveld, J. Kooiman and T. van der Tak, *Elite Images of Dutch Politics*, Ann Arbor, 1981.
23. Daalder (1975), p. 229.
24. See Chapter 4.
25. K.R. Gladdish, 'Two Party versus Multi-Party: The Netherlands and Britain', *Acta Politica*, VII, 3, 1972.
26. 'Kiezen of Delen' (Take it or leave it), *Nederlands Juristenblad*, 1964.
27. The Cals-Donner Committee, which issued three reports, in 1968, 1969 and 1971.
28. 'Democracy in The Netherlands', *Acta Politica*, III (1967-8).
29. R. Verboom, 'Implications of PR with 18 Districts', *Acta Politica*, III (1967-8).
30. 'Reaction to the implications of PR . . . J in T'veld, *Acta Politica*, III (1967-8).
31. Daalder (1975), p. 245.

7

THE PARLIAMENTARY ARENA

The Dutch Parliament is unique. Is there another country with a parliamentary system in which ministers are forbidden to be members of Parliament?

— E. van Raalte, *The Parliament of the Netherlands* (1959), Preface

The quotation above, from a work by a distinguished constitutional commentator, draws attention to a central feature of parliamentary operations in the Netherlands, even though it happens not to be unique. Norway has a similar provision,[1] and other European states have variations on the theme of the separation of powers. But from a British standpoint the Dutch division between cabinet and parliament is a striking departure from the stereotype of responsible democratic government, and one which has profound consequences.

To present an intelligible account of the Dutch legislature requires some selective ordering of the various dimensions of role, procedure and behaviour. To this end, this chapter will begin with a sketch of the constitutional scaffolding, followed by a *catalogue raisonée* of the main aspects of parliamentary activity. It will proceed to a summary of the more significant recent developments and will conclude with a characterisation of the membership, in terms of their outlook and background.

The constitutional frame

The origins of the modern Dutch parliament, the States-General in The Hague, can be traced back to the first national assembly of 1798 during the relatively brief period of French domination. The term 'States-General' stems from the republic and indeed has its roots in the pre-independence era, although it did not then refer to an elected legislature within a unitary state. The present parliament has a continuous history since 1814 when it was established under the constitution which restored Dutch independence and inaugurated the monarchy. The operation of a parliamentary system of government dates from the constitutional revision of 1848–9. The current mode of composition of parliament was determined by the settlement of 1917–18, while the latest enactment of its provenance and scope was set down in the constitutional re-draft of 1983.

Although the concept is not explicitly affirmed, the Netherlands is governed by the principle of parliamentary supremacy, mitigated only by the fact that certain matters require an exceptional majority in the legislature. The Netherlands has remained an hereditary monarchy since 1814, and acts which affect the throne usually necessitate special proceedings. The political role of the monarch is essentially passive and symbolic, although the perennial need for the formation of coalition cabinets can result in him, or her, having to perform an intermediary task in order to initiate this process.

Articles 50–72 of the 1983 Constitutional Statement set out the fundamental items of the provision for a parliamentary system.[2] They assert that the States-General shall consist of two chambers, a First Chamber (the ratifying house) with seventy-five members, and the Second Chamber (the effective legislative house) with 150 members. The parliamentary term shall be four years, but each chamber may be dissolved before a term is completed. Each chamber shall be elected by proportional representation and by secret ballot; the First by the members of the provincial councils, and the Second directly, by all adults of and above the age of eighteen, with two forms of disqualification (convicted prisoners serving one year or more, and mental incompetents). No one may sit in both chambers simultaneously; and no minister, state secretary, state councillor, state auditor or certain judicial figures can be a member of either chamber. Sittings of parliament must be held in public, but there are provisions for sessions *in camera*.

There are further constitutional provisions, under Articles 81–111, which deal with parliamentary procedure and competence. In the broadest terms these are the outcome of the decisions of parliament itself over the past 140 years. For as Article 120 roundly states, 'The constitutionality of Acts of Parliament and treaties shall not be reviewed by the courts'. There is thus an express exclusion of any form of judicial review, so that it can be said, like Britain, that the constitution of the Netherlands is what parliament, over time, has decided it should be. Therefore in both law and practice, the States-General is at the summit of the governmental pyramid; its powers are embodied in a written constitution, but that constitution it and only it can change.

Parliamentary operations

The States-General conforms to the familiar model of West European parliamentary operations, embracing the four basic functions of a democratic legislature. Firstly all legislation requires parliamentary enactment, without exception. This extends to the approval of treaties (Article 91) though this approval may be tacit under certain circumstances. It also extends to declarations of war and the ending of war. It includes, as one would expect, all financial provisions undertaken by the state, pre-eminently the annual budget. Legislation in enacted by a simple majority in both chambers, though matters affecting the throne (Articles 29 and 30) or the financial remuneration of MPs (Article 63) require a two-thirds majority in both chambers. Since the overwhelming preponderance of bills are introduced by the cabinet,[3] the legislative task of parliament is essentially that of the discussion and, if necessary, amendment of government proposals. To accomplish this task, there is an extensive committee structure which divides the field of legislation into subject areas.

The second function of parliament is the generation of policy proposals, which may inspire further legislation, in the form of motions. In common with most other activities, the tabling of motions has increased enormously in frequency over the past twenty years. Indeed it could be said that this form of policy initiation has become almost a new dimension of parliamentary participation since the latter 1960s.

The third function, which has also assumed far greater proportions over the same period, is that of the scrutiny of government. Procedurally, the process of scrutiny takes three possible forms: questions, interpellations and commissions of inquiry. The last, which is the most searching and elaborate of the forms, is an extremely rare operation, engaged in only when the other forms seem likely to prove inadequate. It may be regarded as the last resort in the case of massive scandals, as with the furore over government subsidies to the RSV company of Rotterdam in 1985–6, or where a major vein of public policy has to be opened, as with the Commission which sat from 1947–56 to enquire into the conduct of the governments in exile during the Second World War.[4] The rarity of this procedure is illustrated by the facts that the latter case led to the first Commission in sixty years, while the former was only the next occasion.

Interpellation, which is a grand investigation of ministerial conduct by an MP with the approval of the respective Chamber, is a more frequent affair than a commission of inquiry, although its frequency has not increased as much as other forms of parliamentary activity in recent years. By far the most common form of parliamentary scrutiny is the question addressed to ministers, and this has soared in popularity since the early 1960s. Since ministers normally only attend either chamber when presenting or defending legislative proposals, questions are usually put and answered in writing.[5]

The fourth and final basic function of parliament is the elective function. Dutch cabinets are not, as has been noted, part of the legislature; nor do they need to consist of members who have been elected to either chamber. Nevertheless, both the formation and the survival of cabinets are dependent upon the support of a majority in both chambers, so that parliamentary groups play the principal role in the establishment of new governments after each parliamentary election.

The legislative process can be viewed in two perspectives – the procedural and the political. The procedural mechanisms in the Netherlands, set out in a systematic, comparative form, are available in English in the compendium *'Parliaments of the World'*, produced by the Inter-Parliamentary Union.[6] An in-depth historical survey up to 1959, also in English, is provided by van Raalte.[7] There are numerous accounts in Dutch, notably those by van Schendelen,[8] Visscher,[9] and in the symposium edited by Franssen.[10] The starting point of the legislative process is normally the introduction of a bill by a minister, though measures are occasionally sponsored by an MP. Before a bill is presented to parliament, it is usually submitted to the Council of State, a body which advises on possible constitutional implications. The Social and Economic Council is also consulted on matters which fall within its sphere of expertise.

The consideration of bills begins in the Second Chamber, where, after a first reading, they are passed to the most appropriate committee for detailed scrutiny. The committee structure of parliament, in 1986, consisted of a framework of thirty permanent subject committees in the Second Chamber, and twenty in the First Chamber. There were in addition about sixty special committees in the former (reduced to fifteen in 1987), and three in the latter. If a bill falls within the ambit of a subject committee, it will be directed to it. Otherwise it will be referred to either an existing or a newly-formed special committee.

The composition of committees is determined by the Chairman of each Chamber with respect to the overall party arithmetic. Committees elect their own chairmen, but this too is arranged to accord with the distribution of party strengths. Committee hearings are usually open, journalists may attend, and proceedings may be broadcast, either directly or in summary form, on radio and television. At the committee stage amendments may be proposed, discussed and incorporated in bills. When the examination of a bill by a committee is completed, the results are presented to the Second Chamber for plenary debate and discussion clause by clause. There may be a further reading if the plenary discussion has resulted in significant changes.

The processes of amendment are carefully invigilated by the minister or ministers concerned. Parliament has complete control over its treatment of legislation and sets its own agenda and timing for this.[11] Given the separation between cabinet and parliament, the States-General is less overtly dominated by the executive than in most European states, above all Britain. But legislation is nevertheless executive-directed, and, as elsewhere, governments seek to get their measures through with a minimum of alteration in the legislature. Ministers may therefore refuse to accept amendments, and in extreme cases may prefer to withdraw a bill. Cabinets expect to be able to rely upon their supporting parties in parliament to ensure that their proposals are not mutilated to the point of nullity; and there is extensive consultation behind the scenes to prevent this happening. The success of these consultations is revealed by the fact that virtually all government measures are eventually passed, though up to half with amendments agreed between ministers and the Second Chamber.[12] One interesting feature of the amendment process is that in each case it is a matter of whether MPs decide to endorse or reject. There is no tradition of abstention in the Dutch parliament, though spokesmen can cover the absence of individual MPs by delivering the party vote.

Once an acceptable outcome has been achieved in the Lower House, bills are then passed to the Upper House which examines them by means of a plenary debate. The First Chamber has no powers to amend legislation. It must either accept or reject measures in their entirety, and the latter course is extremely unusual. After ratification by the First Chamber, bills are submitted for the royal assent and for counter-signature by the appropriate minister. The annual budget follows the same course as other legislation. There are standing committees in both chambers to examine the budget, and all members receive an annual report on the economic situation prepared by the Central Planning Bureau.

Parliamentary anatomy

It is sometimes assumed, when characterising parliaments, that their basic dynamics can be judged according to how the chambers are physically arranged. Thus the British House of Commons with its rows of confronting benches seems clearly designed for adversarial politics, while the practice in other European chambers of arranging the seats in a semi-circle, facing a central rostrum, suggests a different style, either more consensual or conceivably ministerially dominated.

The two houses in the Dutch parliament are, in these terms, arranged in a manner which might mislead the intuitive. For they are in fact set out according to the British plan, with the parties supporting the government on one side, and the non-governing parties on the other. This implies an adversarial model, but parliamentary operations in the Netherlands are not conceived in strictly oppositional terms. The underlying reasons for this will be clear from earlier chapters.[13] Despite the similarity of layout, there is of course a vital difference between Dutch and British arrangements in that in the Netherlands, ministers, if they are present at all, sit at a table at one end of the chamber and not on the front bench. This expresses their status as visitors, or invitees. They have the right to attend parliamentary sessions, and may be invited to do so (Article 69), but usually only one minister will attend at a time. The Prime minister, who has no departmental responsibilities, is a somewhat infrequent attender except when major policy is under attack.[14]

Relations between ministers and parliament are a matter of practised understandings between the various agencies. Van Raalte, writing in the 1950s, considered it the responsibility of the Chairman of the Lower House to 'protect the Government', if necessary adjourning sessions until a minister had had time to take stock of the parliamentary input and re-assess his position.[15] This brings out the significance of the Chairman, in each chamber, as both the mediator of parliamentary business and the organisational bridge between cabinet and legislature. The role has gained in importance as parliamentary business has increased. The Presidium in the Second Chamber, which originally comprised the Chairman and two Vice-Chairmen, had by 1984 expanded to the Chairman and six Vice-Chairmen, chosen from the major parliamentary groups.[16].

If the Dutch parliament cannot be presented primarily in terms of government versus opposition, what are its key components? The answer, as one might expect in a multi-party system, is the parliamentary group or *fractie*. There are nine *fracties* in the current Second Chamber (as from 1989), ranging in size from over fifty members (the CDA) down to one-person groups (*Janmaat* and RPF). The larger groups have a collegial character and are presided over by an elected chairman. Relations between the *fracties* and their respective national parties are best described as 'semi-detached'. MPs may owe their position to party managers outside parliament, but this is rarely allowed to detract from their sense of autonomy.[17] Discipline within the *fractie* is not imposed by party whips but depends upon group cohesion. If sanctions are needed to curb dissent they more often come from the group than from the chairman.[18] Dissent does of course occur, and in extreme cases can result in the formation of breakaway groups. Usually such groups are ephemeral though they may develop into distinct parties. Thus the PPR, formed in 1968 when three MPs broke from the Catholic People's Party, achieved a permanent identity and a national base; others, such as DS'70, a breakaway from Labour, though it served in cabinet from 1971–2, had a briefer existence and was dissolved in 1981.

It is within the plenary meetings of the *fracties* that the tactics and strategy of parliamentary operations are decided.[19] All, regardless of size, are officially recognised and have paid staffs and resources to support their activities. Indeed the budget for the parliamentary groups rose from a modest 30,000 guilders in 1965 to a towering figure of 15.8 million guilders in 1985.[20] The *fracties* are thus the building blocks of all legislative behaviour and their independence imbues parliament with a strongly self-determining character. The key point here is that the cabinet governs, to a greater extent than in most systems, with the consent of the parliamentary groups. As a leading commentator has put it, 'Because the key to cabinet stability is in the hands of . . . the parliamentary parties, the Netherlands has become an exceptional case of "rule by Parliament." '[21] He goes on to locate the core of the process as 'the political osmosis between the parties-in-coalition and their cabinet'. But, as will be evident from the logistics of parliamentary activity, parties outside the coalition can make a significant impact upon government policy. In March 1988, the CDA-VVD cabinet presented to the Second Chamber a package of social and economic measures designed to make 'drastic reductions' in social security benefits and to lower personal taxes. The package was substantially amended as a result of opposition from the Labour *fractie* which was able to wrest concessions from the government on a number of items.[22]

Parliamentary logistics

In his paper of 1976, van Schendelen produced convincing evidence that the scale and intensity of parliamentary operations had augmented dramatically over the preceding decade.[23] He concluded: 'The increased parliamentary activism since 1967 has been such that the Netherlands can, in a sense, be said to have got a different type of Lower House.' What is most striking about the growth of parliamentary animation, comparing the early 1970s with the latter 1950s, is that it seems largely autochthonous in that it does not appear to relate to any comparable increase of governmental inputs.

During the parliamentary session of 1956–7, 185 bills were discussed in the Second Chamber. By 1971–2 this number had risen only slightly to 213 bills. Yet committee meetings in the Lower House had trebled in frequency by the end of that period, as had the number of amendments to bills proposed by the *fracties*. So far as policy initiatives were concerned, the number of motions tabled in the Second Chamber had increased ninefold, from twenty in 1956–7, to 176 in 1971–2. Additionally, on the scrutiny front the number of interpellations had trebled, from six to nineteen, and the annual total of questions put to ministers had escalated by a factor of ten, from 211 (1956–7) to 2,092 (1971–2).

In seeking some explanations for this enormous increase of business over a relatively short period, van Schendelen considered three possible avenues: variables affecting the personnel of the chamber, changes in the resources available to the *fracties*, and factors deriving from changes in the political culture. Although he discerns several features affecting what he terms the 'intra-parliamentary variables', the only persuasive factor here is that from 1966 on the number of assistants available to MPs had multiplied, as is reflected in the rising budget for facilities in the Lower House. So he is driven to allocate much of the explanation to changes in the general political climate, though this cannot readily be measured. The breakdown of the settled patterns of accommodation associated with the structures of *verzuiling* seems therefore the most likely source of an acceleration of parliamentary challenge and criticism *vis-à-vis* governments of varied complexions.

More recent data on parliamentary activity have been provided by Visscher who, from the vantage point of the mid-1980s, has surveyed the range of fields in which parliamentary participation has manifestly burgeoned since the 1960s.[24] Dealing first with legislative operations, his figures show a consistent expansion of parliamentary intervention (see Tables 7.1 and 7.2).

Table 7.1
AMENDMENTS PROPOSED TO BILLS IN SECOND CHAMBER

	Submitted	*Adopted*
1963–4	178	62
1973–4	362	81
1983–4	800	225

Table 7.2
AMENDMENTS TO THE BUDGET PROPOSED IN
SECOND CHAMBER

	Submitted	*Adopted*
1964	2	0
1974	41	5
1984	115	38

Table 7.3
MOTIONS TABLED IN SECOND CHAMBER

	Tabled	*Adopted*
1963–4	9	1
1973–4	196	61
1983–4	1214	485

On the score of policy initiatives, as reflected in the number of motions tabled in the Lower House, an enormous increase is evident, although the frequency from year to year is somewhat uneven (see Table 7.3).

In the realm of parliamentary scrutiny, although the number of interpellations increased from three in 1963–4 to seventeen in 1973–4, the figure for 1983–4 showed no further growth. In the case of questions put to ministers, a vast increase occurred over the decade from 1961–2 to 1971–2 and the much higher level was more or less maintained over the subsequent decade (see Table 7.4).

The overall picture shows a startling rise in the three spheres of legislative intervention, policy initiatives and scrutiny. Van Schendelen's endeavour to explain this exceptional growth of parliamentary activism

Table 7.4
QUESTIONS TO MINISTERS

	Second Chamber	First Chamber
1961–2	208	12
1971–2	1689	169
1981–2	1481	37

has been subsequently echoed by Daalder who regards parties as having become more sensitive to public opinion with the loss of their 'special clienteles' post-*verzuiling*.[25]

Parliamentary physiology

The character of a legislature can be appraised in a variety of ways. In this chapter, four aspects of the Dutch parliament have so far been considered: its constitutional status, its operations, its key components, and its record of recent activity. There is one further factor which can help to illuminate its nature, and that is the make-up of its members. It will already be clear that the Lower House is in all respects the effective legislative chamber. Aspiring politicians might therefore be expected to regard it as the prime forum for participation in public affairs. Membership of the First Chamber is essentially honorific and its composition, the result of election by provincial councils, reflects this. Entry to the First Chamber tends to be a reward for national and local figures whose reputation has been made during more active stages of their careers.

Somewhat surprisingly, although the Second Chamber is the central arena of national politics, a large proportion of those admitted to it do not appear to regard it as a permanent base. Despite the many changes in the pattern of parliamentary activity over the past generation, this feature has remained strangely constant. Van Schendelen records that the average tenure of members of the Second Chamber, a mere 5.8 years in 1963, had decreased to 4.9 years by 1967. In 1979 almost half the membership has served for less than four years, while only one-eighth had served for ten years or more.[26]

Explanations of this relative brevity of service are not readily attributable to the dynamics of the electoral system, for, despite the increased volatility of party holdings in parliament since the 1960s, the great majority of MPs can be reasonably assured of re-nomination through the party lists. They certainly do not face the prospect of having to defend their seats in individual contests where a small shift of support may defeat them. The reasons must therefore be sought within the overall context of public life in the Netherlands. Here the most obvious factor is the extent of mobility between the various sectors. Service in parliament may be regarded as an interface between other governmental posts or public offices at national, provincial and local levels. Thus in the 1979 Second Chamber, almost as many MPs had their sights on posts as municipal mayor (appointees of the national government) as upon those of minister or state secretary.[27]

This notion of parliamentary service as an interface is to an extent born out by evidence on the background of MPs. Since the war the number of members who had formerly been government employees has steadily risen from 17% in 1946 to 48% in 1986.[28] This rise had been somewhat at the expense of the professions, which accounted for 30% of the membership in 1946 but only 5% by 1986. In that year only 10% of members had backgrounds in trade, industry or agriculture. At the other end of the line the number of MPs moving into cabinet posts has increased over time. In the period 1946–67, only 47% of cabinet members had previous parliamentary experience; in the period 1967–86 this figure rose to 67%.[29] Of the fourteen cabinet ministers sworn in on 7 November 1989, five had never served in parliament; of these, two were previously members of the European parliament, two were appointed direct from universities and the fifth from an employers' federation. Of the ten junior ministers half had no parliamentary experience; three of these came from local government, one from the Farmers Union and a fifth had formerly been a civil servant.

Relatively high mobility on the part of MPs helps to explain the comparatively low average age of members of the Lower House. In 1952 the average age was a little over fifty years. In 1972 it was down to forty-six, and though it has risen slightly since 1977, it is still low in comparison with other countries.[30] It appears that members of the Second Chamber prefer to move on to other jobs, mainly in government, than to make the House the summit of their ambitions. In the survey of the 1979 Chamber, almost one quarter of the members were either uncertain about or definitely did not wish to be re-nominated.[31]

Yet there are many features of parliamentary life in the Netherlands which suggest that it is both congenial and well rewarded. In the mid-1970s, Dutch MPs had the highest salaries of all national legislators in Western Europe.[32] In the 1980s the method of remuneration was changed so as to encourage MPs to devote their whole time to parliamentary matters by means of a tax-free indemnification for lost income. Conditions of service are likewise of a standard which other parliamentarians might well envy. Each MP is provided with an office, and can engage, at public expense, a personal assistant. As already noted, the budget for facilities for both the *fracties* and individual MPs has increased dramatically in recent years.

There seems little question that Dutch MPs enjoy high public status. They also have high visibility, given that the total membership of both chambers is only 225 and that the media pay much attention to parliamentary business. Further, they enjoy within the *fracties* considerable freedom of expression, and, through the extensive allocation of specialist portfolios, the opportunity to exercise considerable influence within their field of expertise. To complete an attractive picture, they are in practice released, given the electoral arrangements, from the direct pressures of constituents. As observed in Chapter 6, very few Dutch citizens afflict individual MPs with their problems or anxieties, since few regard them as useful targets for lobbying on either local or national issues.

In the matter of lobbying, the position of Dutch MPs *vis-à-vis* pressure groups is of interest. A survey carried out in the late 1960s by Daalder and Rusk threw some instructive light upon the ostensible autonomy of legislators.[33] For although 85% of the MPs canvassed conceded that pressure groups had considerable influence on legislative decision-making, most were aloof to any feeling that they represented any particular groups. The report records that 'only one socialist [MP] mentions workers organisations and not a single liberal mentions employers organisations, even though a close reading of the parliamentary record would easily reveal where effective sympathies go.' The general position appears to be that MPs in the Netherlands regard themselves as above the hurly-burly of arm-twisting by interest groups, in their solemn capacity as 'trustees' of the national interest, albeit viewed from a partisan perspective.

To round off a collective portrait of parliament, information about the education and pedigree of its members is worth summarising. One interesting background variable might be cited here. In the 1979–80 parliament, almost 16% of the Second Chamber had worked in central government, but only 3% in local government. In the First Chamber this imbalance was reversed; only 9% had previously worked at central government level, while 24% had backgrounds in local government.[34] This seems to reflect the method of composition of the Upper House which is elected by provincial councils.

In terms of education both chambers have long been heavily weighted towards university graduates, almost two-thirds of the members of each House.[35] But considerable educational mobility among the most recent generation of MPs is revealed by the fact that the overwhelming proportion of members of both chambers (more than 80%) did not have fathers who had been to university.[36] Most surprisingly, in the Second Chamber only one member was the son of a former MP. Reference to sons prompts a query about daughters. Up till the 1960s, the Dutch Parliament, like most other European legislatures, was a largely male assembly. Even the radical populism of the 1960s was unable to raise the female membership to reach 10% in the Second Chamber or 5% in the First. But the 1970s and '80s have seen a steady if undramatic increase in the number of women MPs. By 1979 the figures had climbed to 15% in the Lower and 10% in the Upper House. And by 1988 the proportion had further increased with the balance altered between the two chambers; the First now contained 24% and the Second 21% women members.[37] This may be compared with the lamentable British record, which in 1988 stood at a mere 6% in both the House of Commons and among the active members of the House of Lords.[38]

It is tempting, though risky, to conclude with some attempt at an impression of the general atmosphere of parliamentary deliberations in the Netherlands. Fortunately a respected Dutch authority has hazarded a view on this. Thirty years ago van Raalte conceded that the ethos of the two chambers tended to be neither dramatic nor flamboyant. 'Debates in the Dutch parliament', he averred, 'are frequently concerned with subordinate and often rather technical aspects of the subject on the agenda.'[39] This seems a cautious, possibly even tactful memorial. He goes on to observe that speeches are usually left to the subject specialists and are mostly read rather than delivered extempore. A high seriousness tends to mark proceedings and there is little place for the antics which frequently grace or mar performances in the British House of Commons. The tone had perhaps become less solemn in the late 1980s than it was in the late 1950s, and certainly the pace of business has hotted up considerably as the figures for increased parliamentary activity clearly demonstrate.

In contrast with the somewhat austere tableau of the formal face of parliament, the style of Dutch MPs outside the Chambers, if the present author's experience is at all typical, tends to be extremely open and informal. They give the impression of being more relaxed and less inhibited by strict schedules than many of their European counterparts. Their forthcoming attitude certainly suggests that they believe parliament should be an accessible forum; and they are mostly happy to discuss its operations with frankness and sincerity. How far the absence of direct constituency pressure may contribute to this *bienfaisance* it is of course impossible to determine.

NOTES

1. See Elder, Thomas and Arte, '*The Consensual Democracies*' p. 108, Oxford 1982.
2. English Translation, Ministry of Home Affairs, Feb. 1983.
3. See van Schendelen, 'The Activism of the Dutch Second Chamber', ECPR Paper, 1976.
4. Van Raalte (1959), pp. 158–9.
5. Ibid., pp. 147–8.
6. 1st edition (prepared by V. Herman), London 1976; 2nd edition, Aldershot, 1986.
7. Van Raalte (1959).
8. *Parlementaire Informatie Besluitvorming – Vertegenwoordiging* (Parliamentary Information, Decision-Making and Representation), Rotterdam, 1975.
9. Compendium (1986) A 0600.
10. *Het Parlement in Aktie* (Parliament in Action), Assen, 1986.
11. Van Raalte (1959), p. 166.
12 Van Schendelen (1975), p. 60.
13. See also Daalder (1966) and Gladdish (1987).
14. Van Raalte (1959) p. 184.
15. Ibid., p. 111.
16. Visscher (1986) Compendium A 0600–15.
17. See Daalder (1987), p. 203 *et passim*.
18. Van Schendelen (1975), p. 45.
19 Daalder and Rusk in Patterson and Wahlke (1972).
20. Visscher (1986) Compendium A 0600–75/6.
21. Van Schendelen and Jackson, 'Political Crises and Parliaments', IPSA 1982, p. 16.
22. *Keesings*, 9/88.
23. See Note 3.
24. Compendium (1986) A 0600–45/61.
25. Daalder (1987), p. 258.
26. Van Schendelen (1981), p. 30.
27. Ibid, pp. 318–19.

28. Daalder (1987), p. 212.
29. Ibid, p. 213.
30. Ibid.
31. Van Schendelen (1981), p. 318.
32. Inter-Parliamentary Union Compendium, p. 236. This was the result of a sharp increase in MPs salaries in 1968. Van den Berg (1983), p. 327.
33. In Patterson and Wahlke (1972).
34. Van Schendelen (1981).
35. Ibid., p. 65.
36. Ibid., p. 41.
37. Information Office, Royal Netherlands Embassy, London.
38. British Parliamentary Information Office.
39. Van Raalte (1959), p. 180.

8
THE POLITICAL EXECUTIVE

Cabinet government

> I urged Lord Rosebery not to bring too many matters before the Cabinet, as
> nothing was decided there . . .
> — Queen Victoria[1]

In his admirably concise account of the development of the English
parliament, Kenneth Mackenzie summarised the origins of the cabinet
in Britain.[2] From its beginning as a commitee of the Privy Council under
Charles II, it survived the decline of the Council to emerge as an
unofficial 'board of government' which included the heads of the major
departments of state who met weekly to deal with national matters. The
appointment of Walpole as First Lord of the Treasury coincided with the
withdrawal of George I from the cabinet's deliberations. Walpole went
on to manage the House of Commons on behalf of the King, earning the
sobriquet 'prime minister', a term devised by his opponents to imply
that he was usurping the position of chief executive.

It took a further half-century before the notion of a collective ministry
surfaced when, with the downfall of Lord North, there was a complete
change of ministers in 1782. A further century elapsed before the
principle was finally established that if the cabinet was defeated in parliament, a general election was required before government could proceed.[3]
By this time party government had conclusively excluded the monarch
from any significant role in political affairs.

Since the 1880s, as the scope of the political executive has exploded,
there has been much to suggest that prime-ministerial government
has gradually replaced cabinet government in Britain. Thus by the
1980s the 'board of government', composed of the holders of the major
offices of state, could be viewed as the entourage of an all-powerful
Prime Minister who, as national leader of the majority party in the Commons, confronts few if any checks upon the exercise of a highly
personal prerogative. Given the particularity of these developments,
and given that the concept of a cabinet was a British invention, it
might be wondered whether the term 'cabinet government' is a useful
one for the purposes of comparative analysis. The Dutch case certainly
raises many questions about how far there is a clear operational

model of cabinet government which can be applied to West European democracies. During the intial phase of centralised government in the Netherlands, from 1814–40, the newly-instituted monarch selected and dismissed his principal advisers at will, and presided personally over their deliberations. With the advent of responsible government after 1848, the ministers gradually detached themselves from royal influence and developed a closer relationship with parliament. But it is difficult to present the operations of Dutch ministries in the latter nineteenth century as conforming to any model of collective cabinet government under the direction of a prime minister.[4]

The reasons for the difficulty are threefold. The most obvious was the absence of a fully articulated party system which could link mass electoral decisions with representative contingents in the legislature. Although government could be said to have taken on a party configuration after 1888, it was not until the 1920s that all major movements acquired a national party structure, and not until after the Second World War that this process was finalised. The second reason was that in a situation where parties in the legislature were still larval, the monarch continued, long after 1848, to play a significant role in the forming of new administrations. Even as late as 1939 the Queen sought unsuccessfully to impose an administration upon parliament.[5] Ministers continued, after 1848, to be appointed and dismissed by Royal Decree, as indeed formally they still are.[6]

Thirdly, as a party system emerged, the inevitability of inter-party coalition governments, given the distribution of electoral support, had pervasive effects on the style of what might be regarded as 'the cabinet'. As advisers to the monarch, the holders of portfolios had formerly regarded their offices as a conferment of personal responsibility, as distinct from admission to a ministerial team. When party government crystallised, these allocations took on the character of sealed compacts between the partners in the formation process, which could not subsequently be varied or questioned. Under these conditions any notion of collective responsibility was slow to evolve. As late as the 1950s, van Raalte was at pains to stress the persistence of ministerial independence,[7] and, as will be seen, certain of the structural conditions which reinforce this remain in place.

Paradoxically, the 'sealed compact' which characterises the distribution of ministerial offices, has been translated, where it suits, into assertions of collective responsibility. For where the composition of cabinets is fixed by inter-party agreements, ministers can accurately claim that the entire ministry depends upon their personal survival. Andeweg gives two recent instances where ministers have employed this argument to escape censure and possible dismissal.[8] In this context, the concept of prime-ministerial prerogative, with its ongoing power to determine the composition of the cabinet, has never become viable. Indeed the whole notion of a premier was a late and reluctant development in the evolution of the modern executive in the Netherlands.

There are considerable expositional problems in the specification of what is meant by cabinet leadership during the nineteenth and well into the present century. From 1848 onwards, cabinets are officially recorded as though they had formal leaders, either single or, until 1877, joint.[9] There were undoubtedly cabinets which were under the influence of dominating personalities. The three governments which included Thorbecke (1849–53, 1862–6 and 1871–2) are presented as his first, second and third administrations. Yet Andeweg points out that formally cabinets had only temporary chairmen until the Second World War, even though in practice it was assumed, after 1874, that the same chairman would be retained through the whole period of office.[10]

The appellation prime minister, or Minister-President, was not officially adopted until 1937 when a Department of General Affairs was established as his office. After 1946 the pre-eminence of a prime minister became an acknowledged fact. But the role remained qualified by three circumstances. The first was that parliamentary party leaders did not, up till the 1970s, ordinarily seek the job; so that it was not generally regarded as the summit of political ambition. The second was, and is, that the perennial necessity for inter-party coalitions meant that prime minsters lacked party control over their entire cabinet. In most cases they did not, before 1977, even have party control over a majority of ministers. From 1948–58, when Willem Drees was continuously and prestigiously Minister-President, only a third of the ministers in each successive cabinet were from his own party, the PvdA.

The third qualifying circumstance is that a Dutch prime minister lacks the powers to shape his team comprehensively, to discipline it if necessary by dismissal, or to offer the incentives of promotion to more senior posts. He will have had a say, conceivably substantial, in the overall distribution of portfolios between the coalition partners, though it is unlikely that he will have been able to select freely the ministerial candidates of the other party or parties in the coalition. Once a cabinet has been formed, a prime minister has little scope to re-allocate portfolios, for this would unravel the complex package which brought the cabinet into being. Even if a vacancy subsequently arises, he will not usually have a free hand in the choice of a successor because any replacements become a matter of intricate bargaining between the coalition partners.

These limitations on the scope of a Dutch Minister-President, which survive the heightened profile of the office since the 1970s, may of course be regarded as testimony to the existence of genuine cabinet government. For it would be very difficult in the Dutch context for a prime minister to usurp the individual provinces of his ministerial colleagues. It might therefore be held that what has evolved is a desirable balance between prime-ministerial influence and ministerial independence, thus yielding an appealingly democratic form of collective leadership. But there is a further feature to be taken into account – the relationship between the cabinet and parliament.

Here there recurs the problem of what is the most appropriate model of cabinet government under modern conditions. There may seem little doubt that one of its most important dimensions is the concerted determination of public strategy through the medium of legislation. Yet it is a fundamental principle of public policy-making in the Netherlands that there should be a clear separation of role between the political executive and the legislature. Under the original circumstances of monarchical government, this separation was a feasible concept which eventually promoted greater democracy in the form of parliamentary autonomy. It still has some salience in this respect, but it also operates as a persistent complication from the standpoint of cabinet government. Since ministers are outside the legislature they must fight their parliamentary corners individually. They must also protect their party positions. Linkages, which in earlier periods could be navigated informally, have become more bureaucratically elaborate as the pressures of office, the activities of interest groups and parliamentary interventions have all augmented. There is therefore a problem of concerted long-term policy-making which the rigidities of cabinet formation do little to dispel.

Cabinet recruitment

Cabinet members have traditionally been recruited from outside the States-General. Of the 334 ministers between 1848 and 1958, almost half never served in parliament and almost a fifth entered parliamentary service only after first being in the cabinet; only slightly more than a third of the ministers had prior experience in parliament (A. Lijphart, *The Politics of Accommodation* [1975], p. 135).

These statistics provide convincing evidence that the separation of cabinet and parliament was historically translated into different spheres of recruitment. Since nearly two-thirds of all cabinet members before 1958 were not drawn from sitting members of the legislature, a much smaller proportion of MPs could expect to become ministers.

Where ministers actually came from has been carefully analysed by Daalder over successive periods beginning in 1848.[11] From that date up to 1918, of 190 cabinet members twenty-four came from the civil service, thirty-seven from the armed forces and twenty from academic posts. Twenty-one came from various other (or no) occupations. Of the remaining eighty-two who had held public office (less than half the total), not all had been MPs. During the period 1918–40 the ratio of political office-holders to other sources was little changed at approximately 2:3, but from 1946 onwards the balance tilted towards politicians. The background of ministers from 1946–84 is shown in Table 8.1.

After 1973 the practice of seeking ministers from outside parliament became less common, which reflected changes in the style of government already discussed in Chapter 4. Nevertheless there is still no particular correlation between length of service and parliamentary prominence in either Chamber and access to ministerial office. Scrutiny of the biographies of the fourteen ministers in the first Lubbers cabinet, formed in 1982, reveals that only half had enjoyed a significant career in parliament. Of the rest, several had been ministers or state secretaries in previous administrations, while others had backgrounds in local politics, the

Table 8.1

PREVIOUS OCCUPATIONS OF CABINET MINISTERS, 1946–84

Political office-holders	89
Civil servants	17
Military	2
Business	9
Education	15
Academics	6
Political, social and economic organisations	4
Other	1
	143

European parliament, the civil service and public national or international organisations.[12]

Even the party connections of ministers up until recently were not necessarily strong. Before 1973 it was possible to encounter ministers, or ex-ministers, whose party credentials were surprisingly tenuous, and often of less account in qualifying them for cabinet office than their particular brands of expertise. There was a disposition to regard ministerial timber as of a different texture to parliamentary skills. This traditional view has not been entirely dispensed with; and evidence of greater continuity in cabinet appointments – nine ministers in the 1986-9 cabinet had been retained from its predecessor – does not serve to strengthen the links between parliamentary service and admission to the executive. Despite important changes in the operational style of government, the institutional separation between cabinet and parliament continues to demarcate the two realms more sharply than in most other European systems.

The evolution of government

As with all modern executives, the Dutch cabinet has steadily grown in size as the demands upon government have proliferated. In 1900 there were eight departments of state, each presided over by a minister. They comprised Internal Affairs, Finance, Justice, Foreign Affairs, War, Navy, the Colonies and Waterways, Commerce and Industry.[13] By 1940 four more departments had been added – General Affairs (the Minister-President's office), Social Affairs, Education and Science, Agriculture and Fisheries. Since the war there have been various re-formulations of the economic and social portfolios. By 1986 the second Lubbers cabinet consisted of the six 'traditional ministries' – Foreign Affairs, Justice, Finance, Defence, Internal Affairs plus the Prime Minister's department. There were in addition eight ministries covering social and economic matters: Economic Affairs; Agriculture and Fisheries; Housing, Planning and the Environment; Transport and Waterways; Social Affairs and Employment; Education and Science; Welfare, Health and Culture; and Overseas Development.

In 1948 State Secretaries, or junior ministers, were introduced to deal with the increased volume of government business. These are not members of the cabinet, although the State Secretary for Foreign Affairs, who handles European matters, normally attends cabinet meetings.[14] The second Lubbers administration included eleven State Secretaries, two in the department of Economic Affairs and one in each of the other ministries except Transport, Agriculture, the Prime Minister's office and Overseas Development. This represented a marked reduction in the number of junior ministers, who in the previous government had totalled sixteen.

Under the circumstances of multi-party coalitions, the appointment of State Secretaries has served as a balancing mechanism in the adjustment of party strengths within the government. It has also been used to ensure that in the most important or sensitive ministries, cabinet members were flanked by junior ministers from another party. In the 1982 government, Economic Affairs, Social Affairs, Defence and Education each had two State Secretaries, one CDA and one VVD.

Writing in the early 1980s, Vis asserts that 'the distribution of Under-ministries is now an integral part of the cabinet formation itself.'[15] This comment leads directly to the elaborate issue of government formation, a subject upon which much ink has been expended in respect of the Dutch experience.

The formation of governments

Despite the intricacies of the electoral system, the processing of election results has long been a highly streamlined operation. Although the final composition of the Second Chamber has to await the manoeuvres of the successful candidates, the outcome of the election in party terms is available in the newspapers the day after polling. The complexion of the next government, however, is a vastly different matter. Indeed the election results can be regarded as a mere deployment of the forces before the battle to decide the configuration of the next cabinet can begin.

Accounts of this often byzantine contest are available in English by Andeweg, van der Tak and Dittrich,[16] and by Vis.[17] Comments on the process have also been made in several publications by this author.[18] The most resounding feature of the processes of cabinet-forming in the Netherlands is the length of time it can take before a final outcome is reached. Since 1946 the average duration of cabinet formations, after either elections or crises leading to a new cabinet without elections, has been sixty-eight days. The record delay so far, in 1977, was 208 days, and on three other occasions the period of negotiations has exceeded 100 days.

Most cabinets in this period have not completed a parliamentary term, indeed only three have served out a full four years. All others, a total of

Table 8.2
LENGTH IN DAYS OF CABINET FORMATIONS SINCE 1946

	1946–67	
Beel I	1946–8	47
Drees-Van Schaik	1948–51	31
Drees I	1951–2	50
Drees II	1952–6	69
Drees III	1956–8	122
Beel II	1958–9	10
De Quay	1959–63	68
Marijnen	1963–5	70
Cals	1965–6	46
Zijlstra	1966–7	38
	1967–1986	
De Jong	1967–71	49
Biesheuvel I	1971–2	69
Biesheuvel II	1972–3	22
Den Uyl	1973–7	163
Van Agt I	1977–81	208
Van Agt II	1981–2	108
Van Agt III	1982	17
Lubbers I	1982–6	57
Lubbers II	1986–9	52
Lubbers III	1989	62

Main Source: Daalder, The Compendium A 0500-32.

fifteen up to 1986, have foundered prematurely and since 1967 this has resulted in fresh elections. The reasons for the breakdown of cabinets are worth examination. Andeweg points out: 'Before 1965, cabinet crises did not result from disagreement among Ministers, but rather from conflicts between ministers and their own party!'[19] The dynamics appear to have changed since the mid-1960s, with subsequent cabinets disintegrating because of discord between ministers on party lines.

A reversion to the earlier pattern of cabinet crises was however evident when the second Lubbers government resigned in May 1989, as a result of a dispute between VVD ministers and the leader of the VVD parliamentary group.

From the care which is lavished upon cabinet construction, one might expect that once in place such an artefact would endure until the next change in the distribution of parliamentary forces. But a structural sword hangs over cabinet stability in the Netherlands: the relentless need to maintain accords at both governmental and parliamentary levels where each are distinct and have their own dynamics. A simple model of the lines of force may help to illustrate this point:

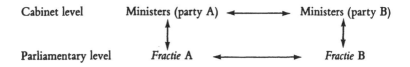

Cabinet level   Ministers (party A) ◄───────► Ministers (party B)

Parliamentary level   *Fractie* A ◄───────► *Fractie* B

Within the most economical coalition – one of two parties – three kinds of inter-relationship must be maintained: between ministers and their parliamentary party; between ministers and their cabinet colleagues from the other party; and between the *fracties* in parliament, which are expected to sustain the government. A serious rupture of any of these three necessary accords will have dire consequences for the continuity of government.

The negotiations for the formation of a new government are set in train by a sequence of consultations in which the monarch plays an important intermediary role. For it is the Queen who, after receiving advice from the Chairmen of the two Chambers of Parliament, the Vice-Chairman of the Council of State, and the leaders of all the parliamentary parties, appoints the person charged with conducting the orchestration of a fresh ministry.[20] Prior to 1951, this task was assigned to a *formateur* who was normally the leader of the largest parliamentary *fractie* resulting from the last election. In that year, because of a conflict within one of the major *fracties*, a more provisional appointment of an *informateur* was made whose job was to make preliminary soundings which could lead to the commissioning of a *formateur*. The complexity of formation negotiations thereafter made the appointment of an *informateur* necessary after each election up until 1981.

Three elements are discernible in the formation process. There is first the overriding question of which parties are able and willing to make a coalition which will command a secure majority in the Second Chamber. Over time the patterns of possibility have crystallised in such a way as to limit the likely outcomes. But the question is accompanied by two further elements. One is how readily a jointly agreed programme can be drawn up for a new government, given that the prior election will probably have been fought on the basis of individual party manifestos. From these differing inputs policy commitments must be selected which will enable a new cabinet to pursue a unified strategy over the ensuing parliamentary term. The other consideration is a mutually satisfactory distribution of portfolios, including the allocation of junior ministers.

The actual strategy of coalition formation in the Netherlands has attracted much analysis, both theoretical and conceptual. The primary objective – the securing of a working majority in the Lower House – is never in question, there being no disposition to risk minority administrations.[21] But for much of the period 1948–73, coalitions were assembled which went beyond the need for the most economical majorities. De Swaan has provided an extended examination of this phenomenon.[22] A more concise appreciation is presented by Andeweg *et al.*, which observes that 'cost sharing' may explain the extension of coalitions beyond the mere avoidance of minority government.[23] The particular configurations of Dutch coalitions have also been viewed in terms of differential partisanship, notably by Daudt who has argued that the confessional centre has mostly preferred to liaise with the Liberals rather than with Labour.[24] This disposition, however, could not in itself determine outcomes freely, if only because of the vicissitudes of the parliamentary arithmetic.

It is possible that the actual outcomes of coalition formation, certainly since 1946, can best be viewed in terms of circumstances and personalities. Thus the four Drees cabinets from 1948–58, all of which were large coalitions, the first two including the VVD alongside the PvdA, could be regarded as expressing a desire for maximum national unity for the purpose of post-war reconstruction. Most coalitions over the past forty odd years have essentially been extensions of the strengths of the Christian parties, either to the left in the shape of the PvdA or to the right via the VVD. Smaller parties – DS'70, D'66 or the PPR – have only been resorted to on three occasions, 1971, 1973 and 1981, and only under special circumstances. So the fulcrum of almost all coalition negotiations since the war has been the balance of compatability between the centre and the major parties to its left and right. Only the den Uyl cabinet of 1973–7 can be said to have temporarily dented the mould.

The most significant fact of cabinet-making in the Netherlands therefore is that, given the distribution of parliamentary forces over the entire period since 1918, coalitions are most readily formed by building outwards from the centre. Even where Labour emerged from elections as the largest single party, as in 1956, 1971, 1972, 1977 and 1982, its sole route to office in a majority coalition was via the centre. And only in 1972 was this route not wholly controlled by the centre. The Liberals, although never matching Labour's strength, have been in an identical position.

So the two main secular parties have in practice been debarred from determining the shape of coalitions unless they were willing to unite. Talk of such an alliance has from time to time been audible in the parliamentary corridors; and a PvdA-VVD coalition would have commanded a majority in the Second Chamber in 1977, 1982 and 1986. But on each of these occasions the Liberals were admitted to office by the CDA, which provided it with a more comfortable outcome than a perilous rapprochement with Labour.

The overall arithmetic of party strengths, it need hardly be said, overrides the matter of relative success at the polls in terms of a party's gains or losses. In 1967, 1971 and 1972, the KVP suffered severe electoral setbacks, yet ministers from the party still entered government, as did those of Labour in 1981. Conversely Labour's significant gains in 1977, 1982 and 1986 did not secure it any places in the cabinet. So long as a majority can be achieved, it matters not at all that its components may have lost ground in the preceding election. Thus in 1986 the Liberals returned to office after having lost a quarter of their former holding in the Lower House.

Views on the part of political analysts of the virtues and vices of coalition-making in the Netherlands range from the resigned 'what else can be expected under these circumstances?', to more iconoclastic positions. As an example of the latter Vis (a D'66 senator) contends that 'vested interests are still preventing attempts to rationalise the formation process,'[25] which hints at sinister resistances and implies that a more streamlined or dignified or just approach is attainable. What this might be is not however clear. The campaign to have cabinet *formateurs* directly elected has been discussed in Chapter 6. The idea of pre-election pacts has also been reviewed earlier in this volume. Within a configuration where pacts must confront either overlapping coalitions or a denial of ideological congruity, even negative commitments – as when Labour tried to exclude in advance a coalition with the KVP – can prove to be unfulfillable.

A profound concern of Vis is that 'there are no rules for the (formation) process itself nor rules regulating the powers of those involved'.[26] As a constitutional lawyer he is unhappy about both the uncertainties of the operation and its costs. As he points out, cabinet formation took up three and a half of the thirty-six years between 1946 and 1982. Also there is the spectre of non-responsible government in the shape of the caretaker administrations which have filled in the often lengthy spaces between elections and the culmination of formation negotiations. Since 1956 no less than four annual budgets have been introduced by out-going cabinets which had no electoral mandate. And finally there is the persistence of confessional, now CDA, dominance in the process itself, illustrated by the fact that 'nine out of ten *informateurs* [have been] affiliated to the confessional party.'[27]

Undoubtedly the prolix nature of cabinet formation and its potential for ignoring the signals of the electorate can be represented as a palpable weakness of the political process. But it remains unclear what solutions are available, other than by means of a re-articulation of the party system so that instead of 'artificial' majorities concocted after elections, 'real' majorities would be directly delivered by the voters.

In the literature dealing with cabinet formation, one aspect of Dutch practice has received relatively little attention. It relates to the *scope* for prolonged inter-party negotiations, as a factor separate from the *problem* of assembling a majority cabinet coalition with a settled strategy and an agreed distribution of portfolios. In most systems, the scope for leisurely discussions is simply not available. The reason for this is that the preceding election may well have changed the party arithmetic in parliament, in such a way as to make it impossible for the previous cabinet to remain in office as a caretaker; thus on the first occasion the caretaker government sought parliamentary approval it would incur defeat. It would then have to resign and the immediate formation of a new administration which commanded parliamentary support would become inescapable.

The fact that in the Netherlands caretaker governments can survive, often for some months, while negotiations for a new cabinet continue, requires assumptions about continuity which are accepted by the major parties. The two major assumptions are firstly that elections are unlikely to effect radical changes in major party strengths, and secondly that new cabinets will continue to be built around the centre. These understandings enable prolonged negotiations to be undertaken without any anxiety about the continuity of governmental and parliamentary business.

The most vivid illustration of the confidence which attends these assumptions is the number of occasions when new parliaments are expected to approve budgets prepared by out-going governments. Thus the den Uyl cabinet, finally assembled in May 1973, did not present its own budget till September 1973. Even though it was a cabinet of a novel and distinctive make-up, its parliamentary supporters were willing to go along with the budget of the preceding cabinet, presented in September 1972, two months after it had lost its majority.

In terms of these logistics, it would seem that there is no clear limit to an indefinite prolongation of the formation process. This of course raises questions about the relationship between the executive and the legislature, in terms of legitimacy and accountability. Given the capacity of caretaker cabinets to soldier on without the risk of a major political crisis, it might be thought that parliamentary control of the executive was inherently weak, and that governments could function without regard to parliamentary pressures. But this is not borne out by the evidence that governments do need the continuing support of their parliamentary parties. The most recent example of this is that the decision of Premier Lubbers, in May 1989, to recommend a dissolution and call fresh elections, was directly triggered by a challenge from the VVD parliamentary leader.

The situation only becomes intelligible in the light of the basic dynamics of the party system *vis-à-vis* the construction of cabinets. The fact that a centre grouping has dominated the complexion of government and politics for over seventy years, imparts a profound inflection to the behaviour of both cabinets and parliament. Continuity has become the armature of the entire system, to such an extent that it would be scarcely too extreme to regard elections as marginal commentaries upon the fortunes of the major actors. No governments can be formed without the active support of the bulk of the Christian centre. Thus parliament would be ignoring this fundamental dynamic if it chose to cavil at the budget of a caretaker cabinet.

Once could extend the point by noting that once a new government is eventually formed, its authority will almost certainly extend beyond the next election. There is therefore a kind of institutional overdrive which, having been built into the system empirically, has become a central feature of the political culture.

The complexion of governments

Tables 3.5 and 4.2 present the pattern of multi-party cabinets since 1946. During the forty-four years up to 1990, the major confessionals, in one form or other, had participated in all nineteen cabinets and had provided the Minister-President in thirteen. Indeed apart from the period

1948–58, there has only been one subsequent government (1973–7) when the premier was not drawn from a Christian party. This continuity of participation by members of a single bloc makes it difficult to construe the subtle variations since the war in the balance of party control of the executive. There have certainly been important changes in the style and character of cabinets. But these changes cannot readily be viewed from the standpoint of definitive transfers of power between the leading contenders.[28]

During the era of post-war reconstruction up to 1958, the Labour party, through its cabinet members, played a significant role in the orchestration of policy. But although the Prime Minister was Labour, most ministers were not, and the confessionals always outnumbered the socialist contingent in cabinet. After 1958 the balance shifted palpably when Labour was replaced by the Liberals as the confessionals' coalition partner, which, with a brief *intermezzo* from 1965–6, remained the pattern until 1973. Confessional paramountcy however began to wane after 1967 as increasing numbers of voters deserted the *verzuiling* profile. In 1971 a five-party coalition was resorted to, including the Labour breakaway, DS'70, in order to achieve a parliamentary majority.

This was the high point of a potential transition as it seemed that the configuration of the party system was about to be re-shaped in a way which would alter the pattern of government.[29] The formation negotiations which followed the election of November 1972 resulted in a partial ascendancy of Labour and its smaller 'progressive' allies, but still with the participation of ministers from two of the major confessional parties. By 1977 the confessionals had regrouped as a single inter-denominational movement, and Labour, despite an unprecedented success at the polls, lost the initiative in the ensuing cabinet formation. Apart from a brief and disastrous coalition between the CDA, Labour and D'66 in 1981–2, the former pattern of a Christian-Liberal partnership, reforged in 1977, survived up to 1989. The parliamentary arithmetic enabled these two parties to form majority executives without recourse to other reinforcements.

In terms of the ideological balance of cabinets since the war, centre-right coalitions have predominated. From 1946–89 Liberal ministers have partnered the confessionals for twenty-three years (excluding the period from 1948–52 when a Liberal minister served in confessional-Labour cabinets), while Labour has participated in cabinet for only seventeen years. This simple statistic does not however accurately reflect the significance of the two secular parties' contributions. When in office

Labour has always been a major partner, backed by a large parliamentary *fractie* and therefore able to exert a very considerable leverage upon public policy. The Liberals played a much less prominent role in cabinets until 1977, when their fortunes soared and their importance increased.

An assessment of the ideological complexion of successive cabinets has also to take account of the spectrum of opinion within the Christian bloc. Up till the confessional merger of 1975, both the ARP and KVP had left wings which expressed, *inter alia*, the worker constituency within each movement. Both Catholics and Calvinists contained within their *zuilen* trade union federations. It was, after all, largely confessional governments in the 1960s which presided over a massive expansion of welfare and social security provisions – commitments which Labour had some difficulty in meeting after the oil crisis of 1973.

Under the economic conditions of the 1980s and the backlash against the all-providing state, CDA-VVD cabinets have taken on more of a right of centre coloration. But the election results of May 1986 signalled some disenchantment with the secular right, and the chameleon propensities of the Christian centre are well able to adjust over time to such indications from the voters. Hence, when in September 1989 Liberal losses at the parliamentary election reduced the combined holdings of the CDA and VVD to the barest majority, the response of Mr Lubbers was to turn to Labour. The resultant CDA-PvdA coalition, which took office in November 1989, ended the long span of centre-right government and   inaugurated a fresh centre-left period.

NOTES

1. Quoted by Ian Gilmour, *The Body Politic*, London 1971, p. 205.
2. Kenneth Mackenzie, *The English Parliament*, Harmondsworth 1950,
3. Gladstone's dissolution of 1886, after the defeat of the Irish Home Rule Bill.
4. See Rudy Andeweg, 'The Netherlands: Coalition Cabinets in Changing Circumstances' in J. Blondel and F. Muller-Rommel (eds), *Cabinets in Western Europe*, London, 1988.
5. Andeweg (1988), ibid.
6. 1983 Constitution, Article 43.
7. Van Raalte (1959), op cit.
8. In the den Uyl cabinet (1973–7) and the first Lubbers cabinet (1982–6).
9. *Parlement en Kiezer*.

10. Andeweg (1988), op. cit.
11. Daalder, The Compendium, A 0500–47.
12. *Algemeen Dagblad*, 4 November 1982. See also Chapter 7, note 31.
13. Daalder, The Compendium, A 0500–10.
14. Andeweg (1988), op. cit.
15. Jan Vis, 'Coalition Government in a Constitutional Monarchy: The Dutch Experience', in Bogdanor (1983) p. 165.
16. In Griffiths (ed.) (1980).
17. See note 15.
18. Gladdish, 1972, 1983 and 'Things fall apart', BBC Radio 3 broadcast, August 1981.
19. 'Centrifugal forces and collective decision-making: The case of the Dutch Cabinet', *European Journal of Political Research*, Vol. 16, No. 2 (1988), p. 135.
20. See Andeweg *et al.* (1980), Griffiths (ed.) (1980).
21. Minority cabinets have however acted as transitional governments before fresh elections, e.g. the Zijlstra cabinet (Nov 1966–April 1967), the second Biesheuvel cabinet (August 1972–May 1973), and the third van Agt cabinet (May–Sept. 1982).
22. A. de Swaan, *Coalition Theories and Cabinet Formations*, Amsterdam, 1973.
23. In Griffiths (ed.) (1980).
24. H. Daudt, 'Political Parties and Government Coalitions in the Netherlands since 1945', *Netherlands Journal of Sociology*, Vol. 18, No. 1 (1982).
25. Vis (1983), op. cit. p. 153.
26. Ibid., p. 157.
27. Ibid., p. 162.
28. See Gladdish (1983), p. 170.
29. See Gladdish (1987), p. 204.

9

PUBLIC POLICY

The Dutch are motivated by the best of democratic intentions. . . .
— Faludi and de Rüijter in Dutt and Costa (eds) (1985).[1]

The policy crucible

The basic structures of post-war policy-making in the Netherlands were reviewed in Chapter 3 under the heading of Corporatist Reconstruction. Essentially the system then adopted combined two distinct approaches to the formulation of public policy, paramountly in the social and economic spheres. There was firstly a corporatist dimension, in the form of a set of agencies which brought together the main producer interests of employers and organised labour, generally referred to as the 'social partners', a term which implied an ideology of social harmony or at least co-operation.

These two overriding interest groups were not however unified but consisted of an assemblage of organisations reflecting the complex structures of the *verzuiling* network. At the summit of official corporatism was the Social and Economic Council. This was a tripartite body, the third element being that of government representatives, and its establishment, under the Industrial Reorganisation Act of 1950, gave rise to a cluster of sub-organisms styled PBOs (*Publiekrechtlijke Bedrijfsorganisaties*).[2] The original intention was that the PBOs should eventually cover the entire field of production, thus endowing the economy with a comprehensively corporatist framework. But, as with other similar ventures (notably in far less democratic systems than that of the Netherlands, such as fascist Italy and Salazarist Portugal, plus Franco's Spain), their ambit remained partial. Nevertheless, the principle of corporatist decision-making became a central ingredient of official national policy-making, and as such had profound consequences for the style of both governmental strategies and political activity.

The second element in the post-war system was the commitment to indicative central planning. This was to be undertaken not by ministers, still less by parliament, but by a set of non-corporate bodies, notably the Central Bank, which was nationalised in 1948,[3] the Central Bureau of

Statistics (dating from 1899) and, above all, the Central Planning Bureau, the flagship of the new order, which was set up in 1945. Conceptually the system could be regarded as an amalgam of rational, pragmatic and strategic inputs into the crucible of orderly, democratic, national decision-making. The rational input was the ostensibly objective process of forecasting, on the basis of carefully compiled data, both the economic weather and the most appropriate responses to it. That was the task of the Central Planning Bureau.[4] The pragmatic input was the outcome of the negotiations between the major economic interest groups as the most authoritative measure of what was feasible in the form of economic and social decisions. The strategic strand was the espousal of a set of aims which would set the course of the policy leviathan through the seas of national reconstruction towards the harbour of social harmony and economic prosperity.

Thus, in the early 1950s, the Social and Economic Council formulated its five general goals which came to be characterised as the 'magic pentangle'.[5] The goals were: full employment, economic growth, reasonable income distribution, a balance of payments equilibrium and price stability. From the standpoint of the late 1980s, such a pentangle of optimistic aims might indeed be thought to warrant the epithet 'magic'. Yet, as the pattern of post-war reconstruction unfolded, the Dutch economy was, for almost twenty years, able to achieve a near approximation of these ambitions. Central to its success was the willingness of organised labour, through its representatives in the various corporate bodies, to accept a saintly degree of wage restraint.[6]

Through the 1950s the restraining of wage costs resulted in price levels advantageously below those of major international competitors. But in 1964 the dam burst. The ship-repairing unions broke away from the central wage negotiations, and the general wage level rose, in one year, by nearly 15%. Retrospectively at least, it was clear 'that the old situation could not be restored'.[7] Near universal compliance with the annual verdicts of the economic planners and the social partners, on which successive governments had relied since 1945, could no longer be taken as a fact of public policy. Looking back, with a clear implication of regret, the OECD economists recorded in their survey of May 1973:

> Wage behaviour appears to have changed some time around the mid sixties. From that time onwards, labour no longer seemed prepared to accept the policy of relative wage restraint, followed, with varying degrees of success, since the war (p. 15).

But in fact the central determination of wages continued to be, for the bulk of the next fifteen years, a cause which successive governments endeavoured to follow. In 1970, when the annual wage settlement once again foundered, a new Wages Act gave the government powers to intervene directly in wage agreements. This was certainly central determination, but without benefit of corporatist benediction. The result was an outbreak of unofficial strikes and an official wage freeze.[8]

Wage policy entered a new phase of difficulty after the oil crisis of autumn 1973. A cabinet with seven Labour ministers, presided over by the PvdA leader den Uyl, struggled to re-impose order in the labour market by a succession of policies based upon authoritative central regulation. The corporatist institutions were clearly flagging, but their structure remained virtually intact. When, in 1980, Richard Griffiths edited his important volume on the policy-making process since the war, the emphasis was still on its corporatist character.[9] But the dissonance between the anatomy of corporatism and the real world of policy options was fast becoming a strategic dilemma. The most crucial factor was that the competitive position of the Netherlands had changed radically since the 1960s. After the crises of the 1970s – which had affected all Western economies, especially those as open to external pressures as the Dutch – the commitments to sustained economic growth, full employment and price stability had become impossible to fulfil.

In the Netherlands the level of public expenditure had produced an alarming gap between consensus and feasibility. If corporatism had seemed the best means for reconciling the twin objectives of economic prosperity and social harmony, by the mid-1970s this philosophy was facing potential failure on both fronts. The sharp end was that the bills were mounting beyond what any budget could realistically deliver, as the share of net national income absorbed by public commitments rose precipitately. The scale of the increase from the early 1950s to the mid-1970s is shown in Table 9.1. The escalation of public expenditure as a proportion of national resources was to continue into the 1980s, as can be seen in comparative terms from Table 9.2.

The most resounding increases of public commitment from 1955 to 1975 had been in sectors whose contribution to production were indirect and long term. Net national income over the two decades had grown by a factor of 2.3; but public expenditure on education, science and culture had risen by a factor of 4.6, and on housing and physical planning by

Table 9.1
SHARE OF THE COLLECTIVE SECTOR AS PERCENTAGE
OF NET NATIONAL INCOME

	1953	1963	1973	1975	1977
Social Security premiums	5.2	10.9	18.3	20.3	19.7
Taxes	26.3	25.2	29.8	30.6	31.6
Total	31.5	36.1	48.1	50.9	51.3

Source: Griffiths (1980) p. 31.

Table 9.2
TOTAL GOVERNMENT OUTLAY AS PERCENTAGE OF GDP

	1973	1984
Netherlands	49	63
Sweden	45	64
Italy	38	57
France	37	53
West Germany	45	47
Britain	21	42

Source: OECD *Economic Survey of the Netherlands*, July 1987 (Diagram 8, p. 32).

5.6.[10] Developments of a similar kind were of course visible in other advanced industrial countries during this period and up to the latter 1960s the Netherlands had not seemed much out of line with its neighbours in the way it deployed its national income. By the latter 1970s, however, over the relatively short span of a decade, the balance of public expenditure had swung towards Scandinavian proportions.[11] Over and above the difficulties of budgeting, this was to have an effect upon the character of the polity and to raise questions about the structures and mechanisms of public policy.

The impact of party politics

One of the key problems of exegesis here is to determine what precisely triggered the escalation of public commitments which, in the 1960s, moved the Netherlands from a relatively low-spending to a high-spending state.[12] Certainly the circumstances were inducive to an expansion of public provision. After some twenty years of restraint the economic situation seemed highly favourable, and the exploitation of natural gas promised to transform the energy supply. There had also been an implicit notion that the sacrifices of the post-war reconstruction period, in which the appeal had been to constraint for the sake of future betterment, would result in a distribution of benefits once affluence had been attained. Corporatism was, *inter alia*, an ideology of wide consultation, which implied that there would ultimately be rewards for all sectors of society. But these are very broad brush considerations. Much more specific to the Dutch case was the traditional practice of endorsing private, i.e. non-state, communal initiatives, which were to become the matrix of comprehensive welfare provision.

This is particularly germane to the timing of the escalation of commitments undertaken directly by the state; for it was precisely in the 1960s, as the voluntaristic pattern of *verzuiling* undertakings began to lose its grip, that a more generic form of state involvement gained ascendancy. Put very generally, it could be claimed that Dutch society had long been paternalistic. But religious mobilisation had made the sub-cultures the focus of that paternalism. With deconfessionalisation, the focus of paternalism rapidly became that of the secular state. The prior apparatus was by no means dismantled. There is a perhaps inevitable tendency on the part of outside observers to see the 1960s as too absolute a watershed in social organisation. Nevertheless, it was within that decade that the state increasingly became a direct provider of services and welfare, and the processes of equalising benefits made for greater and greater public costs.

One point which must be stressed is that despite the superficial similarity with Scandinavian developments in the ascendancy of state paternalism, the Netherlands has never reflected the long-term dominance of a social democratic movement. Indeed the position of the Dutch Labour party has always been relatively weak by West European standards. It played an important role in the process of post-war reconstruction, but it never came within sight of exercising exclusive authority and its role was reconciliationist, not redistributionist. Equally, when a cabinet with a strong Labour component held office from 1973-7, its performance was largely characterised by a desperate struggle to sustain commitments, already undertaken by governments without a social democratic presence, against a down turn in economic fortunes.[13]

Thus, when looking at party political inputs, one has to probe the complex matter of how a policy consensus developed, in the 1960s and early 1970s, which cannot easily be presented in terms of any single overriding ideology. At the heart of the problem there are two distinct elements. One is the nature of policy reconciliation within a centre-based coalitional polity. The other is the extent to which central planning, and the various forms of corporatist consultation and recommendation, created a policy climate which propelled social and economic strategies outside the frame of direct management by the cabinet and parliament.

Policy reconciliation was the inescapable leit-motiv of the Rome-Red coalitions which ran from 1946 to 1958. The Labour party was ostensibly a new formation but its direct progenitor, the SDAP, had no significant experience of cabinet membership. It was therefore vital that it should be able to demonstrate its ability to work co-operatively with the major confessionals, notably the Catholic People's Party. The exit of Labour from government in 1958 did have some consequences for the inflection of national policy.[14] But the confessional-dominated cabinets of the 1960s retained the basic attributes of previous post-war coalitions in so far as their clienteles still included the range of key producer groups in the shape of confessional employer, farmer and trade union organisations. The religious parties therefore remained committed to both corporatist bargaining and the satisfaction of the demands of the various socio-economic echelons.

The emphases within particular party programmes varied somewhat, but not to the extent that commitments could be reversed or more hard-edged policies plausibly canvassed. When the challenges of radical political groups confronted the governing élite, from the mid-1960s, the response was a strategy of accommodation which served to incorporate further claims for increased public outlay. As Table 9.1 illustrates, the share of net national income represented by social security premia rose from 10.9% in 1963 to 18.3% by 1973. There was little direct input from the Labour party during this period since it was in office only briefly during 1965–6 with five ministers out of a cabinet of fourteen. But there was no antipode within the cabinets of the decade to resist the escalation of public commitments. As the author observed in the early 1980s, 'The dynamics of a centre-based system, certainly in the Dutch case disclose a propensity for the centre to absorb and accommodate the contentions of the time, apparently without ideological brakes or the need for ideological accelerators.'[15] That may now be less true, because since 1980 the Christian centre has been a single party with a conceivably greater capacity to adopt clearer stances. But it was certainly a feature of the preceding period.

An orchestra with no conductor?

The policy formulation linkages, from the latter 1940s on, rested as much upon institutions which had no clear political accountability as upon governments and parliament. The planning and forecasting agencies, especially the Central Planning Bureau, were of paramount importance in the calculation of policy feasibility, but they were independent of ministers, not subordinate to them. The principal corporatist bodies, such as the Foundation of Labour (a non-governmental agency) were equally autonomous. The Social and Economic Council which constituted the top level of corporatist reconciliation, though it contained governmental representatives, was also not subject to ministerial direction. Indeed its recommendations, for much of the 1950s and 1960s, had a status which even the cabinet as a whole could not readily contest.

So far as the organisation of government itself is concerned, there were, and still are, institutional features which had effects upon the capacity of ministers to oversee, direct and co-ordinate the policy process. The first thing to note is the historic circumstance of a non-unified civil service. Two recent commentaries on this fact highlight both its significance and peculiarity. Daalder puts the point with characteristic cogency: 'There are *no* general competitive examinations . . . There is *no* real central recruitment of higher civil servants. There is *hardly* anything like conscious career planning within, let alone across departments. There is *no* rotation of posts. . . . In short there is *no* national civil service.'[16] Andeweg, meanwhile, wittily depicts the 'signs of distinct departmental cultures in jargon and dress, ranging from corduroy at Welfare, Health and Culture to blue blazers at Internal Affairs or pin-striped suits in the Foreign Office', summing up the consequences thus: 'Lawyers sometimes refer to "fourteen legal families" because departments have different legislative traditions and there are no non-departmental Parliamentary draftsmen to iron out the differences.'[17]

The departmental autonomy of officials is of course directly matched by the autonomy of ministers within the cabinet referred to in Chapter 8.

A second feature of the governmental dimension of the policy process was the growth of sub-corporate advisory bodies to departments (*adviesorganen*) whose history goes back to the early part of the century. Attempts to control their proliferation date from the 1920s, but as the less formal inputs of the *verzuiling* network gave way to more structured consultation, their number increased inordinately. By 1975 there were almost 400 permanent advisory bodies, plus many more which were ad hoc, 60% of which had never been sanctioned by parliament, and 40% of which had been assembled since 1965.[18]

In addition to the web of corporatist and advisory organs, interest groups also had some purchase within the cabinet itself. Van Putten described this phenomenon in the early 1980s as 'sectorisation'. He exemplified it by observing that the Minister of Agriculture is normally recruited from the agricultural sector, the Minister of Social Affairs is often a former trade union leader, while the Minister of Economic Affairs is 'always a confidant of the employers organisations'.[19] He concludes that 'sectorisation' further contributed to the extreme departmentalisation of government and exacerbated the weakness of the cabinet as the supreme policy-coordinating body.

It is against this complex background that what Scholten has called the 'neo-liberal backlash' against corporatism has emerged.[20] Before examining these recent developments, several further observations are pertinent. One is to make clear that although the policy process since the war has been heavily inflected by corporatist and allied practices, it is not entirely governed by diffuse extra-political inputs. More traditional 'orthodox' procedures have remained the norm in the 'older' ministries, such as Justice and Finance, where civil servants prepare policy for ministers without substantial external intervention.[21] Secondly, as will be evident from the analysis in Chapter 7, parliament has not remained a passive instrument in the policy armoury, but has massively increased the range and frequency of its challenge to proposals. The efficacy of its challenge may be a matter for debate, but there is no doubt of its vigour.

Finally, if a summary of the elaborate inputs into policy-making in the Netherlands carries any hint of incoherence, then that would be to regard the system in isolation from its counterparts. All advanced democratic states are, towards the end of the twentieth century, embroiled in labyrinthine policy exertions. A scaling down of multiple inputs to facilitate more command approaches by ministers does not necessarily improve either the quality or the coherence of public policy, as recent experience in Britain may aptly illustrate.[22]

Changing policy-making styles

As will be clear from the preceding section, any attempt to characterise the dominant style of national policy-making in the Netherlands, in the latter 1980s, would confront the problem of what has actually survived from the era of corporatism and centralised indicative planning. Since their presumed heyday in the 1950s, a number of changes have taken place affecting both their visibility and salience. The 1960s saw the growing intervention of the state in areas formerly governed by voluntary institutions within the *verzuiling* network. By the 1970s corporatism seemed to be increasingly residual, as governments resorted to statutory wage determination, and the Social and Economic Council, though still deferred to, became less and less central to strategic decision-making. In the 1980s the emphasis has certainly been more upon ministerial policy-making, with the Prime Minister playing a far more central role than that of most of his predecessors.

In a recent analysis, Ilja Scholten dates this latest approach from 1982 when the first Lubbers cabinet 'abandoned the approach of corporatist policy-making with respect to industrial relations and simply by-passed the corporatist advisory channels (including the SEC)'.[23] He notes, however, both that proposals to override the corporatist structure were already emerging in the late 1970s, and that (in 1987) the structure had still not been dismantled. It would, therefore, be difficult to offer a conclusive verdict on how far the Netherlands should no longer be regarded as even a partially corporatist entity. The difficulty is corroborated by the fact that although Scholten gives prominence in his title to the 'neo-liberal backlash', his text is mainly about corporatism.

Van Schendelen, in a recent book on politics and business,[24] confirms the trend, from 1982 onwards, towards more direct ministerial decision-making. But he also throws doubt upon the importance accorded to corporatism, even in its prime, contending that in its formal guise it was always partial and limited, and that it was interwoven with, and often confused with, the processes of consultation which were part and parcel of *verzuiling*.[25] This latter is an important point which links with his further view that corporatism has attracted more interest outside, rather than inside the Netherlands. That thought could be challenged, but there is little doubt that corporatism is often less than meticulously defined, and that the concept is perhaps over-appealing to scholarly expositors.

But of course no interpretation can be wholly definitive because of the

mass of evidence to which it must relate. From a more public administration perspective, Fritz van der Meer has informally drawn attention to
modes of decentralisation as a further dimension of changing policy
styles.[26] He points out that the confessionals, within their comprehensive
verzuiling provisions, made functional decentralisation the dominant
policy style of the 1950s, whereas their relative decline in the 1960s and
'70s saw a switch to territorial decentralisation in terms of a devolution
of decision-making to the provinces and most particularly the
municipalities. In the 1980s he sees a recrudescence of functional
decentralisation under the direction of CDA-led governments. Above all
he stresses that the character of policy-making varies enormously from
field to field and issue to issue.

A.J.M. Bekke, in an anthology published in 1985,[27] provides a further
schematisation of the history of corporatism which he dates not from
1945 but from around 1920. His initial period therefore runs from 1920
to 1960, within which he discerns interest groups operating relatively
autonomously *vis-à-vis* the state. In the following period, that of the
welfare state from 1960 to 1980, he finds interest groups functioning
increasingly within the official structures of public policy-making. After
1980 he notes the various efforts by government to control, rationalise
and generally reduce the influence of interest groups. It is of course of
some significance in such a broad characterisation to be clear what
precisely is meant by interest groups, and how far they operate as
informal pressure groups, or within official bodies such as the PBOs, or
as part of the network of advisory organs.

As an illustration of changing policy styles, Bekke cites the example of
health care. In the late 1940s the British model of a state-managed
national health service was considered in the Netherlands, but was
discarded in favour of a 'mixed' formula which deferred to the then
prominence of *verzuiling*. Thus under the Health Care Law of 1956, the
operation of health services was bestowed largely upon private, or *zuil*
organisations. A quarter century later, a new Health Law, in 1982,
retained the structure of non-governmental hospitals and clinics, but
ostensibly increased public control, albeit by decentralising planning and
co-ordination down to regions and municipalities.

In the same volume, H. Versnel makes the point that in terms of
public policy the Netherlands can be best regarded as a 'decentralised
unitary state', in which a strong decentralist lobby proclaims local
autonomy 'a high good'.[28] But he observes that this conviction on the
part of interest groups is not always endorsed by the public, which,

while professing support for local initiative, actually prefers more equitable policy implementation at national level.

As a final strand in the evolution of policy-making, the post 1982 espousal by CDA-VVD governments of styles which take more account of market forces will be discussed in the last section of this chapter. But before that, in order to put some flesh on the bones of a stylistic analysis, the actual record of socio-economic policy, under successive governments since 1971, will be reviewed.

The record of socio-economic policy

Over the past two decades, socio-economic policy at macro level has inevitably confronted a sequence of changing internal and external conditions. It has also, given the nature of the polity, been in the hands of a succession of varied coalition governments. In terms of broad ideological stripe there have been five distinct governmental phases:

1. centre-right   July 1971 to May 1973
2. left-centre   May 1973 to December 1977
3. centre-right   December 1977 to September 1981
4. centre-left   September 1981 to November 1982
5. centre-right   November 1982 to November 1989

The precise dating must be mildly qualified by the fact that each government operated as a caretaker during its final months of office, pending the formation of a new cabinet after a Second Chamber election. A further caveat is that the three-party centre-left coalition of 1981–2 scarcely got off the ground as a cohesive administration. Its term could therefore be considered an interregnum in a long period of Christian-Liberal rule from 1977 to 1989.

Apart from transfers of control, each coalition has constituted a different balance between the participating parties. The space between the parties has also changed somewhat over the years. At the start of the period, according to a survey of 1972,[29] the major confessionals were rather nearer to the left than to the right. But as Labour strove to distance itself from the centre, the confessionals, unified after 1977, slowly gravitated towards a closer accord with the Liberals. This reflected the pragmatic fact of a prolonged partnership in government, rather than a change of the position of party activists on broad issues.[30] Since 1973 it is tempting to discern something closer to a left-right dichotomy than had been the case in the preceding thirty years. But this does not yield a clear polemical frame in which socio-economic strategies can be viewed. Instead the policy inflections within each governmental phase need to be assessed in specific terms.

Of the innumerable indicators which might be deployed to chart the fortunes of the economy since the early 1970s, three have a particular salience as measures of economic felicity. One is the rate of growth of the gross domestic product, another is the rate of inflation and a third is the level of unemployment. In Table 9.3 these three factors have been plotted both annually and by averages in each governmental phase (taking the period from 1977–82 as a unity under the same Minister-President, van Agt). It need scarcely be said that the effects of government policies upon the broad features of an economy are inherently hard to compute. The table therefore illustrates what successive governments had to confront as much as what they might be held to have achieved. This is especially so in the case of a relatively small, open economy such as the Netherlands. Nevertheless, when problems reach a certain magnitude, governments are expected by both their supporters and the populace to find means of redressing the situation.

The essential scenario confronted by the makers of socio-economic policy from around 1970 on is summed up in the following excerpt from a report of the mid-1980s:

> Over the post-war period successive Dutch governments constructed one of the most extensive social welfare systems in the OECD area. Education was expanded, access to medical care was improved and attempts made to ensure that adequate housing was within the reach of lower income groups. This was accompanied by an impressive array of income support schemes for those facing difficult economic circumstances. There was a general consensus that the finance of this system should be equitably distributed such that the heaviest burden would be borne by those best able to pay.[31]

The report goes on to point out that these features contributed to a rapid growth of the public sector through the 1970s, 'based upon the expectation that output would continue to rise at historical rates'. This expectation was not however fulfilled, with the result that by 1982 the budget was in deficit to the tune of nearly 8% of the gross domestic product.

Taking office in July 1971, the Biesheuvel cabinet inherited both an economy and a fiscal picture which were beginning to give cause for concern. Wages were rising at a disturbing rate (12–14% in 1970-1) along with consumer prices. Government expenditure was also accelerating as the social commitments of the 1960s required expanding

Table 9.3
KEY ECONOMIC INDICATORS, 1971–88

	1971	2	3	4	5	6	7	8	9	1980	1	2	3	4	5	6	7	8
GDP change %	4.5	4.0	4.3	3.3	-1.1	4.5	2.4	2.5	2.9	0.8	0.8	-1.4	0.9	1.7	2.1	1.1	1.4	2.7
Average change %	4.3	*		2.7						1.1			*			1.7		
Inflation change %	8	8	7.5	9.6	10	8.9	6.8	4.1	4.2	6.5	6.5	5.9	2.8	3.3	2.2	0.2	-0.3	0.8
Average change %	8		*	8.6						5.5			*			1.5		
Unemployment %	1.5	2.5	2.6	3.0	4.3	4.7	4.5	5.2	5.3	6.5	8.9	12.4	15.0	15.4	14.4	14.0	12.6	12.5
Average %	2.0	*	*	3.8						7.5			*			14.0		

Source: Data compiled by the author from the OECD's *Economic Surveys of the Netherlands,* 1971–89.

public outlays. In 1970 the arrangements for central wage settlements had foundered and the de Jong cabinet had responded with a six-months wage freeze. It also raised VAT from 12 to 14% and imposed a surcharge on taxes to reduce demand and curb inflationary pressures. By 1972 further problems were emerging. Unemployment, though less than 3%, had almost doubled in a year, inflation had stuck at 8%, against an average of 4% from 1965–70, and indexation clauses now covered almost all wage-earners, compared with a mere 10% in 1970. Business investment had slackened, there was a net capital outflow and conflict between the 'social partners' over wage claims was deepening.

The 1973 budget had to provide for a rise in public expenditure which represented a 50% increase over the original estimate for 1972. By the time a new tripartite agreement between employers, trade union federations and government had been secured in December 1972, the cabinet was in its terminal phase. DS'70 had defected from the coalition in September and fresh elections in November had made a centre-right majority in the Lower House no longer possible. The next government (after formation negotiations lasting 163 days) would take over the agreed package of limited wage and price increases, the gradual introduction of a forty-hour week, a freeze on business profits and a programme to reduce unemployment.

The Biesheuvel cabinet could be regarded as the last of the old-style accommodationist ministries. It had sought to restore consensus with moderate policies as befitted a five-party coalition with a wide ideological spectrum. Its successor was a very different assemblage. Also a five-party combination, its inflection under a Labour premier was intentionally left-wing. But it had been compelled to include confessional ministers to ensure a working majority in the Second Chamber. Its programme was a melange of social democratic concerns, tempered by confessional constraints. In Labour's election manifesto economic growth was considered subordinate to greater equality, protection of the lower income groups and the democratisation of institutions. Specific objectives included greater public control over investment and finance, co-determination in industry and the direct election of mayors and provincial officers.[32]

The new government's agenda was, however, soon overtaken by events when, in the autumn of 1973, the world oil price trebled and, during 1974, the cost of imported raw materials rose by 46%. *Avant le deluge*, a package to tackle long-term unemployment, had been hastily assembled. It included job creation, retraining, and a wage-cost subsidy.

But the deteriorating economic scene required more drastic measures. In January 1974 a Special Powers Act was put through parliament which gave the government authority to regulate prices, wages, dividends, redundancies, working hours and foreign labour contracts. Central direction had once more relieved the corporatist structure of its obligations to proceed by assent. When the structure was again resorted to in 1975, efforts to achieve a national wage agreement ended in failure. The cabinet resumed a policy of limited wage increases and price controls.

At the government's mid-term, the economic indicators looked bleak. The GDP fell by 1% in 1975, inflation reached double figures and unemployment rose by nearly 50% on 1974. The cabinet's riposte was a U-turn. Christened a strategy of 'selective growth' it set out to improve profits, freeze real wages, encourage private investment and restrict and restrict the rise of public expenditure to 1% per annum. The change appeared to produce dramatic results. By the end of 1976 GDP had recovered from below zero to a growth rate of 4%, while unit labour costs went up a mere 2% against the vertiginous rise of 16% in 1975.

The year 1976 might be regarded as a watershed in post-war economic policy.[33] From then on governments would be committed to restricting public sector growth in favour of private sector expansion. It also signalled a further retreat from corporatism and a realisation that central wage negotiations were no longer an effective method of directing the economy. It did not, however, amount to an abrogation of prescriptive social goals, although it was clear that henceforth they would need continuous adjustment to take account of economic feasibility.

The cumbersome den Uyl cabinet managed to survive almost four years. Pitted against a world recession it had struggled to fulfil its aims of protecting the low paid, women workers and the unemployed. But the inevitable cost had been higher taxes and social security contributions. In the election of March 1977 Labour was rewarded with a gain of ten seats, but failed to secure a deal with the Christian Democrats which would have given it a further spell in office. Instead a CDA-VVD coalition under van Agt took power with a bare majority in the Second Chamber. The programme of the new cabinet was similar to the one canvassed in the abortive negotiations between the CDA and Labour. Its overall aims were the reduction of unemployment and inflation, and tight control of public expenditure and the budget deficit. Specific proposals included two items from Labour's election manifesto – a levy on excess profits to finance a special investment fund, and broader worker participation in management. Thus although the new government contained only two ministers who had served in the previous cabinet, its initial approach carried on from the strategy resolved upon in 1976.

The strategy was further elaborated in 1978 with the issue of a policy document entitled 'Blueprint 1981' which was provoked by an unacceptably pessimistic medium-term forecast by the Central Planning Bureau.[34] The now familiar objectives of stabilising wages and taxes whilst maintaining the purchasing power of the lower-paid were re-iterated. As for unemployment, the aim was to keep this below the CPB's prediction of 7% by 1982 (in the event it topped 12% at that point). It was also decided, in order to conserve energy stocks, to slow down the exploitation of natural gas. Translated into the budget for 1979, the outcome was a reduction of proposed government expenditure, two-thirds of the cuts having been adumbrated by the previous government, with the remaining third to be achieved by 'less generous provisions for public sector wages and social security'.[35]

The record for 1979 suggested that the economy had at least steadied. GDP growth was up to almost 3%, wage increases appeared to have moderated, unemployment had remained around 5%, and inflation at slightly above 4% was lower than that of most competitors. The van Agt cabinet was entitled to feel that, in the jargon of the time, it had given about the right touch to the tiller. But the prognosticians in the OECD were dubious. 'It would appear', they pronounced, 'that the simultaneous pursuit of a large number of economic and social goals has given rise to inconsistencies or self-defeating elements in policy programmes.'[36]

The red light of economic misfortune began to flicker in 1980 as output started to fall. Early in 1981 interest rates rose, unemployment began to climb and the trade balance went into deficit. Again the OECD analysts delivered a gloomy verdict: 'A self-sustaining pattern of behaviour seems to have developed, with generous social security schemes, buoyant public expenditure, an unsuccessful incomes policy and tightening monetary conditions.'[37] The fact, by the early 1980s, was that the Netherlands had joined the rest of the advanced industrial world in what was to be the most severe of the post-war recessions. During 1980–2 Dutch living standards were to fall by more than 6%. In 1981 the GDP growth rate touched a post-war low of minus 1.4%. Yet with the number of citizens receiving public benefit rising by 3% per annum, a growth rate of 4.5% was required to maintain existing benefits.[38]

Unfortunately the recession coincided with a phase of deep political uncertainty. The election result of May 1981 ruled out a continuation of the CDA-VVD coalition. The alternative was a CDA-Labour coalition, but Labour had lost nine seats and relations between the two party leaders were less than harmonious. A prolonged cabinet formation (108 days) produced an uneasy three-party combination of CDA, Labour and D'66. But within weeks disagreements had surfaced and after a year the cabinet foundered when the PvdA parliamentary group refused to endorse cuts in public spending. A further election in September 1982 led in November to the restoration of a CDA-Liberal coalition under the premiership of Ruud Lubbers, by which time the 1983 budget had already been submitted to parliament by the out-going administration.

During a critical period therefore, from 1981–3, economic policy had been lacking in clear political direction, and in 1983 the public sector deficit reached 10.5% of net national income.[39] GDP growth was less than 1% and unemployment had soared to 15% of the dependent labour force – a figure which would have approached 20% had the procedures for registering disabled workers been less munificent. The incoming Lubbers cabinet manifestly faced an urgent need to get the economic and fiscal situation back on the rails. Its programme, largely dictated by the circumstances, comprised: rigorous control of the public sector to reduce expenditure and the budget deficit, the restoration of output and productivity, and measures to combat unemployment.

Under the first heading the policies adopted over the next four years would have some success, notably in the decrease of the budget deficit (see Table 9.4). Indeed by 1986 the economy had ostensibly been shored up, with rises in investment, non-gas output and real disposable incomes. Also, remarkably, inflation had subsided almost to zero. Yet GDP growth had remained sluggish, averageing little more than 1% per annum, and unemployment had defied the various devices, including statistical adjustments, designed to bring it down substantially.

Table 9.4
THE BUDGET DEFICIT AS A PERCENTAGE OF NET NATIONAL
INCOME

1975	1980	1983	1986
5.2	7.7	10.7	7.8

Source: *OECD Economic Survey of the Netherlands*, March 1986, Table 12, p. 35.

The election of May 1986 re-instated the CDA-VVD governing coalition, which adopted four main policy objectives in its programme for the next four years. The first was a further reduction of the budget deficit to 5.25% of net national income by 1990. This would entail the virtual ending of direct public subsidies to private industry, the freezing of salaries of public employees, and a reduction of the funds for health care along with an increase of charges to patients. Secondly, the government gave a pledge not to increase either taxes or social security premiums. Thirdly, it promised to bring the number of unemployed down to half a million (a reduction of 200,000); and fourthly, purchasing power was to be stabilised, thus relying on maintaining near-zero inflation.

The prospects of achieving these ambitions seemed unpropitious. Gas and related revenue were expected to fall drastically from 1987 onwards, which could increase the budget deficit to its 1983 figure. Also no significant improvement in economic growth could be safely assumed, and the prognosis for unemployment was of a plateau of 12–13% through the latter 1980s.[40] The picture by the end of 1988, however, was better than had been expected. GDP growth had moved up towards 3%. There had been a slight fall of consumer prices in 1987 and a rise of less than 1% in 1988, the best record of all OECD countries.[41] The budget deficit had been reduced to a little below the target set in 1986. But unemployment remained stubbornly high and, despite the post-election promise, taxes had been raised by the equivalent of 1.6% of GDP in the 1987 budget.[42]

By the end of the second Lubbers administration, terminated prematurely in May 1989, progress in balancing the books, increasing competitiveness and stimulating growth could be pronounced creditable in terms both of international comparisons and prior domestic history. The government's reputation was certainly one of vigour and astuteness in the eyes of its supporters. The remarkably low levels of inflation in 1986–8 had of course helped greatly to raise public morale. But there had been costs and penalties. The paring down of commitments in the public sector had, almost inevitably, meant a reduction in the level of social benefits. During 1983–8 social security outlay had fallen from nearly 31% to nearly 28% of net national income, and, with relatively low economic growth, this smaller proportion had been spread over an additional 300,000 beneficiaries.[43] The minimum wage, which is the basis for income support payments, had declined in relation to average earnings by some 15% over the same period, and earnings-related benefits had been reduced. But social security provisions still compared very favourably with other EEC members, while unemployment benefits remained the highest in Western Europe (almost three times those of the United Kingdom in 1986[44]), and payments to those off work through sickness were second only to Sweden.

In the 1989 budget, passed by parliament in September 1988, seven items may be highlighted:[45]

1. combating unemployment, which remained 'the principal aim of government policy';
2. a promise to introduce 'substantial tax cuts for the individual tax-payer';
3. a reform of health-care funding 'to enable market forces to function more effectively in the health care sector and to curb costs';
4. a reduction of the standard rate of VAT from 20% to 18.5%;
5. cuts in social security contributions and 'a shift in the burden of con-tributions from employees to employers';
6. additional expenditure on the infrastructure, training, conditions of employment, defence and family allowances;
7. a reduction of financial assistance to students (including a switch of loan provisions from the state to commercial organisations) and of benefits to unemployed young, single persons.

Items 2, 3 and 7 could readily be fitted into right-wing prescriptions for the reduction of public commitments. But the ostensible priority given to item 1, plus parts of 5 and 6, suggested a counter-tendency. Overall the budget appeared to reflect the complexion of a coalition within which the Liberals imparted something of a Thatcherite spin, while the CDA continued to have an eye to its widely spread clientele within all sections of society.

To conclude this review of socio-economic policy since the early 1970s, one might say that policies throughout have been reactive to a relatively fixed scenario in which social commitments have represented one half of the equation, and economic fortunes the other half. In neither sphere has any government had anything like full command over either inputs or outcomes. Perhaps the most general feature of policy styles over the period has been the increasing subordination of corporatist reconciliation to more central direction, culminating after 1982 in an attempt to marry ministerial management with an invocation of market forces.

The state as entrepreneur

Measured in terms of the share of the gross national product which is managed by central and local government, the Netherlands is exceeded only by Sweden in the size of its public sector. Commonly referred to as 'the collective burden', it can be expressed by statistics which suggest an alarming preponderance of public bureaucratic decision-making over private choice.[46] Yet the direct involvement of the state in services and productive enterprises has never had a high profile. The term 'profile' is perhaps the most apposite in this context, because the precise degree of state involvement in the economy and infrastructure is greatly obscured by forms of organisation which make a clear exposition surprisingly difficult.

In a detailed review of the mid-1970s, five species of state involvement were categorised in terms of their legal and organisational structure.[47] But, as will be apparent, these various structures did not necessarily reflect generically differing degrees of governmental control. At that point in time three major undertakings – Dutch State Mines, Dutch Railways and the Dutch Gas Union – were operating, along with other public enterprises, as limited liability companies (*naamloze vennootschappen*, or NVs), a form of incorporation identical with that of many private companies. Their staffs were company employees, not civil servants, and no minister was directly accountable to parliament for their policies or operations. There were also complex linkages between them which further obscured their connection with the State: Dutch State Mines, for example, then owned 40% of the shares of the Dutch Gas Union.

A second form of organisation applied to a number of enterprises, e.g. nuclear fuels and explosives, which were classed as closed companies (*besloten vennootschappen*, or BVs), whose activities required less public disclosure by law. There were, thirdly, non-profit-making enterprises which operated as either associations (*vereniging*) or foundations (*stichting*). The former included organisations which were responsible for water, electricity and gas exploitation and distribution; the latter covered an array of non-profit undertakings and also the Dutch Broadcasting Foundation (NOS).

All three of the above categories were part of the public domain in so far as they excluded private shareholding. But the state also participated in a range of enterprises which were not formally closed to private shareholding, notably Royal Dutch Airlines (KLM) and the steel giant Hoogovens. Finally there was the relatively small sector of direct government units, such as Posts and Telegraphs, the Mint, and the Government Printing Office. These were funded by parliament, to whom the relevant minister was responsible, and their personnel were civil servants.

From this summary it will at least be clear that the state sector is both multifarious and difficult to quantify. Equally difficult would be any attempt to account in general terms for either the range or variety of state holdings, some of which go back to the beginning of the century (Dutch State Mines, for example, was established in 1902). But it is possible to speak of the extent to which state involvement is significant in particular sectors of the economy. In the mid-1970s, public enterprises represented, in terms of total employment, three-quarters or more of activities in the fields of energy and communications, a third in the sphere of transport, and roughly one-twentieth of the industrial and financial sectors. Within the national workforce about 7.5% of employees could be regarded as public, in addition to the civil service. And as a proportion of the whole economy, public enterprises then accounted for around 10% of total investment and production.[48]

In 1982 the first Lubbers cabinet embarked upon a policy of restructuring which included moves towards deregulation, decentralisation and privatisation. Its principal motive was the reduction of direct government expenditure, though other arguments were adduced including the expansion of the market sector of the economy. Given the miscellaneous character of public holdings, however, it was far from obvious what could or should be privatised, or indeed what in many cases privatisation might amount to. The implementation of the policy took two forms. One was the hiving-off of direct government enterprises such as Post and Telecommunications and the Printing Office. The former was split into three companies (which remained for the present government-owned), while the latter was scheduled for eventual transfer into non-public control. The second line of implementation was the sale of shares in major enterprises, such as KLM, Hoogovens and Dutch State Mines, to reduce the proportion of state ownership.[49]

The whole operation, still ongoing in 1989, appears to have attracted little opposition from political parties or trade unions, and little enthusiasm on the part of private industry or investors.[50] But it does represent a new inflection in the direction of public policy which could conform to the notion of a 'neo-liberal backlash' against the tentacles of the state.[51]

NOTES

1. A.K. Dutt and F.J. Costa (eds), *Public Planning in The Netherlands*, Oxford, 1985, p. 46.
2. See J. van Putten, 'Policy Styles in The Netherlands' in J. Richardson (ed.), *Policy Styles in Western Europe*, London, 1982.
3. See W. Keyser and R. Windle (eds), *Public Enterprise in the EEC*, Part VI: The Netherlands (with assistance of H. van der Kar), Alphen aan den Rijn, 1978, p. 43.
4. See R.T. Griffiths, 'The Netherlands Central Planning Bureau' in Griffiths (1980).
5. P. de Wolff and W. Driehuis, 'A Description of Post War Economic Developments and Economic Policy in the Netherlands' in Griffiths (1980), p. 37. This chapter provides an excellent summary of policies and outcomes from 1945 up to the late 1970s.
6. See Windmuller (1969) and S. Wolinetz, 'Socio-Economic Bargaining in the Netherlands: Redefining the Post-War Coalition', *West European Politics*, 12/1 (Jan. 1989).
7. Wolff and Driehuis, op. cit., p. 42.
8. Gladdish (1983), p. 179.
9. Griffiths (1980), op. cit.
10. Wolff and Driehuis, op. cit., Table 2.10, p. 28.
11. Indeed the shift of balance from private to public consumption, between 1955 and 1969, exceeded that of Scandinavian countries. *OECD Economic Survey of the Netherlands*, June 1974, p. 28, footnote 2.
12. An attempt to provide a generic explanation of 'the sharp rise in the share of government after the mid 1960s' in all Western systems is made by N. Roubini and J. Sachs, 'Government Spending and Budget Deficits in Industrial Countries' in *Economic Policy: A European Forum*, no. 8 (April 1989).
13. Gladdish (1983), pp. 181-2.
14. See Chapter 3.
15. Gladdish (1983), p. 177. Karl Popper has put the point even more generally with the contention that multi-party governments are less likely to resist pressure for increased commitments, because they cannot be so easily penalised as single party governments in subsequent elections. Roubini and Sachs, op. cit., pp. 129-30.
16. H. Daalder, 'The Mould of Dutch Politics', *West European Politics*, Vol. 12, No. 1 (1989), p. 8.
17. R. Andeweg, 'Centrifugal forces and collective decision-making: The case of the Dutch Cabinet', *European Journal of Political Research*, Vol. 16, No. 2 (1988a), p. 132.
18. Inventory compiled by WRR (Scientific Council for Public Policy) quoted by I.Th. M. Snellen (ed.), *Limits of Government: Dutch Experiences*, Amsterdam, 1985. He notes that in the spring of 1985, as part of the 'great operations' launched by Prime Minister Lubbers, 150 *adviesorganen* were abolished, while others were amalgamated.
19. Van Putten, op. cit., p. 179.
20. Ilja Scholten, 'Corporatism and the neo-liberal backlash in the Netherlands' in I. Scholten (ed.), *Political Stability and Neo-Corporatism*, London, 1987.
21. Van Putten, op. cit., provides the example of the Selective Investment Law of 1974 where 'the formal advisory bodies had little influence . . .'

22. It would be difficult to imagine, for example, a Dutch government enacting policy as ill-considered as the fixed-rate poll-tax (euphemistically styled 'community charge') for the raising of local revenue in the United Kingdom.
23. Scholten, op. cit., p. 121.
24. M.P.C.M. van Schendelen and R.J. Jackson (eds), *The Politicisation of Business in Western Europe*, London, 1987.
25. Conversation with the author, June 1989.
26. Ibid.
27. Snellen, op. cit.
28. Ibid., chapter VI, 'Multi-level Policy'.
29. Gladdish (1983), p. 185, note 5.
30. See Chapter 5.
31. *OECD Economic Survey of the Netherlands*, 1984, p. 29.
32. See Wolinetz in Paterson and Thomas (1977).
33. The *OECD Economic Survey of the Netherlands*, February 1977, concluded: '1976 marked the beginning of an important re-orientation of economic policies in the Netherlands' (p. 5).
34. Ibid., March 1979, pp. 29–30.
35. Ibid., p. 32.
36. Ibid., March 1980, p. 58.
37. Ibid., April 1981, p. 39
38. Ibid., Jan. 1983, pp. 17–18.
39. Ibid., Feb. 1984, p. 7.
40. Ibid., July 1987, Table 13, p. 26.
41. Ibid., 1988/9, p. 9.
42. Survey of the Dutch Economy, *The Economist*, 12 Sept. 1987.
43. *OECD Economic Survey of the Netherlands*, 1988/9, p. 40.
44. Ibid., p. 42.
45. Dutch Ministry of Finance press release, 20 Sept. 1988.
46. Public revenue as a proportion of net national income was recorded as 55% (unchanged from 1983 to 1988), in the *OECD Economic Survey of the Netherlands*, 1988/9. An even higher figure – 70.3% in 1983 – was put forward by Andeweg, 'Less than Nothing? Hidden Privatisation of the Pseudo-Private Sector: The Dutch Case', *West European Politics*, Vol. 11, No. 4 (1988b), p. 121.
47. Keyser and Windle, op. cit., pp. 2–4.
48. Ibid., p. 71.
49. *OECD Economic Survey of the Netherlands*, 1988/9.
50. Andeweg (1988b) op. cit., pp. 119–21.
51. Scholten, op. cit.

10
THE INTERNATIONAL CONTEXT

> The Dutch polity, being itself free from lust for power, is the most impartial
> judge of other nations' lust for power.
> — J.R. Thorbecke, 1830[1]

From old to new testament

From the late 1940s, Dutch governments have pursued a more vigorous
set of external policies than at virtually any point since the early
eighteenth century. This fact may not be widely appreciated outside the
Netherlands. Indeed even the Dutch foreign policy élite is capable of
playing it down – witness a recent remark to the author by an embassy
official that Holland has no independent foreign policy but merely
follows the decision of NATO and the EEC.[2] It is nevertheless the case
that the years since the late 1940s have seen, alongside the commitments
to the Western military alliance and European integration, an enormous
expansion of the Dutch foreign service[3] and membership of a vast
number of international bodies.[4]

The metamorphosis of a state which, for a century up to the Second
World War, played an almost silent part in international power politics
into one which has sought a voice in world affairs at all significant levels,
requires both exposition and analysis. Till recently the phenomenon
tended to be presented in terms of the underlying continuity of a traditional strategy which, owing to post-war circumstances, needed merely
a new frame of tactical expression.[5] This approach had both scholarly and
psychological attractions. On the one hand it offered some long-term
intellectual coherence when reviewing Dutch policy over time. It also,
less consciously perhaps, provided a certain kind of domestic reassurance.

The transformation of the Netherlands, after 1949, from a formerly
neutral state into a military power which would shortly provide a base
for weapons of immense destructive capacity[6], had potentially profound
psychological consequences for the peace of mind of the citizens. These
could be dealt with in a variety of ways. They could even be ignored for
as long as was feasible.[7] But eventually they had somehow to be squared
with the pervasive national self-perception that Dutch society embodied
a love of peace, a belief in the pursuit of international harmony, and a

contempt for military prowess, coercion and the exercise of might. The view that what had happened was a mere re-shaping of earlier preoccupations, and that the old traditions of high principle, order and justice were simply being re-aligned, could be regarded as a way of squaring an otherwise difficult circle.

The case for seeing post-war developments as part of an underlying continuity rested upon several premises. The simplest was the argument of basic geography which ran that since the Netherlands has always been a small maritime state, wedged between larger powers in a strategic corner of North-West Europe, its foreign policy needs had remained essentially constant. What had changed after 1945, under this conception, was not Holland but the world. In the nineteenth and earlier twentieth centuries, Dutch governments, while maintaining their colonial possessions, had been able to stay clear of inter-state conflicts, relying upon a combination of the balance between the big European powers, and the British navy, to keep the peace.[8] In the post-war world these insurances had been swept away, and new modes of self-protection were called for. But these new modes could still be fitted into the old frame of reference. Thus the facts that the Netherlands now sees the need to be present at the world's conference tables, to commit forces and substantial resources to a military alliance,[9] to promote economic and political integration in Europe and to take a significant hand in the development of the Third World – all these can be presented as stylistic variations of traditional stances.

Much of course depends upon how these traditional stances are construed. It might, for example, be thought that they always included certain ambitions – in the realm of empire and in presiding over the cultivation of international peace – and that the studious aloofness to international embroglios was merely one face of a more positive concern with national interest. But this would require a more strenuous revision of history than the issue would seem to warrant. If there is an area in which there does appear to be a degree of continuity between past and present it is the national reluctance to view foreign policy in terms of self-interest. As late as 1989, a leading Dutch analyst felt impelled to record that 'it is astonishing to note that until recently the terms ''power'' and ''national interest'' were hardly ever mentioned in public debates on foreign policy'.[10] Instead the time-honoured disposition to regard moral influence and legal-rational forms of accommodation as the superior forces in inter-state relations seems to have survived.[11]

The most critical and significant phase in the transformation of Dutch foreign policy was the short but intense period of re-appraisal which occurred from 1947 to 1949. As early as 1942, van Kleffens, Foreign Minister in the London government-in-exile, had signalled the need for a new approach to national security.[12] Yet it was not till the end of 1946 that parliament confronted the external circumstances of the post-war situation.[13] By then the Netherlands had joined the United Nations and formulated its demands for reparations and a territorial readjustment at the expense of Germany. But the problem of recovering control in Indonesia was a grave preoccupation,[14] while the Foreign Minister from mid-1946 to mid-1948 was a non-party ex-diplomat who appeared unwilling to take major foreign policy initiatives. By March 1948, however, the Dutch government had signed the Brussels Treaty between Britain, France and the Benelux countries; and by April 1949, the Netherlands was a full and founder member of NATO. The latter event took place against the backdrop of an American embargo on military shipments to the Dutch forces in Indonesia, while the Dutch claims for reparations from Germany were being sedulously ignored.

However this profound change of external orientation is packaged, there can be little question that it represented undertakings of an order which no previous Dutch governments had contemplated since the collapse of the union with Belgium in 1831. Although the Dutch parliament had ratified the Covenant of the League of Nations in 1920, it had rejected the Geneva protocol of 1924 which provided for guarantees of armed assistance. Further, in 1936, the Dutch government signed the Copenhagen declaration opting out of automatic sanctions and the duty to afford a right of passage for forces operating under the Covenant. Indeed there was considerable pressure from political circles in the late 1930s for the Netherlands to withdraw completely from the League.[15] A mere decade later, the Dutch foreign policy élite were willing to bind themselves to an alliance which would dictate virtually all important strategic options over the next forty years. How could this be reconciled with the refusal of previous generations to enter into the mildest of military commitments which might prejudice Dutch interests and remove the freedom to stand aloof from international conflict?

There were two very specific reasons for the change of orientation. One was that the policy of high-minded neutrality as a prophylaxis against attack had been irrevocably shattered by the German invasion of 1940. The other was the perception of a Soviet threat which would unite all the invaded former neutrals into a security system guaranteed by the might of the United States. But it was still believed that there was a need to reconcile the new strategy with the old historic position.

This need was accorded its most skilful orchestration by Joris

Voorhoeve in his book *Peace, Profits and Principles. A Study of Dutch Foreign Policy*, complied in the 1970s and published in 1985. He discerns, through Dutch history, three dominant tendencies: maritime commercialism, neutralist abstentionism and internationalist idealism. The first he sees as promoting 'a strong reliance on treaties and orderly legal regulations, an aversion to nationalism and a craving for international order and peace.[16] The second he traces back to the loss of the Belgian provinces in 1831 and a subsequent identity crisis in the Netherlands although neutralism can be traced back to dispositions after the Peace of Utrecht in 1713. Dutch neutrality during the century of dedicated abstention from inter-power conflict, from 1840 to 1940, Voorhoeve regards as having had certain biases. Thus it was anti-French up to the 1860s, anti-German up to 1900, and briefly anti-British during the Boer War and its aftermath.

This second historic tendency feeds into the third – internationalist idealism, where religious pacificism melded with the Calvinist tradition of rule-ordered behaviour to promote 'contempt for the wicked struggle among nations'.[17] This theme was later reinforced by the socialist belief in internationalism as a channel for the class struggle, while an unwillingness to engage in military investment (other than in the East Indies) fuelled the conviction that the Netherlands should become what Vandenbosch has called a 'Peace Laboratory'.[18] In his cool and at times ironic presentation of foreign policy pretensions, the latter author has plotted persuasively the various ways in which 'small power and isolationist policy was developed by the Dutch to a point little short of perfection'.[19]

When, for example, in 1863 the government delivered a temperate note to Russia over its actions in Poland, this was censured by the Second Chamber for departing from the accepted position of neutrality. Progressively, as Vandenbosch recounts, a symbiotic relationship developed between the policy of clinical neutrality and the aspiration to the role of world intermediary. From the 1890s on, a series of conferences at The Hague, initially devised to codify private international law, led to the establishment of a Permanent Court of Arbitration there. Upon this foundation was later erected the League of Nations' Permanent Court of International Justice, which, under the United Nations, became the International Court of Justice.

During the nineteenth century, therefore, a carefully-shaped ideology of constructive neutrality became the chief pillar of Dutch foreign policy. It was gravely tested in the First World War when the maintenance of territorial integrity 'was little less than a miracle'.[20] But it was shattered in May 1940. It would verge on the absurd to contend that the former policy might or should have been resurrected after 1945. The case is instead that what did finally emerge by 1949 was profoundly different from what had gone before, and that it cannot plausibly be passed off as a retuning of the old postures. There is admittedly some risk of the argument becoming metaphysical; because there were inevitably some continuities – most obviously at the general level of political culture, with its attitudes to nationalism, the persistence of transactional styles and so on.

But it is more illuminating to view post-war Dutch foreign policy as a sea-change which cannot be phrased in terms of the long prior addiction to international law, peace and morality. The most palpable point to make is that the whole concept of national security changed. Whereas before it had consisted largely in remaining inconspicuous, a position which could be clothed in ethical and legal vestments, after 1949 its central column became a military alliance with the United States. And however much that alliance may be regarded as the safeguard of democracy, decency and justice in the world, it cannot readily be erected into a universal moral principle. Between pacifism and nuclear deterrence there is a pretty deep moral and political gulf, as Dutch citizens came increasingly to realise in the latter 1960s.

Setting the post-war mould

There is an unquestioned consensus on the part of commentators that up to the German invasion of 1940, although the Netherlands had significant external interests, its leaders strove for a nearly immaculate abstention from active involvement in international power politics. This was reflected, *inter alia*, in the almost risible unimportance accorded to the Foreign Office within the governmental and parliamentary networks.[21] External relations were also a concern of the Ministries of Economic Affairs and the Colonies, but even the latter's responsibilities were deliberately played down in order to avoid any undue international complications.[22]

The first intimation of new thinking about foreign policy came in 1942–3, when, as already mentioned, the Foreign Minister in the Dutch government-in-exile proposed an abandonment of neutrality in favour of some form of collective security in alliance with the major Western powers – Britain, France and the United States.[23] Undoubtedly the

experience of being a member of a wartime alliance helped to shape this
notion, its immediate objectives being security against Germany in
Europe and Japan in Asia.

When peace came there was however something of a vacuum in clear
thoughts about external policy. 'Everyone was agreed that the old
cherished policy of neutrality was dead and buried,' affirms Schaper.[24]
But precisely what followed from that conclusion was uncertain. Subsequently it was considered that an active foreign policy 'was a matter of
course' which required little debate and could simply be instrumented by
the policy élite;[25] but that seems a view conditioned by hindsight.

The first task in 1945, before indeed the country was fully liberated,
was to take a decision about participation in the emerging United
Nations Organisation. The Dutch delegation in San Francisco –
despatched before any parliament could be assembled – was concerned
about maintaining the principles of international law and the rights of
small powers within the new consortium. When, in the autumn of
1945, the provisional Dutch parliament was asked to approve the UN
Charter, Vandenbosch records that it 'was a foregone conclusion, but
that there was little enthusiasm for the step'.[26] The main anxiety was
that the arrangements were more oriented to big power influence than to
formal juridical provisions for the settlement of international disputes.
But van Kleffens was still Foreign Minister, and his view that isolation
was an untenable option prevailed. This verdict can be seen as a watershed in post-war Dutch positioning. It led, among other things, to direct
Dutch participation in the UN military action in Korea in 1950, by
which point the Netherlands was allied to the United States under the
umbrella of NATO.

Entry into the UN did not, however, precipitate any clear or specific
thoughts about foreign policy by the newly-reconstituted political
parties, whose pronouncements in the run-up to the first post-war parliamentary election, in May 1946, were both vague and brief. External
relations were by then in the hands of a largely reactive ex-diplomat, van
Boetzelaer, who saw the UN as a flawed assembly though one which
offered some prospect of international salvation 'in accordance with
God's plan'.[27]

The sequence of events which would draw the Netherlands into
military pacts, first within Western Europe and soon after on a transat-
lantic basis, began to unfold from January 1947 onwards when Dutch
concerns about the treatment of Germany prompted a memorandum to
the 'great powers',[28] then comprising the United States, the Soviet

Union, France and Britain. Its main thrust was that a treaty between Germany's neighbours was essential to ensure the former enemy's permanent demilitarisation. At the same time it was stressed that German economic recovery was vital for the regeneration of the West European economy. Two novel lines of post-war Dutch policy were thereby adumbrated: regional military security and European economic co-operation.

When the London conference of the four 'great powers' in November-December 1947 broke down, the British Foreign Secretary Ernest Bevin countered, in January 1948, with a proposal for a Western European Union which would embrace economic, diplomatic and military interests. The Netherlands, operating within the Benelux association which had been formed in 1944, responded positively; and the remarkably rapid outcome was the Treaty of Brussels, signed in March 1948, between Britain, France and the Benelux countries. This was the second watershed in the Dutch external reorientation; 'it meant that the Netherlands was prepared to form a political alliance for the first time in more than a hundred years' and represented the 'end of the policy of neutrality and non-alignment'.[29]

The third step, and the one which was to be the most crucial for both security policy and international posture over the ensuing forty years, was Dutch membership of NATO.

The Atlantic Alliance

The Brussels Treaty provided for military aid and assistance by all five powers if any were attacked,[30] and its preamble allowed for its extension to other states.[31] Approved by the States-General in April 1948, by the time it took effect in August negotiations had begun for the inclusion of the United States and Canada. In less than a year the Treaty was thus expanded into a North Atlantic alliance which was ratified by the seven founder members, including Holland, on 4 April 1949. The alliance – which would be extended to seven further states including, in 1955, West Germany – constituted a mutual defence pact centred upon US military capacity and directed against the Soviet Union. For the Netherlands it amounted to a comprehensive commitment to a foreign policy based upon a military alignment, a move to which only the Communist members of the Dutch parliament objected.[32]

Understandably a great deal of analysis has since been lavished upon the nature and consequences of this commitment from the standpoint of

Dutch interests, needs and outlook. Several aspects of these concerns are worth special attention. The first is that although the Atlantic Alliance emerged out of a regional European security pact, and would thereafter run concurrently with Dutch participation in and active promotion of Western European integration, it can be regarded as the keystone of all subsequent security policy in the Netherlands. This reflects the signal fact that since 1949 the Netherlands has consistently placed its obligations to the United States above the various proposals for a more independent security policy on the part of Western Europe.

A second aspect is that although much effort has been expended upon developing a rationale for this stance which accords with the historic Dutch reputation for upholding international law and morality, the elements within it which reflect national self-interest seem manifest. Indeed the semantics of the term 'moral' in this context have been stretched even by otherwise clear-minded commentators.[33] In a subtle characterisation of the effects of United States protection, Voorhoeve has sought to retain the flavour of traditional Dutch positioning, arguing that by becoming the 'faithful ally' of a superpower, the Netherlands has been able to opt out of 'the cruder forms of [international] politics'.[34]

A third aspect is that the change from passivity to activism, which has been the hallmark of post-war external policies, has carried with it both a certain unease and the realisation that the strength of even a small diplomatic hand can be increased if the right strategic choices are made. In these terms the key dispositions of Dutch strategists in the late 1940s have conferred upon the Netherlands a highly favourable set of cards with which to play in the international arena. In the most immediate theatre, that of Western Europe, Dutch governments have had to contend with the proximity of much larger powers, notably France and Germany, whose strength could best be countered by an appeal to supranational decisions in which votes were at least formally equal. Within NATO the Dutch role has perforce been very different. As Voorhoeve shrewdly puts it, 'the Netherlands, like the other small European powers, preferred the gentle hegemony of a remote Atlantic superpower over . . . less credible leadership but more immediate domination by Britain, Germany, France . . .'[35]

The effects of the Atlantic Alliance upon the Netherlands has prompted much scholarly assessment of the role of small powers within the international system.[36] A central issue has been the apparent paradox that although membership of a powerful military organisation affords the Netherlands both security and status, its scope for independent decision-making is effectively occluded by that membership. NATO has been interpreted as a 'feudal alliance' in which there is no prospect of any counter-alignments by its smaller components,[37] and as a 'loose system of domination' within which the Netherlands, as a minor player, has no balancing capacity.[38] Further, by having to identify so closely with American policy, governments could be regarded as having sacrificed Dutch traditional impartiality and thereby forfeited any role as a potential mediator in international disputes. The usual counter to this implication of vassalage is the claim that the Alliance was a 'choice by the Dutch government based upon considerations of national interest, not a manifestation of dependency upon foreign powers'.[39]

If we examine the record since 1949, it may be possible to judge how far the Netherlands has been dominated by its adherence to NATO, and how far it has been able, on occasions, to be a dissenting ally where either a sense of excessive cost or pressure from domestic opinion has produced a clash of interest. Often, however, the record is uncertain and many different factors have contributed to outcomes. The case of Dutch decolonisation in Asia is an apt illustration of this. Although United States pressure was applied to hasten the exit from Indonesia in 1949 and from New Guinea in 1962, there was little scope anyway for a last stand by the Netherlands in a region where it could bring no more military resources to bear.

More fertile as an issue is the Dutch position on disarmament and nuclear deterrence which have been continuing themes in external policy over the past four decades. The country's historic pro-peace stance, revived in the latter 1960s and thereafter by the clamour of peace lobbies at home, has constituted a recurrent source of tension within the foreign policy system. NATO has of course engaged periodically in disarmament moves as part of a multi-track approach to combating the perceived threat from the Soviet bloc. But the Netherlands has remained a very small voice in these overtures, and Dutch governments have been keenly aware that the cultivation of more pacific approaches to East-West relations carries the risk of undermining the kinds of assurance the Atlantic pact provides.

Thus the official attitude towards nuclear weapons early took on the character of having to swallow the possibility of mass destruction as part of the commitment to a consolidated Western defence. In 1957 the deployment of United States tactical nuclear missiles in Holland (the first European country to receive them) took place, according to Walraven, 'without any discussion'.[40] And in 1962 Prime Minister de Quay made it clear that the use of atomic weapons would require 'all possible co-operation demanded of it.'[41]

This quasi-fatalism would later be challenged, notably as the more critical wave of public opinion of the late 1960s confronted the unpalatibilities of the Vietnam War. Between 1967 and 1970, parliamentary debates on foreign policy increased both in frequency and controversy. But this was a mere prelude to the potential change of outlook and orientation represented by the den Uyl cabinet of 1973-7, when both foreign and defence matters came under the direction of Labour ministers. This interlude was of profound interest from the standpoint of the conflict between left-wing rhetoric and policy continuity. For the cabinet faced opposition to the *status quo* from party activists, elements within the churches, and its supporting parliamentary groups.

In 1975 parliamentary motions proposing the delineation of nuclear-free zones in Europe were supported by the Labour *fractie*,[42] and the Labour party congress was extremely critical of many aspects of NATO strategy. But in its Disarmament Memorandum of the same year, the government backed the continuation of nuclear deterrence, and the Foreign Minister, van der Stoel, rejected demands for a no first-use declaration and the withdrawal of United States tactical nuclear forces from Holland.[43] It seemed that the fear of unsettling the Atlantic Alliance remained paramount, and that a quarter-century of adherence to NATO had conditioned the extent to which Dutch governments of whatever political stripe would be willing to rock the boat.

The debate over medium-range nuclear weapons, which was to dominate the early 1980s, took on a somewhat different complexion, however.[44] In part this extended episode was an exceptional case in that the United States was itself uncertain how best to respond to what had begun as an initiative from European leaders, notably the West German Chancellor Helmut Schmidt. Thus the length and range of the debate promoted by United States policy-makers offered unusual scope for the opinions of its NATO allies. The CDA parliamentary group was therefore able to take a stand on what it thought Dutch public opinion would endorse, and argue for a postponement of the deployment of the new missiles. Divisions within the CDA-VVD cabinet, and wide-ranging popular opposition to accepting the weapons, thus resulted in the deferment of a final decision on installation until late in 1985. It was then decided by the cabinet and endorsed by a narrow majority in parliament that installation should proceed. By 1988 the superpower agreement on the mutual withdrawal of medium-range missiles made the whole matter redundant. But the episode stands as a singular example of foot-dragging by a faithful ally which had repercussions within Europe as well as upon United States-Netherlands relations.

Western Europe

A number of strands are discernible in the Dutch involvement, post-war, in Western European integration. An early precursor was the formation of the Benelux Customs Union in September 1944, undertaken by the respective governments-in-exile in London.[45] Of its various features, two are worth attention. One is that it represented the first effective collaboration between the Northern and Southern Low Countries since the separation of 1831 – previous attempts up to the 1930s having ended in failure. The other is that it operated as an inter-government organisation, largely because a supranational format would have given the micro-state of Luxembourg the casting vote. Progress with the dismantling of inter-state tariffs was however relatively slow, the abolition of duties coming into effect on 1 January 1948.

By then other developments within Western Europe were already in train. From mid 1947 the Dutch government was reacting to the Marshall Plan and the moves which led to the formation of the OEEC. The failure of the East-West London conference in December 1947 would be quickly followed by the British initiative which resulted, by mid-1948, in the Treaty of Brussels. The following year the Dutch Foreign Minister, Stikker, put forward a plan for tariff reductions in Western Europe,[46] which was succeeded by the French Schumann plan proposing a European Coal and Steel Community. At this point the concept of supranational institutions became a central theme in Dutch foreign policy thinking.

The case against this was obvious; it would mean a derogation of sovereignty which would in turn mean relinquishing the option of abstention from unwelcome commitments. The case in favour – which received overwhelming support in the Second Chamber of parliament in April 1948[47] – was that supranational decision-making would give the Netherlands a greater opportunity for parity with its larger neighbours. The Coal and Steel Community came into existence in 1951, with both inter-governmental and supranational provisions. Thereafter Dutch governments would support, wherever it did not seem wholly detrimental to specific national interests (as in the transport sector) the principle of supranationality.

In the long lead-up to the Treaties of Rome in 1957, Dutch governments played an enterprising role, as evidenced by the plan of Foreign Minister Beyen, in 1952–3, for a customs union between the members of the ECSC. Parliamentary support for Dutch EEC entry was withheld only by the Communists, and by sectarian Calvinist MPs who feared the prospect of a Catholic dominion in Western Europe.[48] The advantages of Dutch membership of the Common Market seemed widely apparent. The Dutch economy was tied to regional prosperity, especially on the part of West Germany, its largest trading partner. After three years of membership, Dutch exports to other EEC countries had risen by 80%. Politically the Netherlands now had a seat in a continental forum which enabled it to challenge the most influential participant – France – given the relative passivity of the two other large members, Italy and West Germany.

There was also the bonus that EEC decisions did not affect Dutch security policy, which was firmly tied into the United States alliance. This fact was used consistently by Dutch governments to resist all attempts at closer defence co-operation on a European basis, on the grounds that with two European nuclear powers the Netherlands would be easily out-manoevred if American protection were diminished. However, at least one writer, in the mid-1960s, detected that 'a certain uneasiness has continued to pervade the Dutch attitude towards Europe'.[49] Four grounds for this unease were offered: uncertainty about becoming a 'completely continental nation'; unhappiness about the inherent protectionism of the EEC; a distrust of the mounting strength of West Germany; and an aversion to immersion in power politics. These anxieties seemed not, however, to affect popular enthusiasm for EEC membership, which into the 1970s regularly won the support of over 70% of opinion poll respondents.[50]

From the outset of the negotiations which led to the Rome Treaties, Dutch governments had taken the view that West European integration should be on the widest possible basis.[51] In part this arose from the belief that the benefits of freer trade were proportional to the size of the market, and that the formation of separate associations such as EFTA would damage that concept. But it also had a strongly political element in that the smaller the EEC base, the greater the danger of dominance by either France or West Germany or a concordance of the two. Thus the principle of 'openness' was asserted which, as Suzanne Jones pointed out, was 'a euphemism for British participation'.[52] She further observed that this exemplified a tendency of Dutch negotiators to wrap their desires in envelopes of principle (this author's paraphrase), which one might speculate had Calvinist undertones.

Through the 1960s the debate about enlarging the Community to include the United Kingdom provoked the fitful opposition of de Gaulle. Much of the political energy injected by Dutch ministers into the debate was directed against the French position. When, after 1969, the dam broke with the exit of de Gaulle, Dutch policy-makers had to face the real prospect of a larger Community in which the Netherlands would have a proportionately smaller voice. With the expansion of members from six to nine, in 1974, it quickly became clear that the presence of Britain dwarfed that of the Netherlands as a counter to Franco-German pressures. It also became apparent that on the question of national sovereignty, the British position was not so very different from the earlier platform of de Gaulle.

After 1986, when the EEC admitted Spain and Portugal to become a twelve-state organisation, the Dutch role did indeed seem much reduced. The Netherlands now had one Commissioner out of seventeen, held only five votes in budget matters out of seventy-six, and sent only twenty-five MPs to a European parliament with 518 members.[53] Voorhoeve, summing up from the vantage point of the late 1970s, considered that whereas special circumstances had given the Netherlands an unusually high profile within the EEC from 1956–73, British entry had 'cost the Netherlands a part of its role'.[54] In the most recent developments towards a single market by 1992, it is noticeable that while Dutch parliamentarians remain committed to the enhancement of the Community's powers, their British counterparts, in both major parties, have grave reservations about any further surrender, as they see it, of national sovereignty.[55]

The wider world

As has already been pointed out, Dutch dealings with the world at large have, since the late 1940s, been more intensive and extensive than in any previous period in modern times. The canvas includes UN participation, concerns with human rights, democracy and the international order, Third World matters, disarmament, ecology and so on. Voorhoeve has attempted to summarise these preoccupations under the heading of *mondiale politiek*, which he translates as 'mundial policy' or more prescriptively 'world-wide co-operation'.[56] The Dutch Foreign Office, since its most recent reorganisation in 1985, has divided up its global tasks between three directorates: Political Affairs; European Co-operation; and International Co-operation. The first deals with the world on a geographical basis; the second, much the smallest, concentrates upon European integration, while the third, much the largest, deals with overseas development.[57] In 1987 the long-standing distinction between the Foreign Office and the Diplomatic Service was eliminated, and the two were integrated.

The complexity of external relations under contemporary conditions, however, even for a relatively small power like the Netherlands, makes it difficult to schematise adequately the entire range of operational issues. Instead it is more useful to highlight areas on which Dutch foreign policy-makers have concentrated in recent years. The two major realms of external concern – the Atlantic Alliance and Western Europe – have already been reviewed. Outside these two frames, the emphasis over the past generation has been upon policy towards crisis areas, such as the Middle East and South Africa, and upon Third World development.

Both spheres impinge upon international and regional associations. Indeed it is hard to extract specific concerns from the web of commitments which affect the Dutch response to particular issues. In their selection of case studies of Dutch foreign policy since the war, Everts and Walraven cite five which arose directly from NATO debates, four which derived from UN participation, two which were aspects of decolonisation, four which concerned specific problems areas and one which was a matter of EEC policy.[58] All sixteen cases could be classified in a variety of ways, according to topic, format, ambit, etc. The Netherlands' accession to the Non-proliferation Treaty of 1968 for example involved its membership of NATO, the EEC and the UN[59] while the question of sanctions against South Africa also fell within the framework of UN and EEC policy.[60]

Leaving aid and development to be dealt with subsequently, what general reflections are possible on the pattern of Dutch *mondiale politiek* in the post-war era? Voorhoeve sees something of an ideology in the Netherlands' approach to world order and, hopefully, decency. 'Mundialist idealism', he observes, 'has become an important drive in Dutch foreign policy – though certainly not the main one'.[61] The main goals have, in his view, remained national security, prosperity and identity. But he believes that they have proved 'compatible with mundial idealism',[62] at least up to the 1980s.

What is perhaps being said here is that Dutch foreign policy exponents have been able to subscribe to, and on occasions promote – as with the UN Convention against torture[63] – measures designed to improve international conduct, after having secured, through pacts and alliances, the main needs of national interest. Such a strategy is doubtless what all civilised nations would seek to be able to achieve. In the Dutch case the two distinguishing features would appear to be, firstly, a deep concern for international ethics with its roots in convictions, both religious and secular, about justice and harmony; and secondly, the capacity to deal with material self-interests by making shrewd choices in the international sphere.

The Netherlands has long been a state which has promoted the cause of peace, and has done little in its recent history (if one overlooks the 'police action' in Indonesia in the late 1940s) which could be thought in any way to threaten peace. But it has never been charged with, nor could ever be cast in the role of, keeping the international peace. The modesty of its size and resources precludes such a responsibility – which has profound consequences for the ability to combine the preservation of national interests with the pursuit of enlightened international causes.

Development aid

Aid to the poorer countries of the world—in the terminology of the 1980s, development co-operation—has become an important theme of the Netherlands' role on the world stage. Its significance as a dimension of external policy took root in the mid-1960s when a minister without portfolio was appointed to promote overseas assistance. In the de Jong cabinet of 1967–71, under Minister Udink, the volume of aid was doubled and a goal of 1% of net national income (NNI) was set for this purpose.[64] In the 1970s the target was raised to 1.5% of NNI, and under Minister Pronk in the den Uyl cabinet, the Netherlands became a leading aid donor in terms of the proportion of national resources committed to this end.

The policy was expounded in a set of principles which referred to the structural imbalances of the world economic system, the importance for peace of harmonious North-South relations, the need to promote an energy programme less dependent upon oil, and the strengthening of economic co-operation under the aegis of the United Nations.[65] In adopting a policy of high profile development assistance, the Netherlands was in tune with a similar outlook on the part of the Scandinavian states. If an element of national interest can be discerned, it is in the mild sense that this is a field in which affluent small powers can achieve some international visibility. Also small country aid can pardonably be directed towards regions which may be of special interest to the donor. Thus in the 1970s three of the principal destinations of Dutch aid were Surinam, the Antilles and Indonesia, with each of which the Netherlands had a special relationship.

The selection of countries to whom aid is to be channelled also confers, at a not inordinate cost, a sense of affecting the fortunes of chosen parts of the world, which can be linked with objectives of a broadly humane kind. In a very interesting exercise, Peter Baehr has examined the targeting of aid by the Ministry of Development Co-operation in relation to the recipients' record on human rights.[66] His theme was the problem of determining whether the performance of governments in the field of human rights should be a criterion for development assistance. He points out that, in a policy memorandum of May 1979, the Dutch government officially rejected 'the idea that aid should be used to reward countries which respect human rights and conversely withheld to punish countries which disregard those rights'. The operating principle was instead to be that 'Aid should relate to the needs of the people and not to the conduct of governments.'[67] Nevertheless the ministry did attempt to assess progress on human rights in aided countries, though Amnesty reports revealed discrepancies between official evaluations and the ostensible facts.

By 1980 India had become the leading beneficiary of Dutch development assistance, followed by Indonesia, Tanzania and Bangladesh. In that year 0.8% of the Netherlands' GNP went into overseas aid, compared with a range from 0.27 to 0.39% in the cases of the United States, Japan, and Britain. By 1986–7 Dutch aid was greater in volume than that of the Britain and as a proportion of GNP was exceeded only by Norway.[68] The importance given to overseas development assistance by successive Dutch governments varied only slightly from the mid-1970s to the latter 1980s. In 1985 there was a drop in the total amount, though this was balanced by a cancellation of all debts due from the least developed recipients. In 1986 asistance was boosted to almost 1% of GNP.[69]

The record over the past fifteen years is thus an extremely impressive one in comparative terms. The strategy is endorsed by all mainstream political parties, though perhaps receiving more emphasis from those on the left, and appears to be popular with the vast majority of voters. Its execution may not be wholly immune from trade and allied considerations, but it is certainly not regarded, as it is in Britain, as a direct expression of the national economic interest. Over 90% of bilateral aid takes the form of outright grants. In 1987 only the United States, Japan, France and Germany exceeded the Netherlands in the sheer volume of aid provided. In that year the Dutch outflow of development assistance was $50 million greater than that of Britain, and more than three times the British effort as a proportion of the respective GNPs.[70]

Participation in foreign policy

Up till the Second World War two factors made foreign policy in the Netherlands a matter of miniscule participation. The historic circumstance of the royal prerogative in external affairs confined them to the executive rather than the legislature, and the tradition of ministerial independence gave the Foreign Minister a very free hand in determining what the policy ought to be.[71] But the long-term stance of neutrality meant that very little happened which required extensive discussion or consultation. Thus the oversight of foreign relations tended to be restricted to what a later writer has called the 'small band of diplomats and other professional insiders' who patrol 'the exclusive happy hunting-ground' of foreign policy deliberation.[72]

In so far as this scenario has changed over the past half-century, the changes have perhaps been more expressive than instrumental. The band of advisers has been expanded to include academics and commentators upon foreign affairs; parliament has increased its voice in external matters, chiefly through the operations of the Standing Committee on Foreign Policy in the Second Chamber; and public debate has become more lively, largely as a result of 'determined efforts by committed single-issue groups'.[73] On the political party front the general tendency since the war has been for opinion, often strongly phrased, to be submerged in the continuum of policy which the foreign affairs establishment has successfully maintained.

This last point is best illustrated by the conformity of the ostensibly left-wing den Uyl cabinet with the policy goals and practices already well-charted by the early 1970s. For the effects of coalition government, which in themselves made for considerable continuity, were reinforced by the remarkable longevity of Mr Luns, Catholic Foreign Minister from 1956–71, who managed to resist virtually all efforts to make foreign policy more accountable.

Yet much attention has been addressed by writers in the 1980s to the role of public opinion and of domestic factors generally in the shaping of foreign policy.[74] It is certainly the case that from the late 1960s on, public and party controversy about the direction of external policies became much more evident than during the previous two decades. The unpopularity of the Vietnam War is commonly cited as the watershed in public acquiescence to official strategy. The development of critical opposition is also linked to the effects of the 'cultural revolution' of the 1960s, which opened the whole field of government policy to wide-scale challenge. In the 1970s one of the chief targets of the iconoclasts was the unwavering adherence of successive cabinets to the NATO nuclear position.

With the orchestration in 1977 by the Inter-Church Peace Council (IKV) of the campaign to 'rid the world of nuclear weapons'.[75] beginning with the Netherlands, a major conflict developed which put severe pressure upon Christian Democrat ministers and parliamentarians. This reached a crescendo over the issue of deploying Cruise missiles in Holland – a matter which was postponed by three successive governments until the decision in November 1985 to go ahead with the installation.

Since that episode is the most vivid of all the conflicts over security policy in the post-war period, the critics' ultimate lack of success in influencing the outcome may be taken as a conclusive demonstration that governments have been able to ride out all storms in the sphere of foreign policy. This fact is sometimes presented as evidence of a high consensus in the realm of external affairs and over security policy in particular, but the division of opinion about the acceptance of Cruise indicates that this is not comprehensively the case. The reason why governments have consistently held the line against public discord, party resolutions and parliamentary opposition seems more to do with their lack of autonomy inside an alliance structure, and the sheer impossibility of pursuing an independent foreign policy. In those circumstances virtually no amount of public disaffection can be allowed to sway those responsible for dealing with the outside world.

Yet again the processes of coalition-making make their own contribution to the defusing of differences between the major parties over foreign and defence policy. The need of coalition cabinets to produce a common programme, in this as in all other fields, inevitably promotes compromise, continuity and conformity with the long-established lineaments of external relations. In the manifestos produced by the leading parties for the election of September 1989, there were some differences between the programmes in this area.[76] Labour proposed a small reduction in defence expenditures and no modernisation of Lance missiles. The Liberals advocated a 1% increase in the defence budget and modernisation. The Christian Democrats suggested some reduction in nuclear armaments to be balanced by a small increase in the outlay on conventional forces; while Democrats '66 argued for a freeze of defence costs and the retention of nuclear weapons.

But the differences between the programmes were not such as might inhibit, let alone stymie, coalition negotiations; and since all four parties sought office it was clear that they had been designed so as not to do so. In any case the question of modernising short-range weapons would not be decided in or by the Netherlands, and defence received little attention during the election campaign. Security policy has not always had such a low electoral profile. But the fact remains that no cabinet formation has ever been disrupted by persistent differences over foreign or security matters, and that no cabinet has ever broken up as a result of a conflict over external affairs. The nearest a government has come to a breakdown of accord was when Defence Minister Kruisinga resigned over the neutron bomb in 1978. In the first Lubbers cabinet of 1982–6, it was known that the Defence Minister – de Ruiter – did not favour Dutch acceptance of Cruise missiles. But he did not resign when the cabinet decided to deploy them, and parliament narrowly endorsed the decision.

In its firm control of foreign and security policy, the position of the Dutch executive is probably little different in practice from that of its West European counterparts. If there are differences, then they are perhaps noteworthy in two respects. One is the extent to which external affairs are regarded as largely the preserve of the Minister for Foreign Affairs – a circumstance which conforms with the general pattern of ministerial independence within cabinet. The other is that during the 1970s and '80s public dissent from official policy has achieved at times massive proportions but yet has failed to influence outcomes.

NOTES

1. Quoted by J.C. Heldring, 'Between Dreams and Reality', in Leurdijk (1978), p. 310.
2. A similar remark is recorded by Robert Russell, 'The Atlantic Alliance in Dutch Foreign Policy', in Leurdijk (1978), p. 169.
3. Voorhoeve (1985) reports a mere sixty professionals in the department and eighty

in the foreign service in 1939. By 1977 these numbers had soared to 1,500 employed in the department and 2,100 abroad (p. 71). Walraven records a rise in personnel from 0.7% of the national civil service in 1950 to 2.33% in 1980. Everts and Walraven (1989), Table 6.1, p. 55.

4. Riemersma counts 900 organisations in 1960, rising to over 2,000 in 1983. Everts and Walraven, p. 23.
5. Thus Heldring, op. cit.: 'The new foreign policy drew its intellectual and moral inspiration from the same sources as the old one' (p. 312).
6. Van Staden: 'In 1957 the Netherlands, under the centre-left Drees cabinet, was the first West European country to allow American nuclear weapons on its territory'. 'The Changing Role of the Netherlands in the Atlantic Alliance', *West European Politics*, Vol. 12, No. 1 (1989), p. 100.
7. It was not till the 1960s that the full implications of the American nuclear guarantee entered the arena of political debate. See Leurdijk (1978), p. 195.
8. See Vandenbosch (1959), pp. 4 and 56.
9. Defence accounted for 19% of the national budget in 1962, reducing to 13% in 1972 and 9.5% in 1982. Up to 1968 defence expenditure averaged 4.4% of GDP, reducing to 3.4% thereafter. In citing these figures Riemersma points out that they are 'well ahead of other small countries such as Belgium, Denmark and Norway'. Everts and Walraven p. 20–1.
10. Van Staden, op. cit., p. 103.
11. E.g. Heldring, op. cit.: 'Dutch moralism and legalism now seized upon the notion of European integration, and this satisfied the Dutch need of an international rule of law' (p. 312).
12. Voorhoeve, op. cit., p. 102.
13. Ibid., p. 103.
14. See Walraven: up to 1949, 'The problem of Indonesia require[d] much of the energy of the top of the ministry.' Everts and Walraven (1989), p. 51.
15. Vandenbosch (1959), pp. 181–6.
16. Voorhoeve, p. 43.
17. Ibid., p. 49.
18. Vandenbosch (1959), p. 164.
19. Ibid., p. 56.
20. Ibid., p. 108.
21. Ibid., p. 38.
22. 'In their determination to adhere to a small power policy, the Dutch at times found the possession of extensive and important colonial territories . . . a source of embarrassment'. Ibid., p. 191.
23. A 1943 circular to diplomatic posts advocated 'closest co-operation with powerful well-disposed countries whose interests were most closely interwoven with . . . the Netherlands . . .' H.A. Schaper, 'The security policy of the Netherlands 1945–1948' in Leurdijk, p. 90.
24. Ibid., p. 89.
25. Everts and Walraven, p. 40.
26. Op. cit., p. 295.
27. Schaper, op. cit., p. 95.
28. Ibid., p. 99.
29. Ibid., pp. 107 and 113.

30. Vandenbosch (1959), pp. 302–3.
31. Voorhoeve, pp. 106–7.
32. Ibid., p. 108.
33. Van Staden, for example, translates Dutch gratitude and respect *vis-à-vis* the United States into 'moral overtones'. Op. cit., p. 100.
34. Op. cit., p. 119.
35. Ibid., p. 118.
36. See the chapters by Van Staden, Russell and Leurdijk in Leurdijk (1979), op. cit.
37. Robert Rothstein, *Alliances and Small Powers*, New York, 1968.
38. Van Staden, 'The Role of the Netherlands in the Atlantic Alliance', in Leurdijk (1978), p. 147.
39. R.W. Russell. 'The Atlantic Alliance in Dutch Foreign Policy, in Leurdijk (1978), p. 169.
40. Everts and Walraven, op. cit., p. 41.
41. Quoted by Leurdijk, p. 194, op. cit.
42. Ibid., p. 234, footnote 117.
43. Ibid., p. 220.
44. See R.B. Soetendorp, 'The Nato Double-track Decision of 1979' in Everts and Walraven, pp. 149–60.
45. For a thoughtful extended account of the Benelux Union and its effects upon subsequent wider integration, see Voorhoeve pp. 154–60.
46. Ibid., p. 160.
47. Ibid., p. 161.
48. Ibid., p. 164.
49. Suzanne Jones, 'The Denial of Grandeur: The Dutch Context' in Leurdijk, p. 250.
50. Voorhoeve, Table VIII-I, p. 185.
51. Ibid., p. 173.
52. Leurdijk, pp. 257–8.
53. Van Staden, 'Decision-making in International Organisations' in Everts and Walraven, pp. 69–70.
54. Voorhoeve, p. 289.
55. A view based upon discussions at the Anglo-Dutch conference on 'The Future of Europe' at the Clingendael Institute, The Hague, June 1989.
56. Op. cit., chapter IX, pp. 197–250.
57. Walraven in Everts and Walraven, Figure 4–1, p. 54.
58. Op. cit., Pt. II.
59. Everts and Walraven, p. 119.
60. Ibid., pp. 310f.
61. Op. cit., p. 248.
62. Idem.
63. See Baehr in Everts and Walraven, pp. 296–309.
64. Voorhoeve, p. 256.
65. Summarised in the pamphlet *Foreign Policy* published by the Ministry of Foreign Affairs, 1983 edition, pp. 8–9.
66. 'Concern for Development Aid and Fundamental Human Rights: The Dilemma as faced by the Netherlands', *Human Rights Quarterly*, vol. 4, no. 1 (Spring 1982).
67. Ibid., p. 45.
68. *OECD Development Co-operation Report*, 1988, Table IV-I, pp. 60–61.

69. OECD *Development Co-operation Report*, 1987.
70. OECD *Development Co-operation Report*, 1988.
71. P. Baehr, 'The Foreign Minister is unquestionably *the* dominating figure in the field of Dutch external relations', *Government and Opposition*, vol. 9, no. 2 (Spring 1974), pp. 172–3.
72. Van Staden, 1989, op. cit., p. 104.
73. Ibid.
74. See P. Everts (ed.), *Public Opinion, the Churches and Foreign Policy*. Leiden 1983; P. Everts (ed.), *Controversies at Home: Domestic Factors in the Foreign Policy of the Netherlands*, Dordrecht, 1985; J.E. Siccama, 'The Netherlands depillarised. Security policy in a new democratic context' in E. Flynn (ed.), *NATO's Northern Allies*, London, 1985.
75. Van Staden (1989), op. cit., p. 105.
76. See summary of party programmes in *Algemeen Dagsblad*, 4 Sept. 1989, compiled by A.P.D. Lucardie, Netherlands Documentation Centre for Political Parties.

SELECT BIBLIOGRAPHY

The works listed are primarily those cited in the notes. Most are in English.

J.G. Abert, *Economic Policy and Planning in the Netherlands*, New Haven, 1969.

R. Andeweg, *Dutch Voters Adrift: On Explanations of Electoral Change, 1963-1977*, Leiden, 1982.

——, 'The Netherlands: Coalition Cabinets in Changing Circumstances' in J. Blondel and F. Muller-Rommel (eds), *Cabinets in Western Europe*, London, 1988.

——, 'Centrifugal Forces and Collective Decision-Making: The Case of the Dutch Cabinet,' *European Journal of Political Research*, Vol. 16, No. 2 (1988a).

——, 'Institutional Conservatism in the Netherlands: Proposals for and Resistance to Change', *West European Politics*, Vol. 12, No. 1 (1989).

——, 'Less than Nothing? Hidden Privatisation of the Pseudo-Private Sector: The Dutch Case', *West European Politics*, Vol. 11, No. 4 (1988b), p. 121.

R. Andeweg, K. Dittrich and Th. van der Tak, 'Government Formation in the Netherlands' in Griffiths (ed.), *The Economy and Politics of the Netherlands since 1945*, The Hague, 1980.

P.R. Baehr, 'Parliamentary Control over Foreign Policy in the Netherlands', *Government and Opposition*, Vol. 9, No. 2 (1974).

——, 'The Dutch Foreign Policy Elite', *International Studies Quarterly*, 24/2 (1980).

——, 'Concern for Development Aid and Fundamental Human Rights: The Dilemma as faced by the Netherlands', *Human Rights Quarterly*, Vol. 4, No. 1 (Spring 1982).

W.E. Bakema and W.P. Secker, 'Ministerial Experience and the Dutch Case', *European Journal of Political Research*, Vol. 16, No. 2 (1988).

H. Bakvis, *Catholic Power in the Netherlands*, Montreal, 1981.

——, 'Toward a Political Economy of Consociationalism', *Comparative Politics*, Vol. 16, No. 3 (1984).

——, 'Electoral Stability and Electoral Change: The Case of the Dutch Catholics', *Canadian Journal of Political Science*, Vol. 14, No. 3 (1981).

J. Bank, 'Verzuiling: A Confessional Road to Secularisation' in A. Duke and C. Tamse (eds), *Britain and the Netherlands*, Vol. VII, The Hague, 1981.

D.J. Barnouw, *The Making of Modern Holland*, London, 1948.

J. Th. van den Berg, *De Toegang tot het Binnenhof* (Access to Parliament) *1849-1970*, Van Holkema and Warendorf, 1983.

J.C.H. Blom, 'The Second World War and Dutch Society', in A. Duke and C. Tamse (eds), *Britain and the Netherlands*, Vol. VI, The Hague, 1977.

K. Brants, 'Broadcasting and Politics in the Netherlands', *West European Politics*, Vol. 8, No. 2 (1985).

L.P.J. de Bruyn and J. Foppen, *The Dutch Voter 1972-3*, 2 vols, Nijmegen, 1974.

S. van Campen, 'How and why the Netherlands joined the Nato Alliance', *Nato Review*, Vol. 30, No. 3 (1982).

Alice Carter, *The Dutch Republic in Europe in the Seven Years War*, London, 1971.

G.N. Clark, 'The Birth of the Dutch Republic', *Proceedings of the British Academy*, XXXII (1946).

H. Daalder, 'Extreme Proportional Representation: The Dutch Experience', in S.E. Finer (ed.), *Adversary Politics and Electoral Reform*, London, 1975.

——, 'The Netherlands: Opposition in a Segmented Society' in R.A. Dahl (ed.), *Political Oppositions in Western Democracies*, New Haven, 1966.

——, 'The Dutch Party System: From Segmentation to Polarization – and then?', in H. Daalder (ed.), *Party Systems in Denmark, Austria, Switzerland, The Netherlands and Belgium*, London, 1987.

—— and J. Th. van den Berg, 'Members of the Dutch Lower House: Pluralism and Democratization 1848-1967' in M.M. Czudnowski (ed.), *Does Who Governs Matter?*, 1982.

——, and J.E. Rusk, 'Perceptions of Party in the Dutch Parliament' in S.C. Patterson and J.C. Wahlke (eds), *Comparative Legislative Behaviour: Frontiers of Research*, New York, 1972.

——and C.J.M. Schuyt, *Compendium of Politics and Society in the Netherlands*, Alphen aan den Rijn, 1986.

——, 'The Mould of Dutch Politics', *West European Politics*, Vol. 12, No. 1, p. 8.

H. Daudt, 'Political Parties and Government Coalitions in the Netherlands', *Netherlands Journal of Sociology*, Vol. 18, No. 1 (1982).

J. Deboutte and A. van Staden, 'High Politics in the Low Countries' in W. Wallace and W. Paterson (eds), *Foreign Policy-Making in Western Europe*, Farnborough, 1979.

DNPP Yearbook [Annual of the Documentation Centre For Dutch Political Parties] (published by the University of Groningen).

J. van Doorn, 'Welfare State and Welfare Society: The Dutch Experience', *Netherlands Journal of Sociology*, Vol. 14, No. 1 (1978).

A.K. Dutt and F.J. Costa (eds), *Public Planning in the Netherlands*, Oxford, 1985.

G. Edmundson, *History of Holland*, Cambridge (England); 1922.

C. van der Eijk, 'Counter-Inflation Policy' in Griffiths, ed. (1980).

——, and B. Niemoller, *Electoral Change in the Netherlands*, Amsterdam, 1983.

S. Eldersveld, J. Kooiman and Th. van der Tak, *Elite Images of Dutch Politics*, Ann Arbor, 1981.

P. Everts (ed.), *Public Opinion, the Churches and Foreign Policy*, Leiden, 1983.

——, *Controversies at Home: Domestic Factors in the Foreign Policy of the Netherlands*, Dordrecht, 1985.

——, and G. Walraven (eds), *The Politics of Persuasion. Implementation of Foreign Policy by the Netherlands*, Aldershot, 1989.

H. Franssen (ed.), *Het Parliament in Aktie* (Parliament in Action), Assen, 1986.

P. Geyl, *The Revolt of the Netherlands, 1955–1609*, 2 vols, 2nd edn, London, 1962.

——, *History of the Low Countries: Episodes and Problems*, London, 1964.

——, *The Netherlands in the 17th Century*, London, 2 parts; 1961, 1964.

K.R. Gladdish, 'Two-Party versus Multi-party: The Netherlands and Britain', *Acta Politica*, Vol. 7, No. 3 (1972). Reprinted in *Parliamentary Affairs*, Autumn 1973.

——, 'The 1982 Netherlands Election', *West European Politics*, Vol. 6, No. 3 (1983a).

——, 'The Dutch Political Parties and the May 1986 Elections', *Government and Opposition*, Vol. 21, No. 3 (1986).

——, 'Parliamentary Activism and Legitimacy in the Netherlands', *West European Politics*, Vol. 13, No. 3 (1990).

——, 'Coalition Government and Policy Outputs in the Netherlands' in V. Bogdanor (ed.), *Coalition Government in Western Europe*, London, 1983.

——, 'The Netherlands' in V. Bogdanor (ed.), *Representatives of the People? Parliamentarians and Constituents in Western Democracies*, Aldershot, 1985.

——, 'Opposition in the Netherlands' in E. Kolinsky (ed.), *Opposition in Western Europe*, Bromley, 1987.

——, 'The Centre Holds: 1986 Netherlands Election', *West European Politics*, Vol. 10, No. 1 (1987a).

R.T. Griffiths, *Industrial Retardation in the Netherlands, 1830–1850*, The Hague, 1979.

——, 'The Netherlands Central Planning Bureau' in Griffiths, ed. (1980).

—— (ed.), *The Economy and Politics of the Netherlands since 1945*, The Hague, 1980.

E. Hansen, 'Depression Decade: Crisis, Social Democracy and Planisme in Belgium and the Netherlands', *Journal of Contemporary History*, Vol. 16, No. 2 (1981).

M. de Hond, *Hoe Wij Kiezen* (How we vote), Amsterdam, 1986.

J.H. Huizinga, *Dutch Civilisation in the 17th Century*, London, 1935, 1968.

G.A. Irwin, 'The Dutch Party System' in P. Merkl (ed.), *Western European Party Systems*, New York, 1980.

——, 'Patterns of Voting Behaviour in the Netherlands' in Griffiths, ed. (1980).

J.A. de Jonge, 'The Role of the Outer Provinces in the Process of Dutch Economic Growth in the 19th Century in Britain and the Netherlands' in J.S. Bromley and E.H. Kossmann (eds), *Britain and the Netherlands*, Vol. IV, The Hague, 1971.

——, and B. Pijnenburg, 'The Dutch Christian Democratic Party and Coalition Behaviour in the Netherlands' in G. Pridham (ed.), *Coalitional Behaviour in Theory and Practice*, Cambridge (England), 1986.

W. Keyser and R. Windle (eds), *Public Enterprise in the EEC*, Part VI: 'The Netherlands' (with assistance of H.J. van der Kar), Alphen aan den Rijn, 1978.

R. Kieve, 'Pillars of Sand: A Marxist Critique of Consociational Democracy in the Netherlands', *Comparative Politics*, Vol. 13, No. 3 (1981).

P.W. Klein, 'The Foundations of Dutch Prosperity' in Griffiths, ed. (1980).

J. Kooiman, 'Departments under Pressure: Governing Problems of Ministries in the Netherlands', *European Journal of Political Research*, Vol. 11, No. 4 (1983).

R.A. Koole, 'The Modesty of Dutch Party Finance' in H.E. Alexander (ed.), *Comparative Political Finance in the 1980s*, Cambridge (England), 1989.

——, and M. Leijenaar, 'The Netherlands: The Predominance of Regionalism' in M. Gallagher and M. Marsh (eds), *Candidate Selection in Comparative Perspective*, London, 1988.

E.H. Kossmann, 'The Crisis of the Dutch State 1780–1813' in J.S. Bromley and E.H. Kossmann (eds), *Britain and the Netherlands*, Vol. IV, The Hague, 1971.

——, *The Low Countries, 1780–1940*, Oxford, 1978.

——, and A.F. Mellink, *Texts Concerning the Revolt of the Netherlands*, Cambridge, England, 1975.

P.E. Kraemer, *The Societal State*, Boom, Meppel, 1966.

I. Leonard Leeb, *The Ideological Origins of the Batavian Republic*, The Hague, 1973.

J.H. Leurdijk (ed.), *The Foreign Policy of the Netherlands*, Alphen aan den Rijn, 1978.

A. Lijphart, *The Politics of Accommodation: Pluralism and Democracy in the Netherlands*, Berkeley, 1968; 2nd edn, 1975.

V.R. Lorwin, 'Segmented Pluralism, Ideological Changes and Political Cohesion in the Smaller European Democracies', *Comparative Politics*, Vol. 3, No. 2 (1970).

W.D. Maass, *The Netherlands at War, 1940–45*, London, 1970.

H.J.G.A. van Mierlo, 'The 1981 Netherlands Election', *West European Politics*, Vol. 4, No. 3 (1981).

——, 'Depillarisation and the Decline of Consociationalism in the Netherlands 1970–85', *West European Politics*, Vol. 9, No. 1 (1986).

J. Mokyr, *Industrialisation in the Low Countries, 1795–1850*, New Haven, 1976.

E. Newton, *The Netherlands, 1795–1977*, London, 1978.

Geoffrey Parker, 'Why did the Dutch Revolt last 80 Years?', *Transactions. Royal Historical Society*, XXVI (1976).

——, *Spain and the Netherlands 1559–1659: Ten Studies*, London, 1979.

——, *The Dutch Revolt*, London, 1979.

Select Bibliography 187
Parlement en Kiezer (Parliament and Voter) Annual Official Handbook, The Hague.

N.W. Posthumus (ed.), 'The Netherlands during the German Occupation', *Annals of American Academy of Political and Social Sciences*, Philadelphia, 1946.

J. van Putten, 'Policy Styles in the Netherlands' in J. Richardson (ed.), *Policy Styles in Western Europe*, London, 1982.

E. van Raalte, *The Parliament of the Netherlands*, London and The Hague, 1959.

S. Rokkan, 'Towards a Generalised Concept of Verzuiling', *Political Studies*, Vol. 25, No. 4 (1977).

H.N. Rowen, *John De Witt, Grand Pensionary of Holland, 1625-1672*, Princeton, 1978.

S. Schama, *Patriots and Liberators: Revolution in the Netherlands 1780-1810*, London, 1977.

——, *The Embarrassment of Riches*, London, 1987.

M.P.C.M. van Schendelen, *The Dutch Member of Parliament, 1979-80*, Rotterdam, 1981.

——, 'Disaffected Representation in the Netherlands', *Acta Politica*, XVI (April 1981).

——, *Parlementaire Informatie Besluitvorming - Vertegenwoordiging* (Parliamentary Information, Decision-making and Representation), Rotterdam, 1975.

—— (ed.), 'Consociationalism, Pillarization and Conflict-Management in the Low Countries', *Acta Politica*, XIX (1984).

—— and R.J. Jackson (eds), *The Politicisation of Business in Western Europe*, London, 1987.

C. Schiff, *Industrialisation Without National Patents*, Princeton, 1971.

I. Scholten, 'Does Consociationalism Exist? A Critique of the Dutch Experience' in R. Rose (ed.), *Electoral Participation: A Comparative Analysis*, London, 1980.

——, 'Corporatism and the Neo-Liberal Backlash in the Netherlands' in I. Scholten (ed.), *Political Stability and Neo-Corporatism*, London, 1987.

R.E. Smit and H. van der Wusten, 'Dynamics of the Dutch National Socialist Movement (NSB), 1931-1935' in S.K. Larsen *et al.* (eds), *Who were the Fascists: Social Roots of European Fascism*, Oslo/Bergen, 1980.

I. Th. M. Snellen (ed.), *Limits of Government: Dutch Experiences*, Amsterdam, 1985.

A. van Staden, 'The Changing Role of the Netherlands in the Atlantic Alliance', *West European Politics*, Vol. 12, No. 1 (1989).

S. Stuurman, *Verzuiling, kapitalisme en patriarchaat*, Nijmegen, 1983.

A. de Swaan, 'The Netherlands' in E.C. Browne and J. Dreijmanis (eds), *Government Coalitions in Western Democracies*, Harlow, 1982.

——, *Coalition Theories and Cabinet Formation*, Amsterdam, 1973.

Jan den Tex, *Oldenbarnevelt*, 2 vols, Cambridge, 1973.

Th. van Tijn, 'The Party Structure of Holland and the Outer Provinces in the

Nineteenth Century' in J.S. Bromley and E.H. Kossmann (eds), *Britain and the Netherlands*, Vol. IV, The Hague, 1971.

A. Vandenbosch, *Dutch Foreign Policy since 1813: A Study in Small Power Politics*, The Hague, 1959.

J. Verhoef, 'The Rise of National Political Parties in the Netherlands, 1883–1913', *International Journal of Politics*, Vol. 4 (1974).

W. Verkade, *Democratic Parties in the Low Countries and Germany*, Leiden, 1965.

J.J. Vis, 'Coalition Government in a Constitutional Monarchy: The Dutch Experience' in V. Bogdanor (ed.), *Coalition Government in Western Europe*, London, 1983.

B.H.M. Vlekke, *The Evolution of the Dutch Nation*, New York, 1945.

J.J.C. Voorhoeve, *Peace, Profits and Principles: A Study of Dutch Foreign Policy*, The Hague, 1979.

J. de Vries, *The Netherlands Economy in the Twentieth Century*, Assen, 1978.

W. Warmbrunn, *The Dutch under German Occupation, 1940–1945*, Stanford, 1963.

H.L. Wesseiling, 'Post-Imperial Holland', *Journal of Contemporary History*, Vol. 15, No. 1 (1980).

N. Wilterdink, 'Property Relations and Wealth Distribution in the Netherlands,' *Netherlands Journal of Sociology*, Vol. 21, No. 2 (1985).

J. Windmuller, *Labour Relations in the Netherlands*, Ithaca, 1969.

M. Wintle, *Pillars of Piety: Religion in the Netherlands in the Nineteenth Century*, Hull, 1987.

S.B. Wolinetz, 'The Dutch Labour Party: A Social Democratic Party in Transition' in W. Paterson and A. Thomas (ed.), *Social Democratic Parties in Western Europe*, London, 1977.

——, *Wage Regulation in the Netherlands*, Washington DC, 1983.

——, 'Socio-Economic Bargaining in the Netherlands: Redefining the Post-War Coalition', *West European Politics*, Vol. 12, No. 1 (1989).

P. de Wolff and W. Driehuis, 'A Description of Post War Economic Developments and Economic Policy in the Netherlands' in R.T. Griffiths (ed.), *The Economy and Politics of the Netherlands since 1945*, The Hague, 1980.

H. van der Zee, *The Hunger Winter, 1944–5*, Norman & Hobhouse, 1982.

INDEX

advisory bodies, 145
Agt, A.A.M.van, 60, 62, 63, 129, 137, 153
Andeweg, R., 13n, 41, 47, 49n, 69n, 70n, 96, 124, 128, 129, 131, 136n, 137n, 144, 159n, 160n
Anti-Revolutionaries, 12, 15, 17, 20, 76; see also Anti-Revolutionary Party
Anti-Revolutionary Party (ARP): 17, 21-2, 23, 27, 29, 38, 39, 41, 43, 44-7, 71, 72, 75, 77, 80, 92, 136; religious denomination of supporters, 43; see also Calvinists, confessionals

Baehr, P.R., 176, 181n, 182n
Beel, L.J.M., 40, 41
Bekke, A.J.M., 147
Biesheuvel, B.W., 59, 129, 137, 149, 151
British Conservative Party, comparison with Dutch parties, 83-4
British Labour Party, comparison with Dutch parties, 83-4

cabinet: 17, 22-3, 29, 30, 33, 38, 41, 51, 54, 57-60, 61, 62, 67, 110, 111, 113, 122-34; background of ministers, 125-7; party leadership, 77; Parliamentary relations, 13; Prime Minister and, 122-5; Government and, 122-5, 127-8
Calvinism, 4, 12
Calvinists: 16, 19, 24, 38, 43-8, 55, 68; and representation, 95-6; see also Confessionals, Evangelical People's Party, Political Reformed Party, Reformed Political Federation, Reformed Political Union
candidates: regionalism and localism, 79-80; selection of, 77-80
Catholic National Party (KNP), 39
Catholic People's Party (KVP), 37, 38, 39, 41, 43-7, 50, 53, 54, 80, 92, 113, 132, 136, 143; religious denomination of supporters, 43

Catholics: 16, 17, 19, 21, 22, 23, 24, 26, 27, 28, 35, 53, 55, 68, 76; and representation, 95-6; see also Catholic National Party, Catholic People's Party, Roman Catholic Party, Roman Catholic State Party
central planning, 138-9, 144, 146-8, 156
Central Planning Bureau, 139, 144, 153
Centre Party (CP), 56, 64; see also Janmaat
Christian Democratic Appeal (CDA): 54-6, 58, 60-9, 102, 132, 133, 135-6, 170; aims and programme, 85; CDA-VVD coalition, 61-2, 63, 65-9, 170; defence policy, 179; party activists, 82-4; political profile, 81; resources, 80-1; socio-economic policy, 152, 154; voting behaviour 88-93
Christian Historical Union (CHU): 22, 23, 27, 29, 39, 41, 43, 44-7, 72, 80, 92; religious denomination of supporters, 43
Civil Service, 144
coalitions: 38, 61-2, 63, 65-9, 123, 130-6; and confessionals, 131-6; and foreign policy, 178-9; and public policy, 143, 148-9, 152, 154, 155; see also Christian Democratic Appeal, Democrats '66, Labour Party, People's Party for Freedom and Democracy
Colijn, H., 29-30, 34, 77
colonial policy, 20-1
Communist Party of the Netherlands (CPN): 27, 37, 39, 46, 56, 64, 74, 87; see also Green Left
Communists, 31; see also CPN
confessionals: 16, 19, 21, 24, 27, 28, 29, 34, 35, 36, 37, 38, 41, 42-7, 50, 54-5, 57, 58, 66, 68, 104, 105, 151; and policy-making styles, 147, 148; unification of, 54-6
Conservative-Liberals, 16-17, 20, 23, 40
Conservatives, 16

189